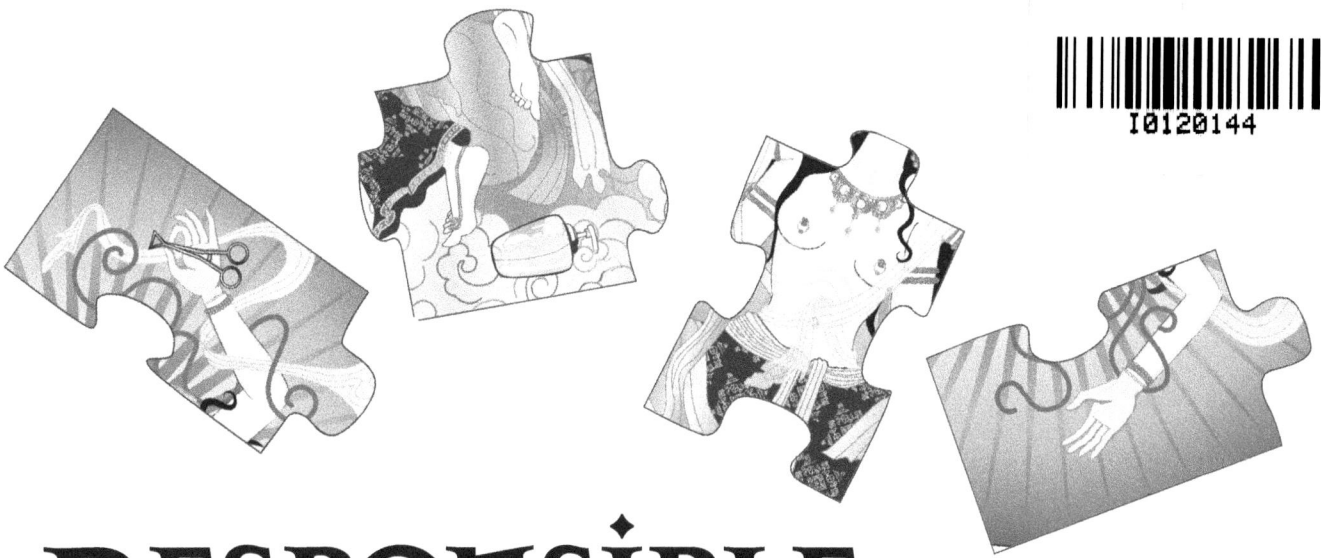

RESPONSIBLE BODY PIERCING

✦ *putting the pieces together*

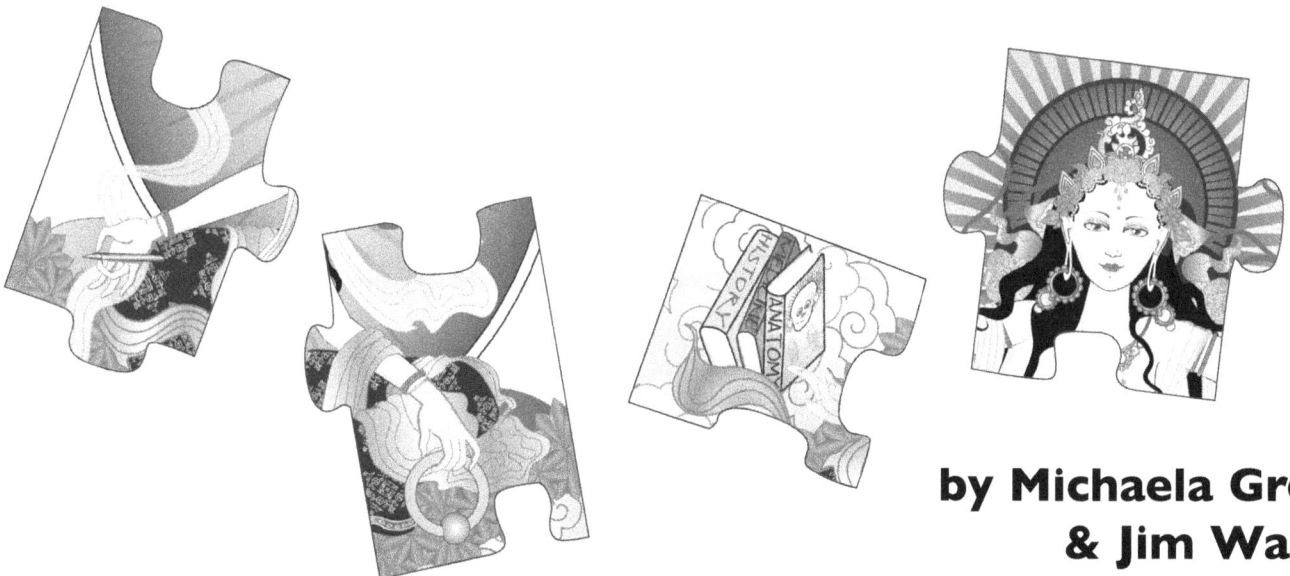

**by Michaela Grey
& Jim Ward**

ISBN: 978-0-9888516-1-0

Gauntlet

ENTERPRISES

A division of Re:Ward, Inc.

Cover image: The Devi of Piercing by Michaela Grey

This book is dedicated to the memory of Doug
Malloy. Without him there would never have
been a Gauntlet, and quite possibly no modern
piercing movement. Had it evolved without him,
it would certainly have taken a far different,
and perhaps less imaginative, form.

• TABLE OF CONTENTS

Preface to this Reprint and a
DISCLAIMER

For almost 25 years, Gauntlet was at the forefront of the body piercing industry. Between 1995 and the company's demise in 1998, it conducted ongoing seminars teaching aspiring piercers the basics of the profession. This was the manual given to all students who undertook the training.

At the time, this book contained the most current information available, but it has been over two decades since it's publication. During the intervening years, there has been an enormous evolution in an ever expanding industry. While the traditional piercing placements have remained largely unchanged and many of the techniques demonstrated herein are still valid and in use by some piercers today, so much else has evolved and changed.

Take a couple of examples: most, if not all, of the cleaning products and aftercare preparations and instructions have been discarded in favor of safer and gentler alternatives. Jewelry standards have also improved dramatically. At the time this manual was written, what was referred throughout as "surgical stainless steel" was the low-carbon alloy 316L. It was considered ideally suited for wearing in piercings. That standard has long since been found inferior and replaced with ASTM F-138. Quality manufacturers are also offering jewelry crafted from ASTM F-136 titanium, a material that received scant mention in these pages.

The authors debated about updating this manual, but aside from the enormous effort, we realized that keeping the information current would be impossible. Thus the decision was made simply to reprint the original with few changes. Michaela Grey has created a new image of the Devi of Piercing who appears on the cover and throughout the manual broken into jigsaw puzzle pieces. I personally considered eliminating the section "A Touch of Heresy" in chapter 13 which I now find of questionable validity. However, in the interest of history, I have left almost all of the text unchanged in terms of content.

There was a contact address on page 119 that has been updated, and I have edited the Supplies & Equipment section of the resouces listed in the back of the book.

a historical curiosity, a snapshot of the prevailing practices and standards of a particular time. Do not accept anything shown or written here without verifying it with an experienced professional piercer who keeps up-to-date with the day-to-day developments in the industry. Gauntlet, its parent corporation, and its officers cannot accept any responsibility for any misfortune that could arise should anyone ignore this warning. Take to heart the title of this document and always act responsibly.

Historic Notes:

Responsible Body Piercing was originally designed and laid out using QuarkXPress, the same software I was using at the time to create Gauntlet's publication *Piercing Fans International Quarterly*. In retrospect, the design, especially the typography, is rather crude. So were the low resolution images.

The original manual was never published in the usual sense of the word. For each seminar, a local copy shop printed and bound as many copies as were needed for that class. A lot of work has gone into the creation of this edition. The specifications of the publisher and the poor quality of the original images made it impossible to reuse the archived PDF files. Consequently, it has been necessary to rescan all of the images at much higher resolution, and the layout has required adjustments to fit within the required margins.

Around 2002, I made the decision to switch to Adobe's InDesign. It has stood me in good stead, but has offered challenges for this project. The application will open QuarkXPress files, but the converted documents are not identical, partially because of improvements in the way InDesign handles typography. Some paragraphs run longer, some shorter. The results are minor, but noticable. No extreme measures have been made to significantly change the design of the book. It remains largely the same as the original.

I hope you enjoy this walk down memory lane, and I hope it will inspire piercers old and new to always act responsibly and with integrity.

Jim Ward
Co-author and Gauntlet founder

It is essential that this document be considered strictly as

• Preface

The history of piercing stretches back thousands of years and has been evident in tribal cultures throughout the world. From New Guinea and Borneo, the Philippines, India, Africa, and Asia to Alaska, the plains of North America, and the mountains and rainforests of South America, people have, from the dawn of history to the present day, succumbed to the piercing urge. Scarcely a corner of the planet has remained untouched.

This urge has taken many forms. For many it springs from a desire for personal adornment. For others it has played an important role in rites of passage marking the milestones in peoples lives. In some cultures it has supplied the means to enhance sexual pleasure and in others to inhibit it.

Not only has piercing touched many cultures, but, in its most recent incarnation in North America, Europe, and Australia it has captured the interest and imagination of people from a wide variety of cultural, vocational, and ethnic backgrounds. From its reawakening in the gay S/M community, it has spread outward. The ranks of the pierced now include people of every gender and orientation (both kinky and not); bikers, bankers, rockers and punkers; accountants and actors; Hell's Angels and housewives; kids with green hair and matrons with blue; college students from the suburbs and people of all colors from the inner cities. Fashion models choose tasteful navel, nostril, and eyebrow piercings, while the queer movement takes to wild facial piercings and the daring opt for nipple and genital piercings. Universally, these people are responding to that inner voice that says, "Decorate your body"! It doesn't matter why a piercing is done; it is still a profound and rewarding experience.

Let us discuss briefly the study which you are about to undertake. For a moment just imagine you have acquired a jigsaw puzzle. On the box lid is a picture of what it will look like when it is finished. That picture is of the piercer you hope some day to become. This text and its accompanying instruction are the pieces inside the box. You will start, fitting piece into piece, to bring your image to life. First will come the simpler parts: the border and areas of distinctive color or texture. Gradually, step by step, you will assemble the more difficult sections.

When you finish your basic instruction, your picture will be far from complete. This is not something you will finish in a few days time. You should, however, find that we have given you all the pieces necessary to finish your puzzle except one...*experience*. That is the piece you must provide.

It will take a lot of time and a lot of experience before you are going to be equipped to undertake some of the more advanced piercings discussed later in this book. We hope to be able to instill in you the wisdom not to attempt these before you are ready. Keep working on the simpler parts of your puzzle and you will find that the more difficult ones will fall into place. The day will come when that image of an accomplished piercer will spring to life. Be patient and keep on working, and you will achieve your goal.

No project of this scope happens in a vacuum. The authors would like to acknowledge and thank the many people whose invaluable assistance and input have helped not only bring this book into being, but to hopefully have kept it from becoming just another dry, dull textbook. Our gratitude to John Stryker for his initial groundwork, Billy Douglas for his outstanding photography of often dull material, Phoebe Gloeckner and Fish for their wonderful illustrations, and Annie Sprinkle for an inspiration. We would also like to thank all of the friends who modeled for us and all of the Gauntlet staff, especially Karen Hurt, who made suggestions and have been there for us, whatever our need. We couldn't have done it without you.

A Piercee's Bill of Rights

Every person being pierced has the right...

• to be pierced in a scrupulously hygienic, open environment, by a clean, conscientious piercer wearing a fresh pair of disposable latex gloves.

• to a sober, friendly, calm, and knowledgeable piercer, who will guide them through their piercing experience with confidence and assurance.

• to the peace of mind which comes from knowing that their piercer knows and practices the very highest standards of sterilization and hygiene.

• to be pierced with a brand-new, completely sterilized needle, which is immediately disposed of in a medical sharps container after use on the piercee alone.

• to be touched only with freshly sterilized, appropriate implements, properly used and disposed of or resterilized in an autoclave prior to use on anyone else.

• to know that ear-piercing guns are NEVER appropriate, and are often dangerous, when used on anything other than ear lobes.

• to be fitted only with jewelry which is appropriately sized, safe in material, design, and construction, and which best promotes healing. Gold-plated, gold-filled, and sterling silver jewelry are never appropriate for any new or unhealed piercing.

• to be fully informed about proper aftercare, and to have continuing access to their piercer for consultation and assistance with all their piercing-related questions.

CHAPTER I—
✦PROFILE OF
A RESPONSIBLE PIERCER

• AN INTRODUCTION

When Gauntlet first came into being in 1975, who would have imagined the phenomenal popularity body piercing would be enjoying less than 20 years later? In response to the huge demand, people calling themselves "piercers" have been springing up all over. From tattoo shops to beauty salons, almost every city and town now has at least one so-called piercer in residence. A few of them are good; some do poor piercings but are at least clean, and some are just plain dangerous.

Presumably you are reading this because you want to become a piercer yourself, and it is hoped that you wish to become a responsible piercer. We have chosen to call this manual *Responsible Body Piercing*, NOT *Professional Body Piercing*. It is very important for you to understand that NO ONE can make you into a professional after a short course of study, and, in fact, we make no such claims. Experience has proven it takes between a year and a half and two years of supervised training for someone with aptitude to become a fully-qualified piercer. Anyone who leads you to believe that you are ready to start a piercing business after taking a weekend seminar and doing a few piercings is dishonest, irresponsible, and unethical. Professional piercers, like good health care workers, good hair stylists, or any other professionals, are not created overnight. They must all train and practice under the supervision of someone with more knowledge and experience. In time they will gain the skills and confidence necessary to win the trust of their clients and make the piercing experience as untraumatic and painless as possible.

So what if you won't be a professional by the time you finish this book. What is far more important is for you to start right now to be a responsible piercer. We encourage you to learn and practice your craft in an ethical, responsible, and, yes, professional way. Form in your mind an image of the professional you wish to be, and in time you will become that image.

This training manual is intended to provide a broad overview of the world of piercing, to teach the fundamentals of sterilization and hygiene, and to help you begin developing a safe and solid technique. It is beyond the scope of this text to make you a good piercer. That can only come with aptitude, practice, time, and patience.

The information herein is based upon the combined experience of nearly 20 piercers over a period spanning almost 20 years. And while these techniques are used daily in Gauntlet's establishments, our piercers constantly seek ways to refine and improve them.

We all know there is a vast difference between just being able to do something and being able to do it professionally and well. Becoming a professional, "master" piercer—a title rapidly becoming meaningless because it is so abused these days—requires more than learning some basic information and techniques. A true "master" piercer always acts responsibly, i.e. safely, knowledgeably, and professionally. These are the traits and qualities you should cultivate and strive to assimilate. Unless and until they have all become an integral part of your being, you cannot consider yourself a professional, much less a "master," piercer.

The Knowledgeable Piercer

No matter what profession you pursue you will have to gain whatever knowledge is unique to it. Piercing is no different. Here are some of the things you will be required to know:
- The names and locations of the various traditional piercings.
- The best jewelry designs and materials for each.
- How to prepare and mark them.
- The appropriate piercing tools and techniques for each.
- Their healing times and appropriate aftercare.
- When a particular piercing isn't a good choice for a particular individual.
- Sterilization from A to Z.
- How to deal with people, gain their trust, put them at ease.

The Safe Piercer

Without question safety is the single most important requirement of any piercer. You simply must not put your clients or yourself at risk in any way.
- Sterilization and hygiene must be strictly observed.
- Never do a piercing that could endanger the piercee or install a piece of jewelry that is not appropriate even though the client might want it.
- Never use an ear piercing gun to pierce anything. Period!
- Absolutely never do piercing under the influence of drugs or alcohol. Likewise never pierce anyone who is intoxicated.

The Professional Piercer

With a solid knowledge of ones craft and safe techniques and procedures, it is possible to be an acceptable piercer. To be a truly professional, "master" piercer requires the highest standards of character and conduct, qualities that go beyond the basics.

• A professional piercer is ethical and honest. It is very important not to pretend to be something you're not. Your clientele deserves the truth. They have a right to know the extent of your training and experience. Studying this manual does not entitle anyone to claim that they are "Gauntlet-trained."

• Arrogance and a know-it-all attitude are incompatible with professionalism.

• The quality of a piercer's work has a definite correlation to their motivation to pierce. Just as a physician who becomes a doctor for the prestige and money will make a poor caregiver, the piercer who is in it for a quick buck, or because it's "cool" will probably not be very good at it.

• Piercing requires patience and a willingness to listen to the fears of a client and respond to those fears in a way that will allow that person to relax and enjoy the experience. Although a good piercer will not always be able to connect with a client, they should make every effort to try and make the experience as positive as possible, or, if that isn't possible, refer the client to another piercer. Whenever you are going to pierce someone, you should ask yourself, "Is this how I would want to be treated? Would I be comfortable in this situation"? Nothing will drive away business faster than a bad experience with you. And word of mouth can be your best or worst advertising.

These then are some of the most basic requirements of a responsible, professional piercer. Let's now begin to look at these in greater detail.

• CONDUCT OF A PRO

Ask your grandmother and she will probably tell you that there was a time, not that many years ago, when a "nice" girl wouldn't pierce her ears. Applied to both sexes and to body piercing, that attitude has very much persisted into the present. It is perceived by much of the public as something uncouth and barbaric, and, unfortunately, many so-called professional piercers are only too happy to make this perception accurate. The surly, mocking, overtly hostile behavior of many involved in the body art professions has seriously hurt our credibility with legislators and health officials. Throwing "cooler-than-thou" attitude at people is NOT cool. It fosters ignorance and fear of the practices which should be respected as valid personal adornment and expressions of individuality.

Composure

A truly "cool" piercer is friendly, open, and available. In response to even the most frequently asked, tedious questions ("Doesn't piercing hurt?"), s/he is able to give a realistic, personal reply. If someone inquires about his/her sterilization procedures, s/he is proud to answer their questions and show them the autoclave, rather than be insulted that a potential client has concern for their health and well being.

It is practically guaranteed that you will not relate to everyone who walks through your door. Clients can be picky, whiny, mean, belligerent, stupid, drunk, immature, or remind you of your ex. No matter what the circumstances, it is very important to remain professional at all times. Try to remember that the attitudes which people project are often the manifestation of their fear and apprehension. If you find that you simply cannot deal with them, perhaps you can tactfully turn them over to a coworker. Perhaps you need to take a short break. Perhaps you just need to grit your teeth behind your smile and deal with the situation as best you can. Remember that every person who walks in the door is going to carry away an impression of your business based on their encounter with you. Unfortunately, their friends and acquaintances are much more likely to hear about a negative experience than a positive one.

This does not mean that you need to stand for verbal, emotional, or physical abuse. It actually feels better to calmly and clearly state your need for respect than to yell, insult, or sulk at a difficult client. In many cases the misunderstanding can be cleared up and a positive relationship can ensue.

Demeanor

The qualities that make a piercer seem professional can be very difficult to define. Obviously it is desirable for your own personality to shine through, and to avoid falseness. But a person about to be pierced is in a peculiar vulnerable state, and you will need to meet their emotional needs to assure a smooth piercing.

Oops! I just stuck myself with your needle... Oh, well.

If you can't calm the piercee into a receptive place, you face the risk of a botched piercing, a hysterical client, and even a serious needle stick.

Knowing Your Limits

A professional piercer is always projects calm and confidence. This does not mean that you can't joke and laugh with your clients, or that you are supposed to have all the answers. A professional piercer never gets into a situation that they aren't fully capable of handling. We all have a little voice inside of us that, if we listen, will steer us clear of potential disaster. If you have a funny feeling about a particular situation, stay away from it! A big part of professional confidence is being able to say, "I don't think I'm ready to do that particular piercing yet. Next year I will be a lot more experienced. Let's wait and look at it then." Your clients will respect you all the more for not attempting what you know is out of your current range, and you will avoid potentially embarrassing, and dangerous accidents. There is no place for cockiness or false pride in a piercing studio. Many lives depend on your knowing your limits and respecting them.

• ANTICIPATING PROBLEMS

Try as hard as we may to avoid them, minor mishaps occur in the piercing room. You might spill antiseptic all over your piercing table, or drop the jewelry on the floor. Our immediate response is to mutter "oops"! or its equivalent. Rest assured that if you do, the piercee will assume the worst. S/he may even jerk or make a sudden movement away from you which could result in an accidental needle stick.

To avoid such possible disasters, discipline yourself never to say anything resembling "oops." And, of course, take steps to protect yourself and your piercee from a potential stick. Cork the needle. Where necessary, explain calmly what has happened. In the case of the jewelry that has dropped on the floor, pick it up. Remove and dispose of your gloves, get a fresh piece of jewelry, disinfect it, put on a new pair of gloves, and continue where you left off. Apologize for the delay.

Wherever possible try to anticipate problems. Someone may faint and slump to the floor with the forceps on and a needle through their tongue. Could you have foreseen this and not pierced them? Or taken steps to prevent them from fainting?

• TRUTH IN ADVERTISING

There are many unscrupulous people in the world who see piercing as a lucrative scam. They could care less about the safety or satisfaction of their clients. There are also a number of people who think that because they do tattooing or hair styling or work in a doctor's office, they know enough about the human body to ply the piercing trade. And then there are those who desperately want to make a name for themselves in the field, but have very limited or incorrect information. All of these people will quite seriously intone that they are "professionals" who are "experienced." Many even are able to rattle off a list of exaggerated or patently fabricated credentials. Some charlatans even go so far as to declare themselves "Master" piercers.

For the piercee this is very dangerous. The piercing needle guided by ego can be a lethal weapon. A lofty, snide, or secretive attitude inevitably masks a woeful and dangerous lack of knowledge and skill.

A very skilled piercer may not be able to draw more than a stick figure. But are we to assume that since s/he is a good piercer s/he is qualified to do tattooing? Likewise, tattooing, hair styling, and the medical professions are all skilled, specialized abilities that do not in and of themselves qualify one to be a competent piercer. While all may work with the human body and have overlapping areas of experience that could make learning easier, piercing is a separate and distinct skill.

During the heyday of the snake oil salesman and the medicine show there was an abundance of self-described doctors, professors, and many other titled individuals peddling their dubious wares. The popularity of piercing has

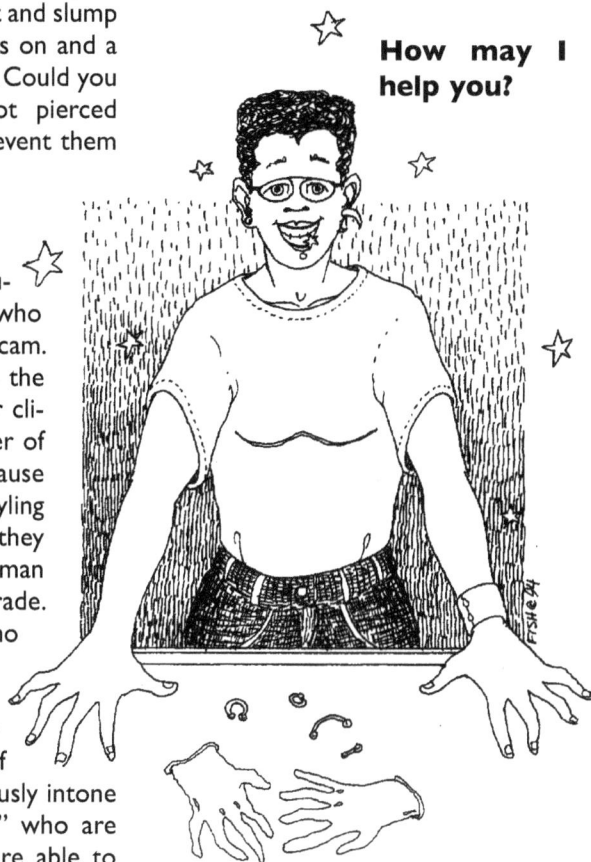

How may I help you?

likewise produced an abundance of individuals wielding a variety of lofty titles—the most popular being "master piercer"—which supposedly describe their accomplishments, but, in fact, are indicative of nothing but their inflated egos.

During the course of Gauntlet's evolution, it became evident that some system needed to be developed for classifying piercers, both trained and in training, and to assign titles which would accurately describe the level of their developing skills. In hopes of encouraging others to adopt similar "truth in advertising," we would like to share Gauntlet's piercer trainee titles and list some of the accomplishments required to merit each title.

Novice: A novice is just that, a beginner; a sponge whose main function is to absorb information, as much of it as possible. There is so much to learn: sterility, bedside manner, appropriate techniques, jewelry, cleaning agents, etc. Simultaneously they take every opportunity to observe piercers as they work, and thus begin to develop the soothing manner so vital in working with the nervousness of people who want to be pierced. Once the novice has a firm grasp of the basic information they are are ready to begin hands-on work. At that time they are considered trainees or apprentices.

Trainee: For our purposes trainee refers to someone who is learning to pierce on their own without the supervision of an experienced professional. Trainees are encouraged to actively seek out as much assistance and information as possible. Ideally, a trainee has attended a seminar or series of seminars at the beginning of their career, to give them some hands-on, supervised experience. If this is not possible, trainees should read the "Pierce With a Pro" series in *PFIQ,* and watch the *PWAP* video series. The *PWAP* series is invaluable as an aid to developing technique, but reading or watching a video does not compare to performing under direct observation and supervision.

Because trainees do not have daily access to an experienced trainer, it is crucial that they make a concerted effort to inform themselves, and ally themselves with professionals who may help them. They are advised to find a piercing-aware doctor. Get a copy of OSHA and local health department guidelines. Use the toll-free piercing information hotline set up by Gauntlet. Speak with other piercers. Because information can be hard to come by, an unsupervised trainee may take much longer to acquire skill than an apprentice. On the other hand, learning on one's own can help one avoid the trap of falling into someone else's bad habits. Unfortunately, if you don't know they're bad, how can you help falling into them?

Trainees have some basic, steadily accumulating knowledge about piercing. They have done some piercings under supervision when and wherever possible. They are able to slowly begin the journey to becoming piercers.

Apprentices: An apprentice is a novice/trainee who has the good fortune to be able to work on a daily basis with a more experienced piercer. They perform their initial piercings under the close supervision of this senior piercer, and can discuss pros, cons, and pointers

as they learn. Because apprentices are supervised, they are able to learn more quickly and smoothly than a lone trainee. Apprentices, if working under ideal conditions, can avoid the poor habits that could come from learning alone.

Apprentices, too, should seek out information from their supervisor as well as doctors, health departments, peers, and other sources. Learning never takes place in just one way, or from only one person. Also, the rule of knowing one's limits applies equally to supervised and unsupervised novices. If you're not ready to do that piercing, no senior piercer standing by is going to magically save you from an embarrassing or dangerous situation. Rather, a trainer or supervisor should help an apprentice assess and nurture their limit awareness skills.

Piercer: A general term for all piercers, but referring specifically to a fully qualified piercer. While not yet a senior or advanced level piercer, a full piercer is completely conversant and comfortable with most of the more popular and common piercings and with appropriate aftercare procedures. By this time sterility awareness should be second nature. S/he has developed a smooth bedside manner and a professional standard. It usually requires a minimum of one to two years for an apprentice, and longer for a novice, to have enough exposure to piercing to reach this level.

A piercer may assist in the training of apprentices, but still lacks the depth of skill to be a primary instructor. Again, the issue of limits is never far from the piercer's mind.

Senior Piercer: A senior piercer has the experience of three to four years of full-time piercing to back up their prodigious body of knowledge and skill. S/he can comfortably and skillfully perform all or most of the forty-odd piercings, offer accurate and current aftercare information, and make judgement calls that less experienced piercers may not be capable of making. A senior piercer is much better equipped to predict the the success of surface-to-surface and other unusual piercings. Senior piercers are qualified to teach others to pierce,

although some may not wish to or be very good at it. Teaching is quite a different skill than piercing.

Master Piercer: The rampant abuse of this title doesn't make defining it any easier. Just as one can learn to play the piano but still not be a concert pianist, many can become competent, professional piercers and not have that innate quality which flowers into mastery. Time spent piercing, even years or decades, does not alone qualify one to be called a master of the craft. A true master piercer does not allow ego to cloud his/her judgement. S/he need not mask inadequacy behind a title. S/he is easily recognized as a master by his/her peers, and the title should be given by them.

There is no shame in remaining senior or even full piercers. What, in fact, could be more fulfilling than just being a first-rate piercer regardless of terminology or experience? While most of us see this as the ultimate title, the real goal is to be the safest, most aware, responsible, professional, and conscientious piercer that we can be. Period!

SUMMARY —
1. Avoid projecting a hostile attitude, no matter how difficult or trying your clients may be.
2. Deal with difficult clients creatively; there are many alternatives to anger.
3. Although occasional mistakes are inevitable, always maintain professional tact and control of the situation. Never make piercees feel anxious, threatened, or frightened.
4. Every situation is unique; find calm, quick, and creative ways to deal with problems.
5. Piercers should always endeavor to act ethically and honestly. They should never misrepresent their level of ability, but know their personal limits at all times.
6. Gauntlet has set levels of piercing mastery which merit the titles novice, trainee, apprentice, qualified, senior, and master piercers. This terminology is presented to help clarify and define personal limits.

• UNPROFESSIONAL BEHAVIOR

While it can be hard to define professional behavior, unprofessional behavior poses no such difficulty. Persons engaging in such conduct are menaces to their clientele and have no place in the craft of piercing.

Drinking & Drugs

Piercing is a complex skill, requiring a sharp and quick mind. Anything less than full attention can lead to deadly mistakes. Piercers operating under the influence are dangerous not only to themselves but to their clients and coworkers. Alcohol, marijuana, and other drugs, legal, illegal, and prescription as well, can severely limit one's judgement and proficiency. A professional NEVER pierces under their influence.

Likewise, s/he should refuse to pierce anyone who is drunk or stoned. Clients under the influence are more prone to bleeding, fainting, vomiting, jerking, and a host of equally unpleasant and/or dangerous behaviors. Don't take the risk.

Personal Health

Fatigue, illness, emotions, and empty stomachs can be a source of many problems, some dangerous. They can effect your judgement and acuity as strongly as drugs. It is essential that you constantly monitor your personal well being. Take an inventory regularly throughout the day. Do you need a short break? A little food? Do you need to go to the bathroom? Piercees are generally most understanding if you require a little personal time to prepare yourself. They usually don't want to be pierced by a tired, sick, angry, or hungry piercer. Never pierce if you can't give100% of your attention in the piercing room.

Sexual Conduct

It is not uncommon for some people to be sexually excited by the idea or experience of being pierced. This is healthy and valid. However, sexual activity in a professional piercing studio can be unsanitary and is unquestionably irresponsible. You are accepting money for the service of performing a piercing and installing jewelry, not for prostitution. If a client requests additional services, send them elsewhere.

It is inevitable that you will be sexually attracted to some of your clients. While it is not our position to tell you how to conduct your personal affairs, we stress that it is crucial that you keep your sexual and professional life separate. Piercees are in a very vulnerable condition. Never use your position as a piercer to take advantage of their state in any way. This includes verbal, physical, or emotional harassments of any kind. Never force your attentions on a client.

More difficult to deal with will be those times when a client attempts to seduce you, especially if the attraction is mutual. We suggest that you again separate your sexual and professional personae. Deal with the piercing like a piercing professional. If you wish to pursue a liaison, make a date to meet outside of business.

Lewd or masturbatory phone calls are a plague of the industry, especially for female piercers since most such callers are male. You may, at first, find these mildly amusing or titillating, but if encouraged they can quickly become an aggravating, time-consuming nuisance. It is usually easy to deter these unwanted calls by not offering any information beyond the most bland. Calmly suggest that the individual come into the store to speak with a piercer. If the caller is a male supposedly wanting information about a female piercing for his wife, ask him to put her on the phone. Repeat offenders can often be repelled by forcing them to speak with a person whose gender does not match their sexual preference. If the problem persists, contact your local police.

Arrogance & Carelessness

There is an epidemic, rampant among piercers, called *Prima Donnaitis*, also known as *Diva Syndrome*. It is a serious occupational hazard. Symptoms are readily apparent: a swelled head, arrogance, I-know-it-all-you-don't-know-anything attitude.

A piercer suffering from Prima Donnaitis can be dangerous. Arrogance can lead to carelessness. A piercer who doesn't pay careful attention to every single thing s/he does is a dangerous piercer.

Since there is no vaccine for Diva Syndrome, you must constantly be alert

to avoid contracting it. Be as cautious wielding your 100th needle as you were with your first. Be as scrupulous about washing your hands now as you should still be 10 years from now. The quality of your life, and the lives of all with whom you interact, is at stake every second of every day. For everyone's sake do not fall victim to Prima Donnaitis. If your clients and coworkers see you becoming arrogant, sloppy, or careless, you are in serious need of an attitude adjustment.

Unethical Competitiveness

At some point you may want to go into business for yourself. With the growing number of people entering this profession, competition is inevitable.

You may be tempted to set up shop across the street from an established piercer. We urge you to resist such temptation. Such behavior is unethical and demeans your stature as a responsible piercer. Develop your clientele on the basis of your skill and ethical business practices. You will be well repaid in respect and client loyalty.

• ANESTHETICS — CRUTCH OF THE UNSKILLED

Nearly everyone wants their piercing experience to be as painless as possible. What few realize is that their best chance for a reasonably pain-free piercing will be found in the hands of a skilled piercer with solid, smooth technique. Issues of legality aside, using an anesthetic (with one notable exception discussed later) is not without some discomfort and carries with it the likelihood of disappointing results and the potential for serious side effects. It has been our observation that, all too frequently, piercers who use anesthetics do so to cover up their own lack of skill. Only with an anesthetic would the piercing be bearable.

The anesthetics which we are discussing at this point are the injectable ones. Topical creams and ointments cannot penetrate skin deeply enough for there to be significant numbing. We sometimes use a topical when doing a Prince Albert piercing. By introducing a small amount into the urethra, which is a mucus membrane and more permeable by the anesthetic, it is possible to achieve some detectable, though not total, numbing of the area. These creams can make the skin greasy and slippery and raise the risk of a misaligned piercing or a possible needle stick.

There are a number of significant reasons why piercers should NOT administer injectable anesthetics:

1. In many countries, the United States included, these are illegal for use by non-medical personnel.
2. Even were this not the case, the area that is injected swells and distorts making accurate placement of the piercing difficult or impossible.
3. There is the possibility that some piercee will experience a severe, possibly fatal, allergic reaction to the anesthetic. Who would want that liability on their hands?
4. The anesthetic injection itself is not without pain, and can, in fact, hurt more than a piercing done without

anesthesia by a skilled professional. In addition when an anesthetic begins to wear off there can be an unpleasant ache or throbbing, whereas there is rarely much, if any, discomfort following a skillful piercing.

Numbing the area to be pierced using cold is another type of anesthesia sometimes used by amateurs. This involves the use of ice or a spray-freezing chemical such as ethyl chloride. Use of the latter carries several dangers: 1) it is not sterile; 2) it carries a risk of causing frostbite; 3) it is extremely flammable; and 4) its fumes can cause dizziness or fainting.

SUMMARY —
1. Piercers should never work under the influence of alcohol or any substance, legal or illegal, which influences their ability. Similarly, they should refuse to work on anyone who is drunk or stoned.
2. Piercers should never work when their ability might be impaired by hunger, illness, emotional or physical stress, or fatigue.
3. Piercers would be wise to keep their business and sex life completely separate. Attempting to seduce a client is unprofessional as well as loathsome behavior.
4. Piercers should endeavor to develop their skills to the point that the use of anesthetics or other numbing agents are unnecessary.

CHAPTER 2 —

◆ THE WELL-EQUIPPED PIERCING ROOM

To pursue any craft seriously requires a place to work and tools with which to work. It also requires that one have a familiarity with those tools. So, if that craft is piercing, what would you expect to find in a respectable piercing studio? You're about to find out.

This chapter will function much like a glossary to introduce you to the equipment which a piercer can reasonably expect to require in the pursuit of his/her craft. Having a familiarity with these items will help you understand what we are talking about when they are discussed in greater detail later in the book.

• FURNISHINGS

A Piercing Table or Chair

If you are going to pierce someone you need something for them to sit or lie on while you do the deed. This can be somewhat problematic since what works well for doing one type of piercing

doesn't necessarily work well for another. Whatever you choose should be vinyl covered to allow for easy cleaning with a hard-surface cleaner. Here are some of the options with their pros and cons:

• **Barber Chair—**
Pros: Somewhat adjustable. Good for piercings from the nipples up though the chair arms may tend to get in your way at times.
Cons: Difficult to gain access to body parts from the waist down.

• **Doctor's Exam Table—**
Pros: A great deal of adjustability from lying down to sitting up. With stirrups, it provides convenient access to the genital area.
Cons: At certain angles the piercee has a tendency to slide off the table, especially when there are no stirrups and when the table is covered with paper.

• **Massage Table—**
Pros: The piercee can sit on the edge for above-the-neck piercings or lie down for body piercings. Table height is adjustable which can save the piercer a sore back. Some models fold up compactly for easy storage or transport.
Cons: Depending on where it is placed in the piercing room, it can be difficult for guiches and some female genital piercings. If the long side is against a wall, a bed cushion, sometimes called a "husband," will allow a woman to sit comfortably with her genitals accessible to the piercer.

A Basic, Armless Chair
When a piercer marks certain piercings the piercee is asked to stand. The piercer then sits to do the marking. A simple chair without arms works just fine for this purpose, though a secretarial-type chair with casters is a bit more convenient if the piercer needs to change position.

Lighting
If you want to do precise work, you have to be able to see what you are doing. This makes good lighting absolutely essential. It should be bright but without harsh glare. A adjustable artist's lamp can be very convenient to provide light to a small area.

Left: **A very workable piercing room. Take note of several features: massage table with "husband" and rolls of exam paper (center), supply cabinet (left), the contaminated instrument area (shelf upper left), and area for customers personal belongings (shelf right).**

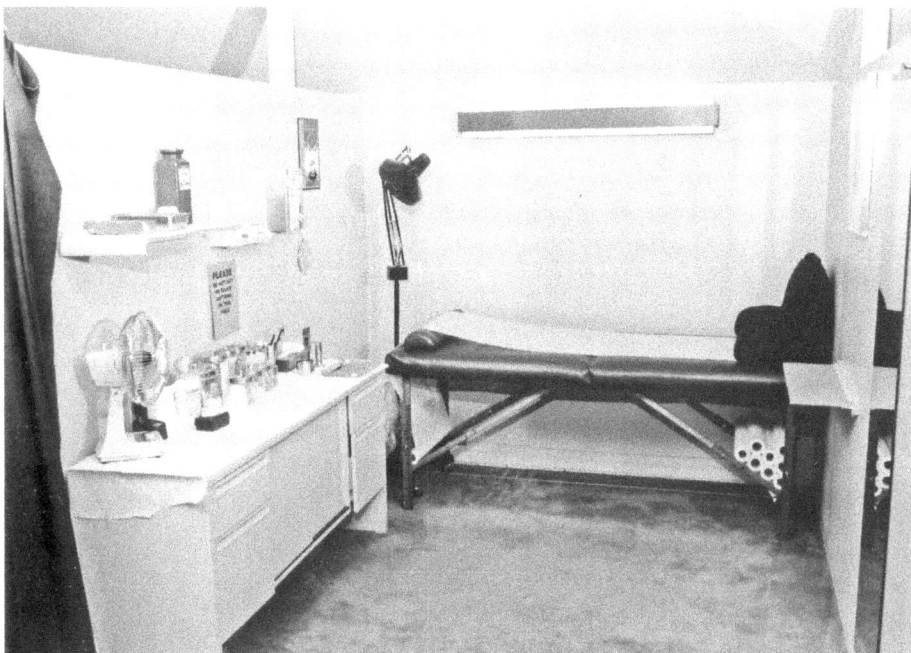

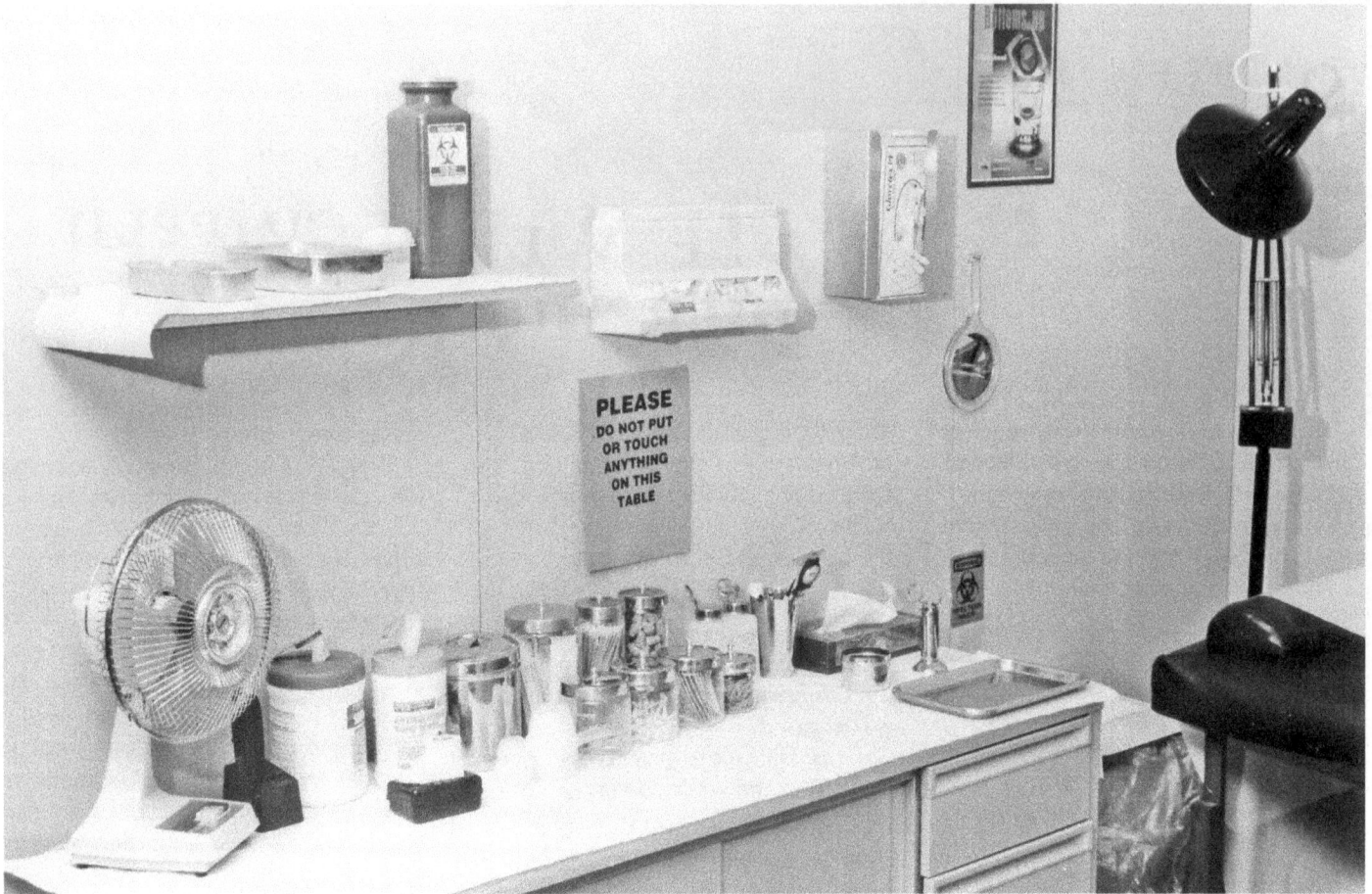

Above, clockwise from upper left: The equipment area: stainless steel trays and sharps container for contaminated instruments and needles; dispensers of gloves; hand mirror; stainless tray for piercing setup; frequently used supplies. *Below left:* piercing setup area and open drawer containing hemostats, forceps, piercing needles, and other supplies. *Below right:* the well-marked trash can.

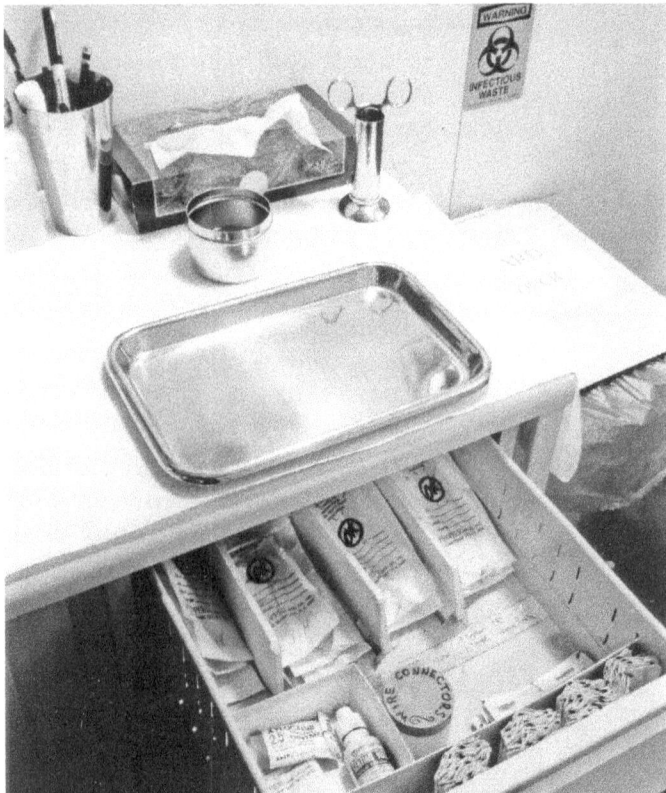

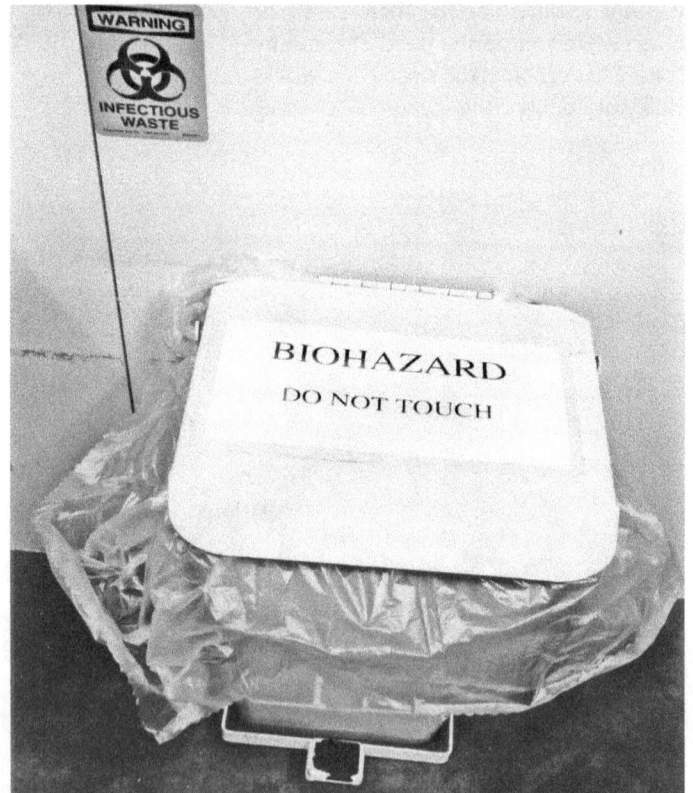

Trash Receptacle

Every piercing area should have its own receptacle for disposing of waste such as table paper, paper towels, tissues, and gloves. This should be marked as a biohazard and have a foot pedal to open and close it. It should never be touched with bare hands by you or your clients. Always use a plastic trash can liner. Piercing needles must NEVER be disposed of in the trash.

Mirrors

Nearly everyone wants to see how their new piercings look. A long mirror mounted on the wall will do nicely. You may also want to keep a small hand mirror close by so the piercee can check out the placement of facial piercings without having to move across the room. These should be regularly cleaned with hard-surface disinfectant.

Shelves

Ideally a piercing room should have a few shelves. One should be away from the piercing equipment and marked or placed so the piercee understands this is a place where they can put their keys, glasses, etc.

The other shelf, also away from the piercing area and marked or placed so clients will not touch or place things on it, can hold a tray for contaminated tools and a sharps container for used needles. OSHA requires that you clearly mark the area with a biohazard designation. Neither you nor your client should touch anything in this area with bare hands. Should this happen, the hands must IMMEDIATELY be washed with an antibacterial scrub.

Coat Hook

Provide a coat tree or a hook on the wall for your clients to hang their clothing. It's cleaner, neater, and much more professional than throwing them on the floor or over the back of a chair.

Implement Storage Space

Needless to say you need some kind of surface on which to place your piercing tools and equipment. This is where you will set up your "sterile" field, so be sure the surface is nonporous and can withstand cleaning with hard-surface disinfectants. The surface should be long enough to set all your most frequently used piercing equipment comfortably without crowding. You will also want storage space underneath to store extra supplies, etc.

• STERILIZATION EQUIPMENT & SUPPLIES

Ultrasonic Cleaner

Thus far nobody has invented the autoclave equivalent of the "pot-scrubber" dishwasher that removes Bacitracin and dried blood and sterilizes at the same time. This appliance is an efficient and safe way to remove matter that accumulates on instruments so that they will come out of the autoclave both clean looking and sterile.

Removing matter manually with a brush can be dangerous because it tends to splatter contaminants. An ultrasonic is worth the investment in safety alone.

Autoclave

One of the most vital and absolutely essential pieces of equipment in a piercing studio, an autoclave is an appliance for sterilizing instruments with steam under pressure. There is no way a responsible piercer can conduct any reasonable amount of business without one.

One can also use a Chemiclave which sterilizes with chemical steam rather than water steam, however, the fumes can be noxious, so if you choose this appliance be sure you have good ventilation.

Pressure Cooker

Autoclaves are very expensive, and people who are just starting out as piercers may not be able to afford one. A *temporary* alternative is a pressure cooker with a vegetable steamer inside to keep the contents above water. Follow the sterilization guidelines later in this book, and get yourself an autoclave as soon as you possibly can!

Sterilization Bags

These are pouches manufactured in a variety of sizes of a special paper which allows live steam to reach their contents but, when dry, keep harmful organisms out. A symbol is printed on them in special ink which changes color when the bag has been subjected to proper sterilization procedures. Bags are used primarily for larger implements such as forceps. Seal with autoclave tape, and be sure to write with pencil on the bag what it contains.

Sterilization Tubing

This is an alternative to sterilization bags which is better suited to small items such as insertion tapers and needle receiving tubes. It consists of a long strip of steam permeable paper adhered along the edges to a strip of clear plastic film. This is handy since it allows you to see the contents. It comes in rolls from which pieces of the desired length are cut, the item to be sterilized inserted and the ends sealed with autoclave tape. Like bags, tubing is also printed with sterilization indicators.

Autoclave Tape

This is a special tape which looks much like masking tape, but has an adhesive which will tolerate the heat and moisture inside an autoclave. It is used to seal sterilization bags and tubing, and, like them, it is also printed with indicators.

Spore Tests

What good is an autoclave if it isn't doing its job. Spore tests are sealed packets of organisms which you autoclave and mail to a lab. The lab cultures the contents to see if they're dead and sends you a report. You should run a spore test at least once a month.

Sharps Container

Your piercing room is not equipped unless you have a sharps container. These are plastic jars or jugs, usually red, made and sold in a variety of sizes specifically for collecting hypodermic needles and syringes. We use them for contaminated piercing needles.

Implement Trays

Keep two stainless steel trays next to your sharps container. In one place contaminated equipment that needs autoclaving, in the other equipment to be disinfected with hard-surface cleaners.

• PAPER GOODS, ETC.

Many of the items in this section are susceptible to being contaminated by ignorant piercees. Should this occur autoclave what you can and throw the rest away. If their contain-

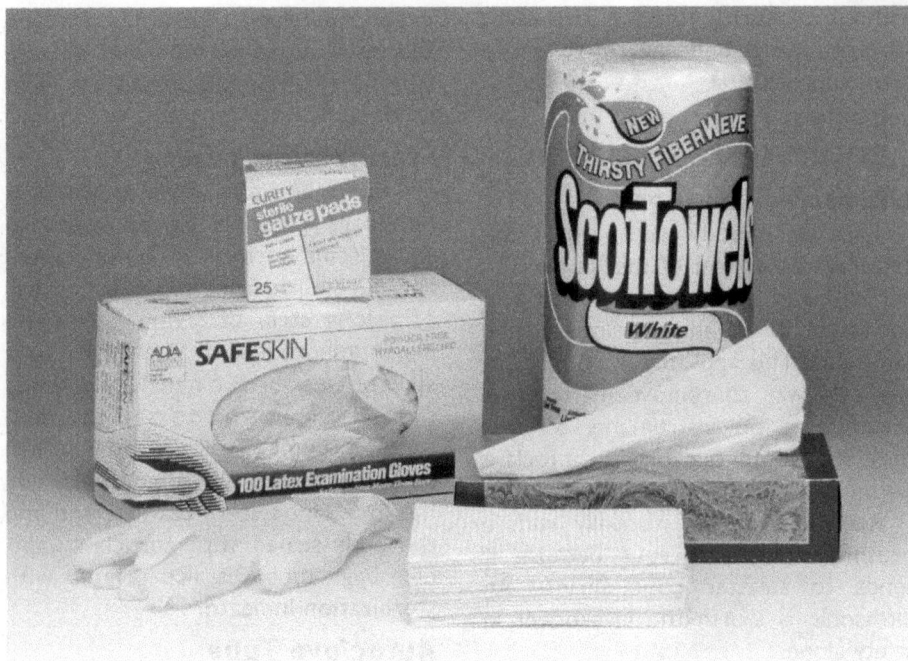

Dental Bibs

These are the bibs the dentist clips around your neck before s/he works on your teeth. They are perfect for lining the tray on which you will lay out your piercing supplies and equipment. Paper on one side, they are lined with plastic film, a convenient barrier against liquids.

Cups & Containers

Small plastic disposable relish cups are very helpful in a piercing studio. Keep some at your front counter and ask clients to place their previously worn jewelry in one. This will avoid contaminating the counter and can be used to sterilize the jewelry without contaminating the main container of jewelry disinfectant. Remember, this type of sterilization is generally fine for jewelry that will be inserted in the same person, but jewelry that has been worn by someone other than the piercee cannot be adequately sterilized by Madacide alone; it must be autoclaved before being reused.

These cups are also handy for single-use quantities of liquid supplies, such as gentian violet, 70% alcohol, marking ink, benzalkonium chloride, and mouthwash. This prevents contamination of the main stock.

Corks

Batches of corks can be placed in large sterilization bags then autoclaved. These can then be stored. As needed, open a bag and place the contents in one of your glass or stainless steel storage jars for easy access. Once autoclaved touch them only with sterile implements or freshly gloved hands.

When performing a clamped piercing corks, provide something solid to support the tissue during the piercing process and to receive the needle. They are also used to shield the needle point while the needle is still in a piercing and thus minimize the risk of a needle stick.

Corks are sold in various grades. Select firm, smooth ones. A crumbly or wobbly cork can lead to a needle stick. Corks are used on only one person and then discarded.

ers are contaminated, autoclave what you can and disinfect the rest. Refill with clean supplies.

Exam Table Paper

This is a paper made especially to cover your exam or massage table. Changing it between clients helps keep your table clean. The paper comes in rolls in several widths and can be purchased from a surgical or dental supply house.

The same paper can be used to cover the surface of your piercing equipment table.

Tissues

Boxes of facial tissues are a boon to cleanliness and an absolute necessity in any piercing establishment. When you are marking a piercing, tissues make great erasers. Fold the tissue in quarters, then roll it into a small, tight, pointed cone. Dip this point into 70% alcohol and remove excess or stray ink. If you anticipate erasing, include a disposable relish cup of alcohol and several tissues in your tray setup.

When people have oral piercings, they tend to drool. You may want to designate a "drool patrol" individual (a coworker, friend of the piercee, or the piercee him/herself) and send them to thoroughly wash their hands with antibacterial soap. Have them wear a pair of fresh latex gloves, and give them several tissues with which to catch any drool that may occur.

Tissues can also be used to pick up things you wouldn't want to touch with your bare hands (as long as the thing isn't wet), they can hold calipers and other dry tools awaiting sterilization, and they spare the need for changing gloves if you need to open a door, close a faucet, switch on or adjust a light. Again, it is important to use a fresh one each time, and it is always better to use too many than to use too few. Keep boxes of tissues everywhere in your studio. In the front area, ask clients to place their previously worn jewelry on one instead of the counter. In the bathroom, they can be used to turn off faucets and open doors. In the piercing room, they can staunch blood from a new piercing, hold piercing equipment (both clean and dirty), and open drawers to retrieve sterile implements. Remember that once tissues have come into contact with contaminants, they are contaminated. Throw them away immediately; handle them with gloves if necessary, but don't touch the contaminated surface.

Sometimes it may be necessary to discard a box of tissues. If a box has been sitting open in a dusty or dirty environment or if it should become soaked with contaminated liquid, throw it out. Again, the risk outweighs the insignificant cost.

Rubber Bands

Small rubber bands about an inch in diameter are a staple in every piercing room. Soak for five to ten minutes in 70% alcohol or hard-surface disinfectant, air dry, then store in a lidded glass or stainless steel container. Rubber bands, once cleaned and stored, are handled only with a pair of sterile hemostats or freshly gloved hands since they will be touched during the piercing and should be as free of organisms as possible.

Rubber bands are used to adjust the grip of forceps used for piercing. They must be removed from the forceps between sterilizations. Use a rubber band during only one piercing session then discard it.

Rubber bands are also used to secure a bandage around the penis after a Prince Albert piercing.

Cotton Swabs

Cotton swabs such as Q-tips serve a variety of purposes. They can be used to clean in tight areas such as nostrils, to clean up after a bleeding incident, or to apply topical anesthetic prior to a PA piercing. You will find them both sterile or just clean. For our purposes it doesn't much matter which we use but it is important to keep them as clean as possible. Remove them from their packaging wearing fresh gloves, and place them directly into a lidded jar. Some medical supply houses carry wood-handled swabs with very small heads which, when dipped in rubbing alcohol, can be used as an "eraser" during the marking process.

Gauze Pads

Gauze pads fill a multitude of purposes; bandaging and protecting new piercings, drying the tongue prior to piercing, and holding wet areas are only a few of them.

Adhesive Tape

Cloth surgical tape is used to apply gauze pads, and to cover the rough surfaces of pliers and other sharp-edged tools.

Bandaids

Always useful, Bandaids can serve many purposes. Try one on a nipple piercing that wants to bleed a little. Use also to pad the rough surfaces of pliers to protect jewelry.

Disposable Latex Gloves

No responsible piercer would consider working without the protection of latex gloves. They protect the piercer from contact with blood products and also help keep the piercing area and equipment as close to sterile as possible.

Latex gloves are available powdered or unpowdered, in several sizes, styles, and brands, and, of course, quality. Experiment to find the glove that is right for you. They should afford maximum protection, comfort, and dexterity.

Many gloves are microporous to one degree or another depending on the thickness of the latex and quality of the glove. This means that there are microscopic holes through which some microbes can potentially pass. For this reason, many lab and healthcare workers choose to "double-bag", i.e. wear two pair of gloves, one inside the other. This can limit ones dexterity while doing a piercing. Consequently, you may prefer to wear only one pair for work requiring precision but use two pairs of gloves when doing other things: taking out the trash, cleaning the autoclave, etc. Also develop the habit of scrubbing your hands using antibacterial soap or surgical scrub before and after wearing gloves.

In cultivating your sterility awareness, it is also important to develop the habit of putting on a fresh pair of gloves before you handle anything that has been sterilized or disinfected. Change your gloves as often as necessary. If you're all set to do a piercing and you simply must blow your nose, go ahead and do it, but do it away from the piercee and your equipment, AND put on a clean pair of gloves before you proceed. Sure you may need to use a lot of gloves during the course of a busy day, but they don't cost more than 50 cents a pair, and you can't put a price on your and your client's well being. It's much easier to contaminate something with a single touch than one might think. So make the frequent and conscious changing of your gloves a religious habit.

• CLEANING AGENTS

Bleach

Common household bleach is an inexpensive, effective disinfectant for which the piercer can find many uses. A solution of 10% bleach and 90% water

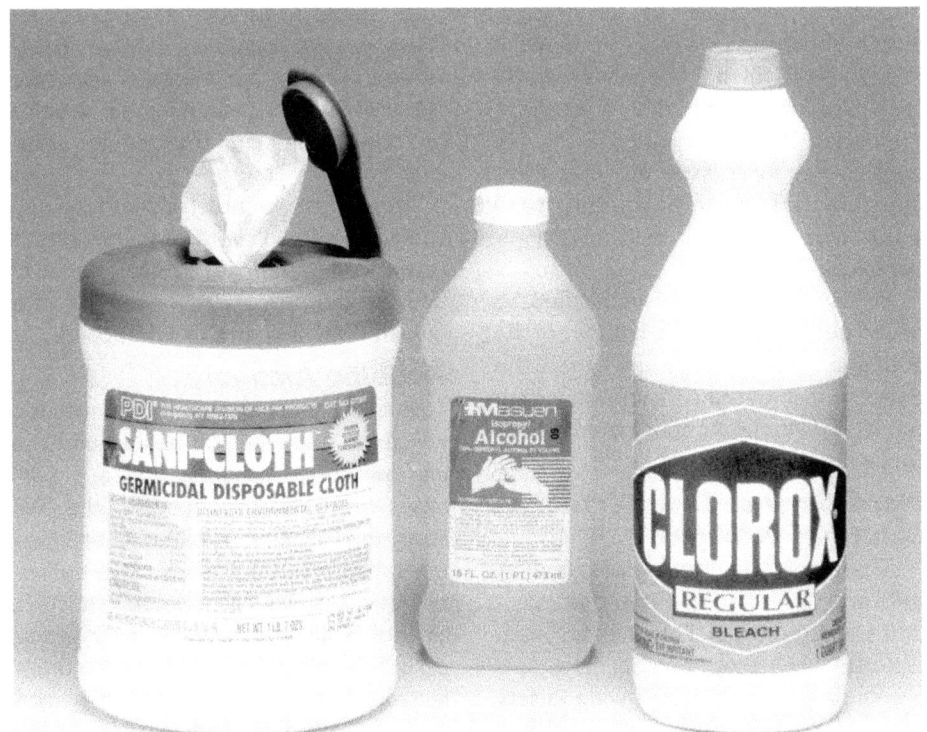

Right: common hard-surface disinfectants.

Left: popular antibacterial soaps and cleaning agents for both hand washing and piercing aftercare.

of alcohol as a cleanser would be swabbing a pair of calipers or a gauge wheel with 70% alcohol for one full minute after it had been in contact with completely unbroken skin or uncontaminated jewelry. It can also be used on a folded tissue or a cotton swab to erase or adjust piercing placement marks.

Keep a small container of 70% alcohol on your "sterile field." Be sure that the alcohol can be accessed without touching the container. Touch the top only with a brand new tissue, never with a used tissue or cotton swab. If you anticipate using any amount of alcohol, pour some into a disposable plastic relish cup as part of your setup.

There is a 70% alcohol gel which may be used as a prep scrub when the sink and antibacterial scrub are unavailable. In this case, vigorous scrubbing with the gel for one full minute is required. This method should be reserved for emergency situations when you can't clean with water and antibacterial scrub.

Hydrogen Peroxide

Though not recommended for general use in the piercing room, in some very specific cases, hydrogen peroxide can be quite helpful. These cases might include cleansing an infected or keloided piercing of any matter (although usually there are more effective options), cleansing jewelry of densely crusted matter before removal, or occasionally stopping persistent bleeding. Hydrogen peroxide is available in liquid and gel form; both can be helpful to piercers, but do NOT use the high percentage liquid used as hair bleach.

Jewelry Disinfectant

New jewelry and jewelry which will be reused on the same individual must be soaked in a surgical disinfectant before insertion. The product preferred by Gauntlet is Madacide. It is a hard-surface, biodegradable disinfectant. A five to 10 minute soak in Madacide will kill any airborne bacteria lingering on the surface of the jewelry. Be sure that the Madacide is completely dried off

makes an excellent hard-surface cleaner. According to current medical standards, the surface must be aggressively scrubbed with this solution and allowed to remain in contact with the surface for 10 full minutes for it to be considered effective. Any matter stubbornly adhering to the surface should be completely removed before the bleach treatment.

It is also advisable to keep a small, disposable container of full-strength bleach in the piercing room to be used in the event of an accidental needle stick. Use it once only, then discard.

Diluted bleach rapidly loses its potency. For this reason, mix up only as much bleach solution as you can use in a few days, and store it in an airtight container.

Bleach can become contaminated, so never pour used bleach back into the container. Also remember that the outer surface of the container of bleach can also become contaminated. Don't touch it with dirty gloves or dirty hands.

Hard-Surface Disinfectant Solutions & Wipes

There are many brands of commercial hard-surface solutions and disinfectant saturated wipes. Designed for institutional use, they contain chemical agents proven to destroy a wide variety of bacteria and viruses. The label will usually tell you which ones. Hard-surface cleaners can generally be used in place of bleach. They work much faster than bleach but must still remain in contact with the surface for one to five minutes. Read the label for exact instructions. Again, be sure the surface is free of any matter.

Commercial hard-surface disinfectant wipes are very convenient for quick sterilization of surfaces and non-autoclavable tools such as calipers and gauge wheels. However, neither hard-surface cleaners nor bleach is adequate sterilization for contaminated jewelry or other implements that require autoclaving.

Neither bleach nor hard-surface disinfectants should ever come into direct contact with human tissue. They will break down protein, of which the human body is primarily composed.

Rubbing Alcohol

Rubbing alcohol is a mild antiseptic which has a number of uses around the piercing room. Ironically, for our purposes it is most effective only in the 70% strength. Higher or lower concentrations render the alcohol much less effective as a cleaning agent. In any strength, alcohol is an inferior cleanser in comparison to bleach or hard surface disinfectants, but is safe for use on human tissue. An example of an appropriate use the jewelry before insertion; though it may be environmentally friendly, it is not something you want to put into the bloodstream.

Madacide is adequate sterilization for jewelry that has not been worn, or for jewelry that is being installed into the same person who has worn it previously (remember not to put previously worn jewelry into your main dish of Madacide!), but it may not be strong enough to kill all the harmful organisms which could be present on a piece of jewelry that has been worn by someone other than the person who will now be wearing it. Such jewelry must first be autoclaved, then placed in a dish of Madacide.

Always ask where jewelry has been before handling and installing it, and always err on the side of caution. Better to make someone wait 45 minutes while the autoclave runs its cycle, than to send that person to the hospital with hepatitis or worse. Many customers will insist that the jewelry was last worn 10 years ago by their aging mother, or was worn by the person with whom they already share bodily fluids. It doesn't matter where the jewelry came from or who has been wearing it; it must be autoclaved before being inserted in another person's body. Period.

Antibacterial Hand Soaps

Check out the shelves of your local pharmacy or supermarket and you will discover a variety of antibacterial soaps. Most, such as Dial Antibacterial, Lever 2000, Softsoap, Johnson & Johnson's No More Germies, and Almay's Unscented contain the chemical triclosan. A few others are povidone iodine based (Clearly Natural and Betadine surgical scrub), and some have chlorhexidine gluconate as the active ingredient (Brian Care and Hibiclens). Since you will be washing your hands approximately 20 or 30 times in the course of an average day, it is important to find something mild and effective. A few people will experience a reaction to one or more of these chemical agents, especially chlorhexidine gluconate. The fragrance in some will bother others. Experiment to find the one that is most compatible with you.

Many of these products come in a dispenser bottle. If yours does not, put it in one. This will prevent contamination of the soap from direct contact with your hands.

Povidone-Iodine Solution

Betadine and other generic brand, povidone-iodine solutions are used extensively for cleaning skin in preparation for piercing. These will be familiar to any healthcare or veterinary workers who come into your shop. A few people are allergic to Betadine—they are also frequently allergic to shellfish—so always ask before using it.

Povidone-Iodine is available in a variety of products and forms. For our purposes use the 10% solution. Because certain types of bacteria can grow in it when it is stored in large quantities, purchase individually packaged wipes or swabs. This will also reduce the chances of cross-contamination.

When stocking your room with these or any other packaged supplies, always wear a fresh pair of gloves.

Benzalkonium Chloride

Benzalkonium Chloride, the active ingredient in many above-the-neck aftercare solutions, is also available in individually packaged wipes. This is ideal for piercing room use. Make it a habit to include one swab with every piercing setup. It can be used to clean up after a bleeding incident, or to remove most of the povidone-iodine after a piercing.

Bacitracin

Bacitracin ointment contains an antibiotic suspended in a petroleum jelly base. It has a variety of purposes but is mainly used to lubricate needles and insertion tapers. There are other ointments containing several antibiotics, including Neomycin to which many people are allergic. This makes Bacitracin safer for general use, but always inquire if a client has allergies to any antibiotic. If so use povidone-iodine ointment unless that too is an allergen. You only need a very tiny amount to get the job done; larger quantities result in messy, greasy and potentially irritated piercings.

The tube containing the Bacitracin can easily be contaminated by a careless piercer or uninformed piercee. Touch the tube only with freshly washed hands, squeeze out a small amount on to a clean tissue, and touch only the Bacitracin you have squeezed out.

Anesthetic Ointment

A very few piercings, primarily Prince Alberts, can be numbed with an over-the-counter topical anesthetic such as Xylocaine 2.5%. Store the tube in a plastic baggie with the cap securely sealed, and handle only with fresh gloves and a new, clean cotton swab.

• MARKING MATERIALS

Marking Pens

Felt tip marking pens are often used to mark piercings. The fine-tip Sharpie is preferred by many piercers. It contains alcohol. This helps keep the tip of the pen adequately clean as long as it comes into contact only with unbroken, disinfected skin. If the point comes in contact with broken skin, a mucous membrane, or an area that has not been thoroughly swabbed with Betadine or other effective antiseptic, it must be discarded. The pen must also be discarded if touched with unwashed, bare hands or contaminated gloves.

Toothpicks

When dipped in India ink toothpicks can be used as an alternative to a Sharpie marker. They are also used with gentian violet for marking oral piercings. Like corks, they should be autoclaved, then stored in a lidded container. Handle only with freshly gloved hands or sterile hemostats.

Gentian Violet

Gentian violet is a bright purple liquid used to treat thrush, a yeast infection of the throat common to children and immunosuppressed people. A sterilized toothpick moistened with it is used by piercers to mark the tongue, lip, and other wet areas that repel ink. Gentian Violet is very quick to stain; it stays on skin for two or three days, and will almost never come out of a carpet or other fabric. For this reason, keep the bottle tightly capped. You may even want to store the bottle in a plastic bag.

Never dispense Gentian Violet, or any other liquid, directly from the bottle onto the piercee. Always pour a few drops into a disposable plastic relish cup.

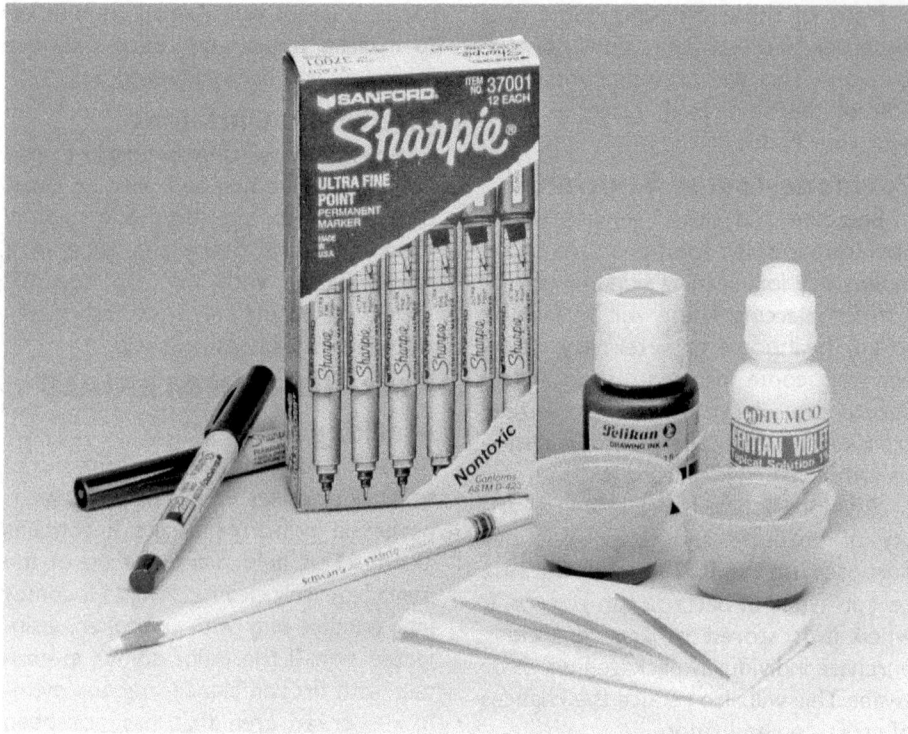

• IMPLEMENTS & TOOLS

Stainless Steel Ware

You will want several lidded glass or stainless steel containers and/or jars on your piercing equipment table in which to stock some of your disposable piercing supplies such as corks, rubber bands, cotton swabs, etc. You will also want a small, shallow stainless steel tray so that before each piercing you will have something on which to lay out the materials you will be using. Wipe it down with a hard-surface disinfectant and line it with a dental bib before each use.

Dial Calipers

Dial calipers are used in many technical fields for accurate measuring purposes. They are absolutely essential behind ones jewelry counter and in the piercing room. While highly precise (and very expensive) metal ones are available, the nonporous plastic ones are much more appropriate. We aren't rocket scientists. Use them at the counter to measure jewelry diameters, lengths, and widths. In the piercing room they can be used to precisely match marks.

Right: **measuring devices— gauge wheel, circle template, and calipers.**

Calipers are made to a variety of measurement systems: thousandths of an inch, fractions of an inch, and millimeters. In the US we prefer the style whose dial measures in fractions of an inch. It happens to also have thousandths of an inch marks on the dial and millimeters along the upper edge which make it very versatile. American piercing jewelry is usually sold in diameters and lengths in increments of $1/8''$ or $1/16''$.

When using calipers be aware of what they touch before, during, and after contact with potential contaminants. Plastic calipers cannot be autoclaved. If they contact broken skin or contaminated jewelry or objects, change your gloves and clean the calipers thoroughly with bleach or hard-surface disinfectant.

Gauge Wheels

Piercing jewelry is not only measured in diameters and lengths but in thickness also. Though some jewelry is manufactured in fractions of an inch, most is sold in gauges. Consequently gauge wheels are essential equipment. With them you can measure the gauge, or thickness, of a piece of jewelry, a needle, or an insertion taper. Gauge wheels are usually made of steel (not stainless, unfortunately) and so, after a certain number of trips through the autoclave or soaks in bleach or other disinfectants, they will need to be replaced.

Be aware that there are several different gauge systems for measuring different things. For jewelry we use Brown & Sharpe gauges.

Artist's Circle Template

Used to measure ampallangs, apadravyas, and healed frenums for properly fitting jewelry.

Hair Clips

A piercee's hair can easily contaminate the freshly disinfected piercing area. Keep some disinfected hair clips handy to pin their hair out of your way before you get started. Be sure to clean

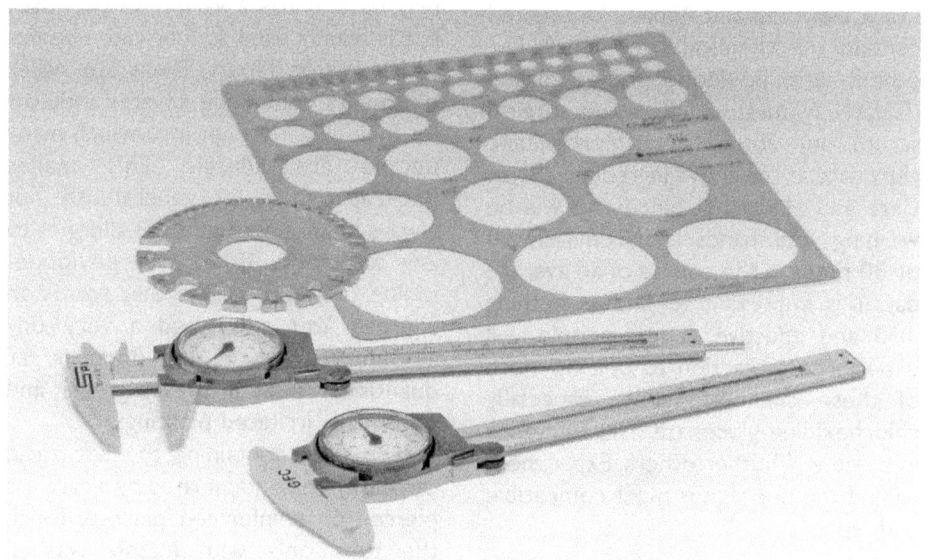

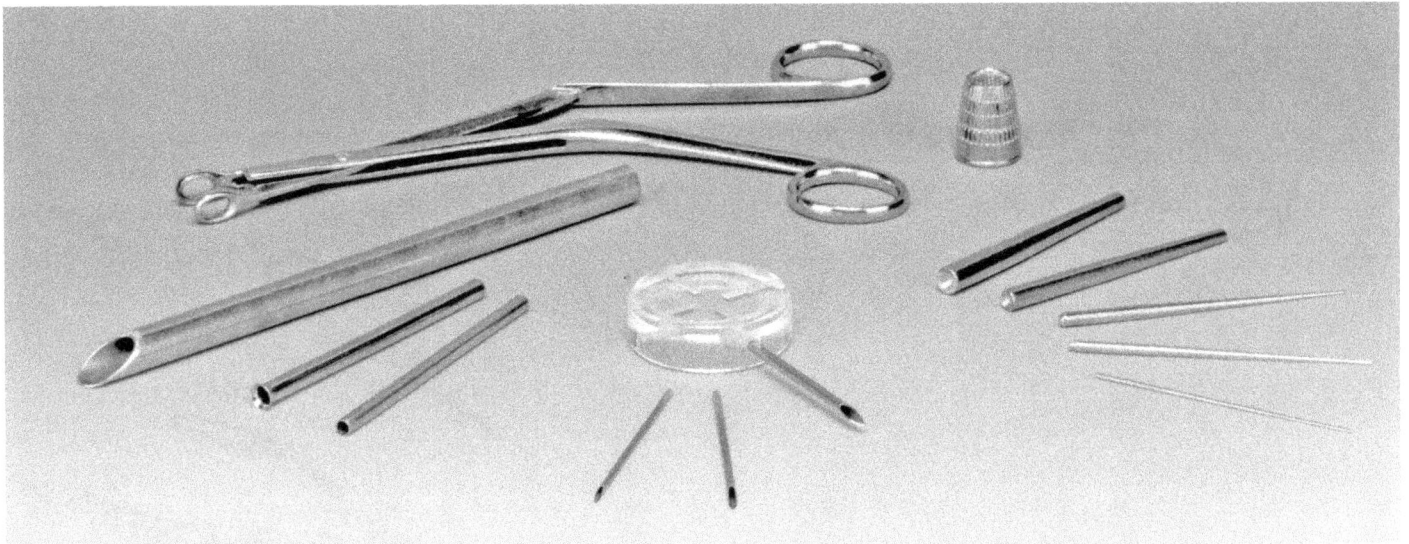

More piercing tools and implements, clockwise from top: "navel" forceps; thimble; insertion tapers; piercing needles and needle pusher; needle receiving tubes and nostril tube.

them between every use. People carry odd things around in their hair, and you don't want to pass them around.

Scissors or Hair Clippers

Dealing with hair is just part of every piercer's day. When preparing for genital piercings and male nipple piercings you may very well need to do a little bit of trimming to get body hair out of your way. This will make marking and clamping more easy and improve the hygiene of the area. Small scissors may be used or electric clippers. Moustache clippers are especially handy.

Forceps

There are many different styles of forceps, all with specialized shapes to make particular piercings easier. These are the most common styles:

Pennington Forceps:

Next to piercing needles, these forceps with the triangular openings at the end of their jaws, are the most commonly used instrument in the piercing studio. They are manufactured in a variety of sizes, each with its own particular uses. Everyone will gravitate to their particular favorites. Quality varies greatly as does price. For general, daily use the inexpensive Pakistani forceps will be more than adequate, but with experience you will find certain situations require the superior characteristics of the German instruments. These, alas, can be quite expensive, but it is worthwhile to at least have a few pair available in the studio for those particular occasions. Here are some of the

various types of Pennington forceps and their most common applications.

1. *Regular*—The openings of these vary from almost equilateral to elongated isosceles triangles. Measurements usually range between ³⁄₈″ and ½″. Used for most nipple, earlobe, lip, and genital piercings.

2. *Mini*—Exactly like Regulars, but with a much smaller triangular head, Minis are used where larger forceps would be awkward or impractical. Most navels, eyebrows, tragi, clits, and clit hoods, and many male nipples, require the use of a Mini.

3. *Small German & Matte Pakistani*—Similar to minis, but vastly superior, are the German and matte-surfaced smaller forceps. The long, narrow, serrated jaws of these assure a secure, comfortable grip. Some experienced piercers would never perform a difficult, precise piercing such as a clit without a small German or a matte Pakistani.

One important note about minis of all varieties: When using them, always manually check before piercing, to be absolutely certain that the gauge of needle you have selected is not larger than the opening in the forceps. This is

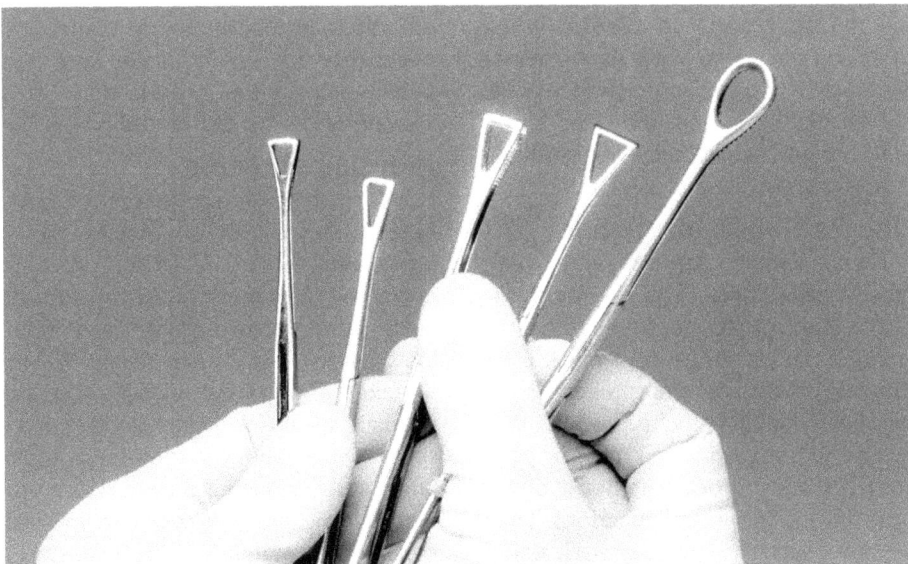

Left: the most commonly used forceps. The first four are Penningtons, mini, small German, matte Pakistani, and regular German. Last is a pair of sponge forceps.

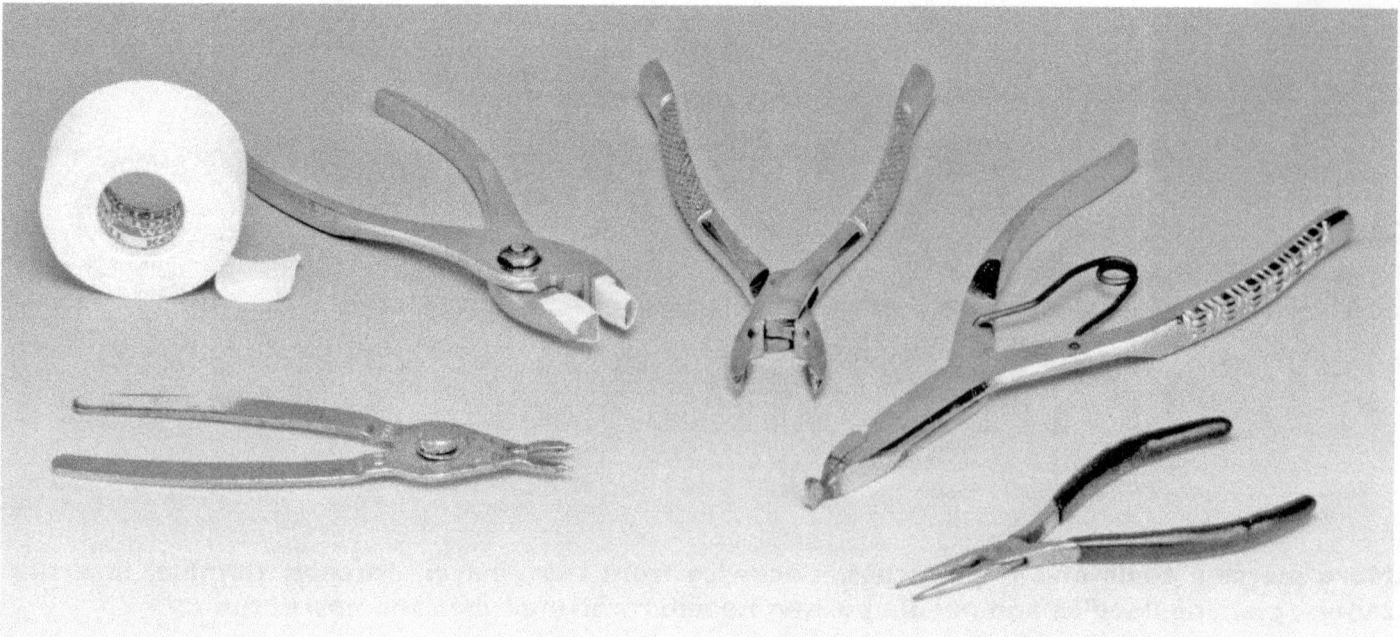

Various types of pliers: left to right, small ring-expanding pliers, regular pliers with their jaws taped with surgical tape, ring closing (hog ring) pliers, large ring-expanding pliers, round needle-nose pliers.

a dreadful, embarrassing, messy, and painful happening for all involved, and is best avoided.

"Navel" Forceps

In a surgical instrument catalog these are actually called "septum cutting forceps." They are preferred by some piercers because they have a slight angle to the jaws and a smallish, oval head. Before they can be used for piercing, the sharp cutting edge must be filed or ground down. Most people do perfectly well with minis that have had the outside angles rounded.

Tongue (Sponge) Forceps

The tongue is second only to the heart as the strongest muscle in the human body and often requires a little taming prior to piercing. The best tool for the task is a large, thick-bodied pair of sponge forceps with an extremely large round or oval head and somewhat larger serrations than usual.

Hemostats & Needle Holders

Many of us who came of age in the 60's remember hemostats as roach clips. No longer confined to hospitals and head shops, they are useful pieces of equipment in the piercing room. Along with needle holders (not to be confused with needle pushers) they come in very handy for grasping small things your hands can't get a secure grip

on and for picking up sterile and clean items. Use them to close tiny rings, screw or unscrew the tiny balls on some jewelry.

Needle Pushers

These are round lucite discs about 1¼" in diameter with a series of holes drilled into the circumference. The holes are sized to comfortably fit 16, 14, 12, and 10 gauge needles. Held securely in the palm of your hand, they can improve your chances of getting a needle through especially tough tissue. Of course, like all reusable implements, needle pushers must be autoclaved between uses. Sometimes the needle will conduct blood into the disc. When this occurs, you may want to throw the disc away. Although autoclaving will kill any harmful organisms, the dried blood will probably never come out resulting in an unsightly piece of equipment.

Needle Receiving Tubes

Prince Albert, septum, and some other freehand piercings require a different approach. To meet these requirements Gauntlet designed, manufactures, and sells needle receiving tubes. These are short stainless steel tubes with one flared end (mostly for septums) or plain (for PA's and vertical clit hood piercings). NRT's fill several functions. They can be inserted where no cork could

ever go, and during the piercing process they first support the tissue then guide the needle point safely clear of the area. NRT's can be bagged and autoclaved just like other tools.

Nostril Tubes

These are specialized NRT's designed just for nostril piercings. Although some piercers use mini Pennington forceps for nostril piercings, most prefer the nostril tube which better protects the inside of the nose. About 8 inches long, approximately ½" in diameter, it is beveled at one end to fit snugly against the inside of the nostril. This tool, too, is a substitute for a cork, which would be difficult to maneuver inside someone's nose. As with NRT's, make sure the needle point is well outside the nostril area before removing the tube.

Piercing Needles

Without these you're out of business. There are many sources for piercing needles these days, so you probably don't have to worry. You'll hear a lot of fancy terms thrown around like "double-beveled" and "super-sharp." Don't be taken in by all the rhetoric. Let the product speak for itself. Buy a few in several sizes and try them out. You'll know soon enough if they measure up.

You may find sources that will sell you piercing needles in bulk, unsteril-

ATTENTION! THIS DOCUMENT IS FOR HISTORIC REFERENCE ONLY!

ized. They may appear cheaper than the prepackaged, presterilized needles, but are you actually saving money when you add in you time and the cost of packaging materials? Improper packaging can result in dull needles, and needle sticks are a risk.

Depending upon vendor, needles can be purchased from 18 gauge to 8 gauge and thicker. We strongly urge you NOT to do new piercings with a needle smaller than 18 gauge or larger than 10. As you gain experience you will understand the reasons for this admonition.

And like all sterilized equipment, new piercing needles should only be handled with freshly gloved hands, sterile hemostats, or needle holders.

While it is theoretically possible to resterilize and reuse piercing needles, DON'T! First of all they get dull rather quickly. Secondly, the time involved in cleaning them properly and resterilizing them, not to mention the risk of needle sticks, makes it not worthwhile. Dispose of them in a sharps container.

• *Insertion Tapers*

Very useful tools for the piercer and piercee, insertion tapers are blunt, tapered needles 3″ to 4″ long in a wide range of gauges. They serve two main functions. When someone has left their jewelry out for a while, the piercing has a tendency to shrink or close up. The blunt point of a taper can often reopen and stretch such a piercing which might otherwise be lost. Tapers are also useful for enlarging piercings so thicker jewelry can be worn.

Thimbles

These are absolutely wonderful for novice and experienced piercer alike as protection from accidental needle sticks. They are used to hold the cork, providing protection against today's super sharp needles especially when performing a piercing where forceful pressure or some angling of the needle into the cork is required. If the needle should happen to penetrate the cork, your fingers would be protected by the thimble. Be sure the cork fits snugly inside the thimble or get a thimble that tightly fits your corks. And always autoclave thimbles between uses. Remove the cork first!

Monofilament Nylon

Most nurserys and hardware stores carry heavy gauge, monofilament nylon, weed trimmer line. This is useful in the piercing room for several purposes. You will occasionally have clients with metal sensitivities whose only hope for a successful piercing is to insert a piece of this nylon line, shape it into a circle and fuse the ends together. There are also some of the newer, less stable piercings which have a greater chance of success when this approach is used.

Matches or Lighter

Use these to fuse the ends of monofilament nylon retainers.

Pliers

You will encounter many different types of pliers, of all sizes, shapes, and materials. If you can find them, purchase stainless steel tools because those made of regular steel or other metals ususally must be discarded after a number of trips through the autoclave or immersion in disinfectants. Autoclaves can also melt or damage the rubber handle coatings of many tools.

1. *Standard Pliers*—These tools, the archetypal "pair of pliers," are used in sets to twist and open 12 gauge and thicker gauge rings. Use them to loosen tight balls on straight and circular barbells. Always pad them with several layers of surgical tape.

2. *Ring-Expanding Pliers*—Pliers which, when squeezed expand outwards. When placed inside a ring, the notches near the end of the jaws spread and open the ring. For large gauge rings use the type of pliers sold by Gauntlet. Take care not to get the ring out of round. You may need to rotate the jewelry to contact with the pliers at several points for even expansion.

3. *Snap Ring Pliers*—You will find these in automotive supply stores. They are a scaled-down version of ring-expanding pliers with two narrow, notched protrusions which hold the ring securely in place while expanding its diameter. Do not use them on rings thicker than 10 gauge.

4. *Hog Ring Pliers*—These can be quite difficult to locate. Gauntlet carries one style of many. Snap-on Tools manufactures several excellent, if expensive, styles. You may also check with an upholstery supply company. These pliers have grooved jaws which hold the ring while closing down its diameter. Again, care must be taken not to distort the ring when you are closing it.

5. Needle-Nose Pliers—Several types exist, some with flat jaws, some with round, some with one of each. The latter two are ideal for bending nostril screws. Many have often-useful wire cutters at the base of the jaws.

Files

Used to smooth the rough edges of a trimmed nostril screw. Remember that files are as subject to cross-contamination as every other tool.

Nail Clippers & Surgical Scissors

To remove nylon monofilament retainers, it is sometimes necessary to use nailclippers or small surgical scissors. Obviously, these should ideally be made of stainless steel since they must be autoclaved after every use.

• *Ammonia Inhalers*

Although you hopefully won't ever have to use one, keep a few of these at hand for fainters.

THE WELL-EQUIPPED SHOPPING LIST

• FURNISHINGS

- ❑ Piercing Table/Chair
- ❑ Armless Chair, preferably with casters
- ❑ Bright, adjustable light
- ❑ Lidded trash receptacle with foot pedal
- ❑ Wall-mounted mirror
- ❑ Hand mirror
- ❑ Shelves (at least 2)
- ❑ Coat hook
- ❑ Implement storage with flat surface & drawers

• STERILIZATION EQUIPMENT & SUPPLIES

- ❑ Autoclave
- ❑ Ultrasonic cleaner
- ❑ Sterilization bags
- ❑ Sterilization tubing
- ❑ Autoclave tape
- ❑ Sharps containers
- ❑ Implement trays
- ❑ Spore tests

• PAPER GOODS & SIMILIAR SUPPLIES

- ❑ Exam table paper
- ❑ Tissues
- ❑ Dental bibs
- ❑ Disposable relish cups
- ❑ Corks
- ❑ Rubber bands
- ❑ Cotton swabs
- ❑ Gauze pads
- ❑ Adhesive tape
- ❑ Bandaids
- ❑ Disposable latex gloves

• VARIOUS CLEANING AGENTS

- ❑ Bleach
- ❑ Hard-surface disinfectant (solutions and wipes)
- ❑ Rubbing alcohol (70%)

- ❑ Hydrogen peroxide
- ❑ Jewelry disinfectant (Madacide)
- ❑ Antibacterial hand soap
- ❑ Povidone-iodine wipes in individual packets
- ❑ Benzalkonium chloride in individual packets
- ❑ Bacitracin ointment
- ❑ Anesthetic ointment (Xylocaine 2.5%)

• MARKING IMPLEMENTS & SUPPLIES

- ❑ Marking pens (Sharpie fine tip) or
- ❑ India ink
- ❑ Toothpicks
- ❑ Gentian violet

• IMPLEMENTS & TOOLS

- ❑ Stainless steel ware: trays, containers, jars
- ❑ Dial calipers
- ❑ Gauge wheels
- ❑ Artist's circle template
- ❑ Hair clips
- ❑ Hair clippers or scissors
- ❑ Pennington forceps in various sizes & styles
- ❑ Sponge forceps
- ❑ Hemostats
- ❑ Needle holders
- ❑ Needle receiving tubes both flared and plain
- ❑ Nostril tubes
- ❑ Pliers of various styles
- ❑ Sterile piercing needles
- ❑ Needle pushers
- ❑ Insertion tapers
- ❑ Thimbles
- ❑ Monofilament nylon line
- ❑ Matches or disposable lighters
- ❑ Nail clippers or surgical scissors
- ❑ Ammonia inhalers

Chapter 3

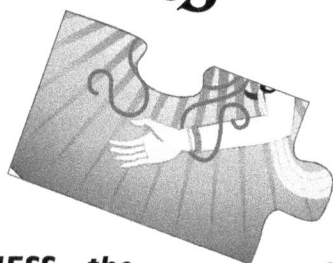

✦ Hygiene, Cleanliness, & Sterility

• AWARENESS—the Cornerstone of Safety

Everything in life involves some kind of risk. With piercing that risk can be significantly higher than many other activities. Piercers work with needles and around bodily fluids, a potentially deadly combination unless some basic rules are followed and and precautions taken. If you are not constantly on your toes you can easily compromise the health and well-being of both yourself and your client. We have seen a piercer become so lost in conversation with his client that cleanliness and sterility were completely forgotten. Such a person is a menace. Anyone who is easily distracted, forgetful, or who loses their train of thought easily, should consider another profession.

• CLEANLINESS—It Can Mean Life or Death!

We live in an ocean of air, and that ocean teems with life. Every cubic millimeter is inhabited by billions of microscopic organisms. They are in every breath we take, in everything we eat and drink, on everything we touch. Fortunately, the majority are either benign or easily dealt with by our immune systems. Still, there are more than enough that can cause illness or even death if they gain entrance into our bodies. Since these organisms can be present anywhere, it is essential that we prevent them from gaining access to peoples bodies through their piercings.

It is of the utmost importance that you, your surroundings, and every piece of your equipment be as scrupulously clean as possible. From a piercee's standpoint, the prospect of being punctured in a disorganized, dirty environment, by a messy, grubby piercer, using tools that appear unsterile, is a quite justifiable cause for alarm. You will (and should) be judged by potential piercees on your appearance and on the condition of, not only of your piercing area, but of your bathroom, waiting area, carpeted surfaces, and other environments not directly piercing-related as well. No one will get to see your sparkling clean piercing room if the disorder of your front area has chased them out the door in search of cleaner premises.

Many people ask their doctors to pierce them because they have heard of or have encountered unsanitary conditions at so-called professional studios. While they may be avoiding disease transmission in doing this, most doctors have not been specifically trained to perform piercings, and frequently install inappropriate jewelry in piercings that are frequently too shallow, too deep, or crooked.

Of course, the vast majority of people have so little consciousness of bacteria and cross-contamination that they will allow themselves to be pierced by incredibly unscrupulous persons operating out of ignorance and greed. Gauntlet has heard numerous reports of people being pierced on street corners, in public toilets, in bar back rooms, hair salons, and over the counter of retail stores. We have also heard of many incidents where people allowed themselves to be pierced with forceps that had just been used to pierce someone else, with needles that had been dropped on the ground at a street fair, with nonsterilizable plastic piercing guns, or after being given tranquilizers, anesthetics, or alcohol by the piercer. As a profession we should be fostering awareness of proper hygiene and technique in our piercees so they can avoid irresponsible and dangerous piercers. The craft of piercing is not, and should not be, a jealously guarded secret. This leads to the proliferation of the incidents listed above. As we discuss the requirements for setting up a safe piercing area, you will gain a clearer understanding of the risks involved if you operate under hazardous and unsanitary conditions.

It is, above all, the responsibility of all piercers to operate at all times with the ideals of safety, professionalism, and sterility in mind, regardless of what the general public may or may not know about these ideals. Keeping yourself, your studio, and your equipment looking clean will impress your clientele, but if you are not religiously utilizing clean/sterile technique, you are a discredit to the profession.

SUMMARY —
1. Every part of your establishment must always be exceptionally clean.
2. Although most people will not be aware of what constitutes proper piercing technique, it is the responsibility of all piercers to adhere to the highest standards at all times.

• MEET YOUR ENEMY

Why is cleanliness so important? While it is hoped that the answer to this question should be self evident to the readers of this manual, at least in its broadest application, take a few minutes to examine it in greater detail.

There is scarcely a cubic millimeter on this planet that isn't populated by billions of microscopic residents: bacteria and viruses and infinitesimal particles of inorganic matter. They are literally everywhere. Even though we bathe, our bodies are covered with them. They are on everything we touch. Fortunately, for us, the majority of them are harmless. However, if an opening into the bloodstream is made available to them, some organisms can quickly take advantage of the opportunity, take up residence, and procreate. Piercings, abrasions, paper cuts—any opening of the skin—can cre-

Mugshots from the Piercer's Most Unwanted List

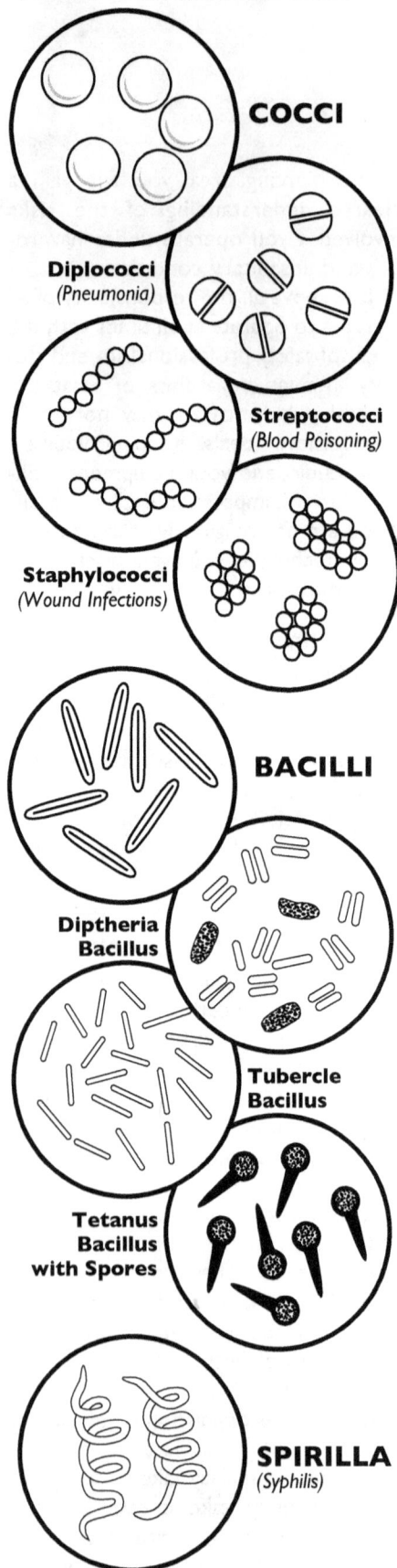

COCCI

Diplococci
(Pneumonia)

Streptococci
(Blood Poisoning)

Staphylococci
(Wound Infections)

BACILLI

Diptheria Bacillus

Tubercle Bacillus

Tetanus Bacillus with Spores

SPIRILLA
(Syphilis)

ate an opportunity for infection. Some of these unwanted guests can, at worst, merely cause temporary discomfort for their hosts, but others can be seriously debilitating or even fatal. Obviously, we want to eliminate these entities from any environment where human tissue is purposely punctured.

Bacteria are tiny, one-celled microorganisms with characteristics of both plants and animals. There are hundreds of different types, but the three most common forms are cocci, bacilli, and spirilla. All bacteria are so small they can only be seen with a powerful microscope. Bacteria are either classified as non-pathogenic (harmless), or pathogenic (harmful). Nonpathogenic bacteria are far more numerous, and many perform important functions in the human body, assisting with digestion, and, in some instances, actually destroying harmful bacteria on or in our bodies.

Although classified as harmless, nonpathogenic bacteria, can still create problems in a new piercing. Any foreign body which finds its way into an opening in the skin slows the healing process by diverting the attentions of the immune system. Even though they are nonpathogenic, our white blood cells will perceive them as invaders and send out the order to attack. This diversion of our immune resources can thus provide an opportunity for invasion by more pathogenic organisms.

Pathogenic bacteria are less numerous, but can inconvenience, sicken, or even kill their hosts. These harmful organisms are classified as parasites, because they require living matter for their growth and reproduction. We will discuss some of the diseases caused by them shortly.

Viruses are different than bacteria. These are submicroscopic bits of DNA—they cannot be seen with the average microscope—which invade living tissue and generate harmful toxins as they reproduce. Due to their near invisibility, the existence of viruses has only been known for a few years. Some viral diseases, such as the common cold, herpes, HIV, and hepatitis are well-known, but many have not even been classified yet, and scientists still have much to learn

about their makeup and behavior.

Unfortunately, it is impossible to completely rid the piercing environment of all bacteria and viruses. Even hospital operating rooms are not completely germ free. However, it is possible, with concentrated effort, to significantly reduce their numbers and all but eliminate the presence of pathogenic strains. Combined with knowledgeable sterile technique and sterile equipment, a scrupulously clean environment greatly minimizes the risk of bacterial and/or viral transmission.

• THE PIERCER'S MOST UNWANTED LIST

Let us introduce you to some of your individual enemies! They may be invisible to the naked eye, but the havoc they can wreak upon the human body makes them adversaries to be reckoned with.

Perhaps the most commonly occurring threat to cleanliness is the bacterium staphylococci. It can infiltrate the body during the piercing or any time thereafter (more on this later). Staph is commonly present in pustules, boils, abscesses, and most average surface infections. Some types of staph are becoming increasingly resistant to antibiotics, most notably the "flesh-eating" staph that received so much recent media attention.

Some of the other pathogenic organisms waiting for a host include those causing tetanus, tuberculosis, pneumonia, diphtheria, and sexually transmitted diseases. They need to be treated with respect and caution, but there is no need to fear them if you act as if everything is contaminated, practice awareness, and utilize clean technique at all times.

The news these days is filled with media coverage about HIV (human immunodeficiency virus) the alleged cause of the progressive disease known as AIDS (acquired immune deficiency syndrome). HIV is an extraordinarily fragile virus. It cannot survive for more than a few hours outside the human bloodstream, and is easily destroyed. Heat, cold, and many cleansers such as bleach or commercially available hard surface disinfectant wipes, will kill it outright. The virus may or may not be the cause of AIDS. This connection is currently under scrutiny and is being debated by some of the world's top authorities in microbiology and virology. In his book *Deadly Deception*, Robert E. Willner M.D., Ph.D has this to say, "It is astonishing and amazing that out of over 2,000 recorded needle sticks amongst health workers, only 20 became HIV-positive, and not one case of AIDS has yet to occur— and this is with direct inoculation! If one dies, look for evidence of drug use, particularly drug therapy with AZT (the drug used to treat AIDS)." Regardless, no responsible piercer would consider risking the transmission of this or any other potentially fatal organism.

Being a bloodborne pathogen, HIV cannot be transmitted through unbroken skin. The ways in which a piercer could possibly contract or transmit HIV are limited: only needle sticks and direct contact between contaminated fluids and mucous membranes or other broken skin would present a serious risk of transmission.

The mortality rate of people with AIDS is very high. To date, about 75% of people with full-blown AIDS die within three years. This does not necessarily mean that HIV infection is fatal—some scientists go so far as to say HIV is not the cause of AIDS. There are many people who have been living with HIV for ten years and longer. And there are people with AIDS who do not test positive for HIV antibodies. These are two reasons why the connection between AIDS and HIV is currently under question.

Whatever the connection between HIV and AIDS, no one has ever died as a direct result of either. People die from any number of common and rare diseases, such as Kaposi's Sarcoma, tuberculosis, pneumocystis carinii (pneumonia), and other illnesses or infections that would be minor for those with healthy immune systems.

The CDC estimated between 1 and 1.5 million infected people in the US in 1991. At that time, there were an estimated 11 or 12 million infected worldwide. This number escalates each year. Many people are infected who do not even know it. You can never make any assumptions about anyone's health or HIV status based upon their appearance.

Early symptoms that may or may not indicate HIV infection include:
1. Very high fevers, lasting for several days
2. A fluid producing cough that lasts for weeks
3. Purplish skin discolorations
4. Persistent, untreatable sores and infections
5. Tiredness or weakness, similar to mononucleosis
6. Swollen lymph nodes
7. Rapid weight loss
8. Unexplained diarrhea
9. Repeated colds and flus
10. A thick or painful whitish coating of the mouth, genitals, or rectum

As scary as it may be to get tested for HIV, you might consider doing so after any incidence of potential transmission. It can take anywhere from six weeks to six months to obtain reliable test results, so mark your calendar for six moths after the incident, and consider being tested at that time.

It may surprise you to learn that a piercer's most dangerous adversary is the virus which causes hepatitis. It is extremely hardy, able to survive several days or even weeks outside the bloodstream, and can kill either quickly, or leave its victim with chronic liver damage that kills slowly over a period of several years.

Hepatitis is a family of viruses (A, B, C, D, and E have been identified) which infect, inflame, and damage the liver. While the damage caused by hepatitis A is temporary, that caused by B is often chronic, and that caused by C and D are much more serious and usually permanent. The symptoms of hepatitis usually appear between two weeks and six months after infection. Many infected persons have no symptoms, and so become carriers. Symptoms include:
1. Fever
2. Headache
3. Poor appetite
4. Nausea & vomiting
5. Tiredness, weakness
6. Jaundice (yellowing of skin or eyes)

Hepatitis A is mainly spread by "fecal-oral" contact and/or sexual contact. Fecal-oral contact, for our purposes as piercers, could also be called cross-contamination. If a piercee has not washed his or her hands adequately after going to the bathroom or touching a mucous membrane or piercing, and then touches a surface or object, they can pass along the virus to anyone who touches the infected thing and then rubs an eye, puts their finger in their mouth, handles their piercing, etc. As hepatitis is very hardy, and can live for up to 10 days outside the bloodstream, there are many potentials for contracting this virus in a piercing studio. This is the reason that regular surface disinfection MUST take place, even when no contamination is apparent.

Hepatitis B is much more serious. This virus is present in bodily fluids, especially bloods and sexual secretions. Any contact with potentially contaminated surfaces, fluids, or objects should be avoided. Hepatitis B is often fatal. Many who survive go on to suffer from chronic hepatitis, or have recurrent problems with their scarred and weakened livers, from which they may later die. Nasty in its own right, infection by hepatitis B also leads to an increased likelihood of infection by hepatitis C and D, unfortunately. There is a series of preventative vaccine shots which protect against both A and B strains.

Hepatitis C is also transmissible through contact with contaminated bodily fluids, mainly through blood transfusions and sexual contact. More than half of those who are infected with this strain develop cirrhosis of the liver and/or liver cancer. There is unfortunately no vaccine for this strain of hepatitis.

Hepatitis D frequently appears in conjunction with the B strain. This form of hepatitis is usually fatal, and no effective vaccine or drug treatment is available.

While fewer than 100 health-care workers have died from AIDS-related conditions supposedly contracted in the work environment, hepatitis B ANNUALLY kills between 4,000 and 7,000 health care workers who contracted this disease on the job. Hepatitis is not always fatal, but of those who survive, approximately 105 each year will go on to suffer from chronic liver damage which can in itself ultimately prove fatal.

You have no way of knowing if one of your customers is carrying one of these viruses. Some people display a passive immunity, and some are carriers without displaying any symptoms. While it is not our position to tell people what to do with their bodies, since you could easily come into contact with bodily fluids, we suggest that you discuss with your doctor the advisability of undergoing a series of hepatitis vaccination shots. If you suffer from certain health conditions, vaccination could be unwise, which is why talking the matter over with your doctor beforehand is a good idea. Hepatitis A and B each require their own vaccine. At this time there is none for C or D.

Not all harmful matter is alive. Dead bacteria or particles of dust or dirt, snippets of hair, or other tiny things floating about in a dirty shop can lodge in the piercing, cause irritation, divert the immune system, and create an opportunity for infection by nastier creatures.

Our most important job as piercers is to avoid transmitting any harmful organism or bit of inorganic debris from one person to another. This is best accomplished by consciously developing what we call "sterility awareness." This is a sixth sense which alerts us when contamination of a clean area or object happens or is about to happen.

Contaminate means, according to the dictionary, "to make impure or unclean; to soil, stain, or infect by contact; to make unfit for use by the introduction of unwholesome or undesirable elements." Those elements which concern us as piercers are the harmful microorganisms we have just discussed. Some of them can float through the air, coming to rest on any surface. Others are brought to us, passing from person to person by casual touch or more intimate contact such as kissing or sexual intercourse.

For example, you might get an itch while standing in the check out line at your local supermarket. You are pushing

the same shopping cart that 10 days ago, someone pushed after touching the ring in their ear. You rub your eye. Assuming that hepatitis or some other tough pathogen were present in the body of the ear-toucher, you could potentially infect yourself.

Developing sterility awareness means training oneself to see how contamination takes place and take whatever steps are necessary to prevent it. It means taking great pains to always remain constantly alert to what is and is not clean in ones environment and thus avoid transferring pathogens from what is not clean to what is.

SUMMARY —
1. Bacteria, viruses, and other harmful organisms exist in the air, on human skin, and on all surfaces.
2. An opening into the bloodstream allows organisms to infect the body.
3. HIV is fragile and cannot survive very long without a host.
4. Hepatitis can survive for many days without a host, and kills thousands of healthcare workers each year.
5. Consult with your physician regarding being vaccinated for hepatitis.
6. Develop sterility awareness to prevent accidentally contaminating the piercing area and equipment with harmful pathogens.

• CLEAN vs. STERILE

Throughout this manual you will frequently encounter the terms *sterile, clean,* and *contaminated*. Every piercer must fully understand these terms. Study the chart on the opposite page. It will help you conceptualize their meaning, and hone your sterility awareness.

• WORK IN A CLEAN ENVIRONMENT

In chapter 1 we discussed personal hygiene. Now let's take a look at our working environment.

This is probably the first thing your clients will see. If you want to make a positive impression, make it shine! Keep it free from dust, dirt, and clutter. If there are rugs or carpets, vacuum them

often and shampoo them regularly. Hard surface floors should be scrubbed down with disinfectant. Glass surfaces can be kept free from smudges with glass cleaner. Expect mirrors, display cases, countertops, and everything else to be touched by your clients, so make it a regular habit to wipe them down with disinfectant.

We've all heard the terms "filthy lucre" and "money laundering." The truth is that money can be very dirty. Consequently, don't touch a person or clean object or surface after handling money without first washing your hands thoroughly.

Make it a habit never to touch contaminated jewelry, i.e. jewelry that has been worn! However well-healed the piercing appears to be, the risk to yourself, your piercees, and your coworkers is too great. Wear a fresh pair of gloves whenever you anticipate any contact with human tissue, used jewelry, or bodily fluids. Keep a supply of antibacterial wipes (benzalkonium chloride or 70% alcohol) on hand to offer to any person you observe touching their piercings or jewelry while at the counter. Have tissues and disposable plastic relish cups available for people to deposit their jewelry in while at the counter. Don't be afraid to politely insist that everyone maintain your standards of cleanliness. You will be protecting yourself, and most people will appreciate your commitment to their well-being.

Common areas such as hallways, waiting rooms, office space, and other common areas must be kept clean and free of debris. Anything which might be tracked into a piercing room must be removed.

Unless you are fortunate enough to have a separate sink to wash up before a piercing, your bathroom will probably have to serve double duty. This is a particularly important occasion for you to practice your "sterility awareness." If you are washing your hands in preparation for a piercing, avoid touching the potentially contaminated faucets or doorknob. Use a paper towel, a tissue, or your elbow instead, and frequently wipe those surfaces down with disinfectant.

From STERILE to CLEAN to CONTAMINATED

Every piercer should thoroughly grasp how their environment and the tools they use pass through stages from sterile to clean to contaminated. The chart below should help your understanding. Visualize sterile as white and contaminated as dark red with several shades in between. Always remember that when a lighter colored item comes in contact with a darker one it becomes that color, and can pass it on, until it is disinfected or sterilized.

Nothing darker than pale pink should ever come in contact with a piercing, directly or indirectly. Bare hands should avoid red items. If red items are touched, hands should be immediately washed. Dark red items should never be touched with bare hands.

•WHITE	•PALEST PINK	•PALE PINK	•PINK	•RED	•DARK RED
Sterile. No living matter. Freshly autoclaved implements, jewelry, needles, etc. in unopened, sterile bags, untouched.	Very clean. Only very small quantities of airborne matter. Sterile implements just removed from their bags. Disinfected implements only touched with freshly gloved hands, trays or surfaces immediately after disinfection/bleaching. Jewelry that has just been removed from disinfecting solution. Bagged "sterile" implements after several weeks in storage.	Clean. Only small quantities of airborne matter. Presterilized corks, rubber bands, nonsterile latex gloves, tissues, cotton swabs, etc. stored in protective containers and only touched with freshly gloved hands. Surface of "sterile" field, only touched with freshly gloved hands if paper is changed daily. Needles, forceps, disinfected jewelry, etc. after several minutes in open air, unused. Surface of skin immediately after Povidone-iodine prep. Hands immediately after washing with antibacterial scrub.	Not clean. Normal levels of airborne matter. Needles, forceps, corks, rubber bands, etc., after extended exposure to open air or frequent handling. Clothing, surfaces, implements, neither contaminated with bloodborne organisms, nor recently disinfected. Unused jewelry prior to sterilization/disinfection. Piercing room furniture, etc.	Dirty. High levels of airborne matter and possible presence of bloodborne matter. Floors, countertops, sinks, doorknobs, light switches, and other areas that may have been exposed to bloodborne contaminants, either directly or indirectly. Unbroken, uncleaned skin. Frequently handled display jewelry. Phones. Money.	Contaminated. High levels of airborne/bloodborne matter- Bodily fluids, new or old. Piercings, new or healed. Broken skin of any kind. Used piercing implements, used disposable piercing needles. Previously worn jewelry.

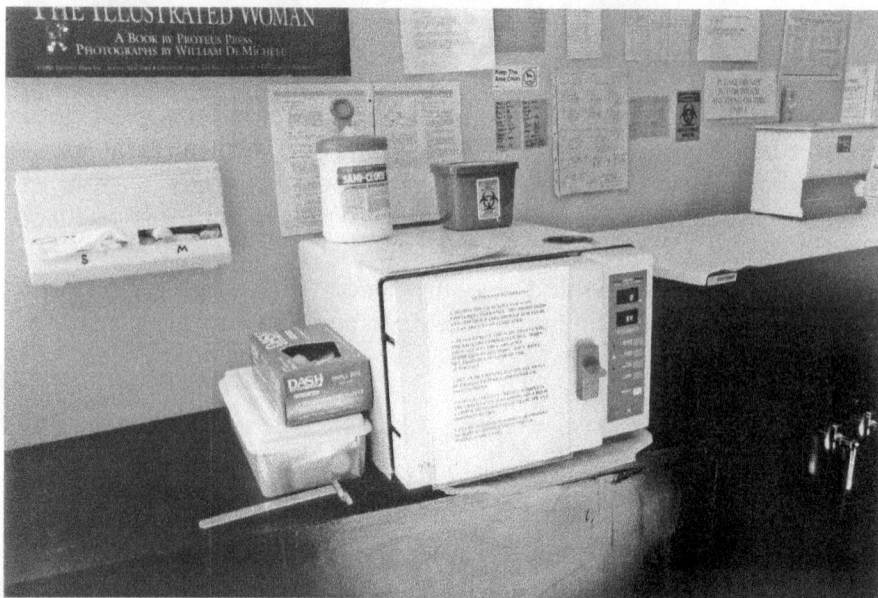

A typical sterilization area: notice glove dispenser and box of the gloves at left of autoclave (center), hard-surface disinfectant wipes and sharps container on top, ultrasonic cleaner on working surface at right.

Every trash container in a piercing studio can be considered contaminated, so never handle the container or its contents without wearing a pair of sturdy latex gloves. OSHA allows a reasonable amount of blood, bodily fluids, and the like in regular household/business trash, and this can be disposed of in the normal fashion. But NEVER dispose of needles in the trash!

Trash cans in piercing rooms need to have secure lids, and a foot-pedal so you don't have to touch the contaminated lid. Mark the lid clearly as a biohazard. In spite of how clearly marked it may be, many, many piercees feel the urge to touch that lid. When this occurs, send them immediately into the bathroom for a thorough antibacterial scrub.

Use plastic trash can liners. This makes disposal easier and cleaner. If possible use clear liners so that any dumpster-rummagers will hopefully avoid your refuse. Unless very little trash has been generated, change the bags daily, and don't let them overfill. Think of all the bacteria living on and in every person who's been in the store that day. Some of it is in those bags.

Wash your hands before and after changing the trash bags, and keep track of what you touch while wearing those gloves. If you open the back door to put trash in the dumpster, wipe that doorknob down with disinfectant when you're done.

SUMMARY —
1. Keep all areas clean, and frequently disinfect all surfaces that are touched with hands.
2. Watch for accidental contamination by hands, piercings, jewelry, or bodily fluids. Disinfect immediately.
3. Ask piercees not to contaminate your areas.
4. Trash containers are contaminated. Touch them only with fresh gloves, use clear plastic liners, change them regularly, and clearly mark them as contaminated.
5. Never throw needles in the trash.

• THE STERILIZATION AREA

While space can often be tight in a piercing studio, it is vitally important that you set aside a space away from client traffic in which to keep your autoclave and other sterilization equipment. Only fully-trained personnel should be allowed in this area. An unknowing person can contaminate some of your sterile equipment and they can also potentially infect themselves with something unpleasant. Keep strangers out!

The area must be clearly marked as a biohazard under OSHA requirements, and for common sense. Gloves must always be worn in this area. Hands must be washed immediately before and after use of this space.

SUMMARY —
1. The autoclave and other sterilization equipment needs to be separate from the rest of the space.
2. Mark the sterilization area clearly as a biohazard.
3. Exercise extreme caution and awareness in the sterilization area.

• THE PIERCING ROOM

The most important area in terms of sterility is, of course, the actual piercing room. Because of the risk of cross-contamination, it is very important that no other services take place in the same room. If the area served double duty as a hair salon, for example, tiny particles of hair could easily find their way into the piercing and lead to swelling, infection, or other problems. Similarly, your piercing activities could present a risk of cross-contamination in the reverse direction.

In addition, the combination of different tools for different purposes cluttering up your work space exponentially increases your chance for careless error, which could be very dangerous for all involved.

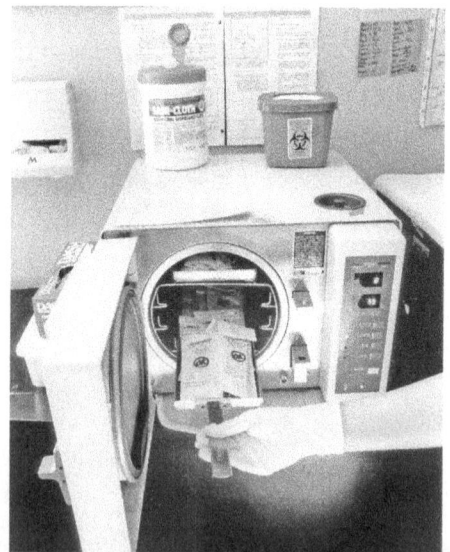

Removing sterilized implements from the autoclave.

The surface on which ones equipment is laid out is commonly referred to in doctor's offices as the *"sterile" field*. The word sterile is actually not accurate since it is in reality a clean field. The paper covering the surface is clean, not sterile. This field should be clearly marked as such, and piercees should be kept from touching anything on it. Make sure your sterile field is located on a sturdy, nonporous surface, preferably a medical cabinet, with protected drawers and shelving underneath. Cover the top of the table with disposable hospital examining paper. This comes in rolls and can be obtained from a surgical supply house. Wipe down the surface and change the paper at least daily, and any time contamination occurs.

Never place anything on the sterile field which is not clean or sterile. If picked up and used, anything touched by a potential contaminant must be either sterilized, disinfected, or discarded. Nonsterilizable items should be thrown away.

Sterilized piercing tools in their sealed autoclave packages should be handled only with freshly gloved hands. The paper helps keep out harmful organisms but is not totally impervious, especially if it gets wet. Keep your sterile packages in a cool, dry drawer away from moisture, light, and air.

Set aside a protected area for contaminated implements. This can be a shelf or a far corner of the table. In keeping with OSHA regulations, it should be clearly marked as a biohazard and treated as such. Keep a stainless steel tray in this area into which you can place contaminated tools. This area is also the appropriate place to store your sharps container.

The trash can in the piercing room is also contaminated, and should be clearly marked as such. Trash cans in this area need a secure lid which can be opened with a foot pedal. For some reason, despite the warning customers invariably seem compelled to touch this lid; if this occurs, insist they wash their hands immediately with antibacterial scrub. And NEVER throw needles in the trash! The proper disposal of needles and other dangerous materials will be discussed at length later.

If your piercing room is carpeted it must be vacuumed daily, shampooed regularly, and kept free of foreign matter. A nonporous surface such as linoleum or tile is more practical and easier to keep clean. All surfaces should be kept immaculately clean with conventional cleansers as well as with disinfectants.

Tables, chairs, or other surfaces where piercees sit or lie require special attention. It is crucial that these surfaces be nonporous. Cover their surfaces with examination table paper. This comes in rolls and can be changed between clients. Should fluids such as sweat, blood, contaminated Madacide, etc. soak through the table paper, wipe the surface down with bleach or hard-surface disinfectant.

SUMMARY —
1. Maintain a room for piercing that is not used for any other activity.
2. The place where equipment and the piercing tray is kept is a "sterile" field. Touch only with fresh gloves or hemostats, and disinfect regularly.
3. All surfaces in the piercing room, including tables, chairs, and the floor directly beneath the piercing area, must be made of nonporous material, in order to clean them thoroughly.
4. Cover chairs and tables with examination table paper. Change this paper between every client.
5. Keep a separate area or shelf for contaminated objects like sharps containers and used tools.
6. The trash in the piercing room is contaminated and must not be touched with ungloved hands. Used needles belong in a sharps container, not in the trash.

• **STERILE TOOLS—Required of Every Piercer!**
There is no single element of responsible piercing more important than using sterile tools! The health and well-being of yourself and your clients depend upon your solid grasp of the information in this section. Please read it through as many times as it takes to completely absorb it. Using it should become second nature.

You cannot practice sterile technique using dirty tools. Sterility awareness is absolutely essential. Be alert! Has the tool come in contact with anything? What have you touched before handling it? Once a tool is used it is contaminated, and once contaminated should be placed in the stainless steel tray in the contaminated area. After use sterilize it as soon as possible, and store it where it will stay clean.

Tools such as forceps, needle holders, hemostats, and insertion tapers that will come into direct contact with open tissue need to be made of surgical stainless steel or other material which will not corrode and is autoclavable. Some insertion tapers are made of nylon, but these are not generally autoclavable, and are considered micro-porous. Consider them one-person tools which can be cleaned with disinfectant between uses.

All reusable implements are autoclaved between each use. Autoclaves are used in hospitals and dental offices to sterilize their surgical and dental equipment. No other method of sterilization is as reliable, and if you are planning on being more than a hobby piercer, an autoclave should be considered essential equipment.

While certain disinfectant chemicals can theoretically sterilize instruments, they should not be depended upon. There may be minute crevices or holes which the solution does not reach. A drop of oily material may keep the chemical from contact with the organisms it needs to kill. When some disinfectant chemicals come in contact with blood it forms a film which actually protects any organisms which may be under it. For these reasons do not rely on disinfectants to sterilize your piercing instruments.

Store used implements in the contaminated tool tray until they can be brought to the autoclave area. Wearing a fresh pair of gloves, remove any rubber bands, tape, or other matter adhering to the tool, and be sure the teeth are unlocked.

An ultrasonic cleaner is an excellent way to remove antibiotic ointment, dried matter, and blood plasma from the tools. The machine should be filled with an approved ultrasonic cleaning

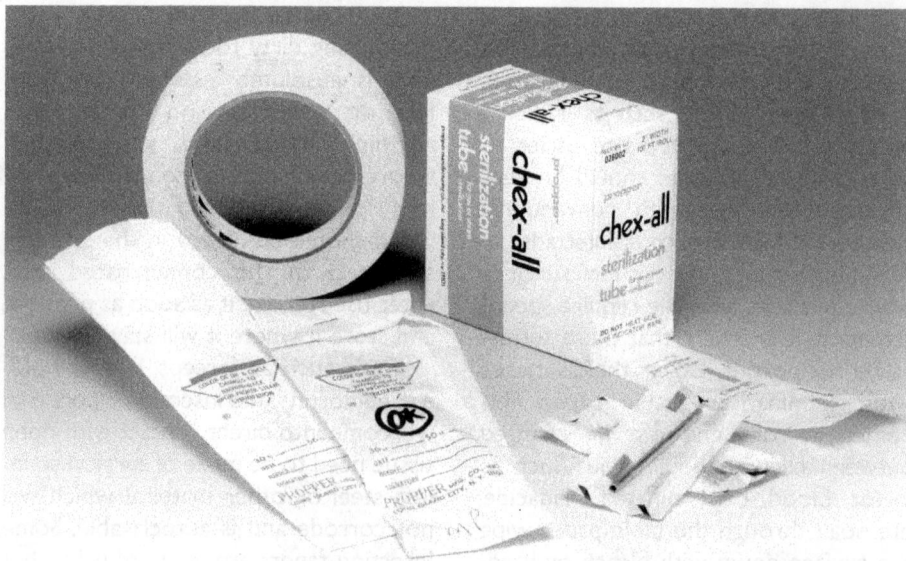

fluid that is changed at least weekly. Follow directions on the label. Bits of tape adhesive can be removed with a little rubber cement thinner on a cotton swab, but don't get any on your gloves. The tools should be left in the ultrasonic for at least 15 to 20 minutes. If an ultrasonic is not available, tools must be thoroughly scrubbed free of all matter with a small brush, pipe cleaner, or mild abrasive, then rinsed in clean water. If you must use this method, be particularly careful not to splatter yourself. Wear protective clothing: in addition to your latex gloves wear a rubberized bib apron, particle mask, and eye protection.

Whatever method is used, tools need to dry completely after this initial cleaning. Remember that they are still contaminated. Do not touch them, or any equipment used to clean them, with bare hands. And be sure to wash your hands immediately after this task is completed.

After the tools have completely dried, don fresh gloves, remove the trays from inside the autoclave, and turn it on. Check that it is on the proper setting. And while you are waiting for the autoclave to warm up you can bag the implements.

Place each individual tool into a clearly labeled paper autoclave bag or length of sterilization tube. These have a light pink "OK" or other indicator printed on them in special ink that will turn grayish brown when proper sterilization occurs. Seal with auto-

clave tape (this will also change color after sterilization). Be careful that no part of the tool punctures the bag or tube. Remember that the stapler, staples, pencil, tape, and anything else you have touched while doing this job is contaminated, so it is best to keep these items set aside for this task alone. Once your implements are bagged, arrange them loosely on the autoclave trays.

Now take a clean tissue and open the autoclave door. Place the bagged tools on their trays in the autoclave. Avoid touching any part of the autoclave other than the interior trays and then change your gloves before touching the surface of the autoclave. Securely close the door and start the sterilization cycle. Wipe down the surface with bleach solution, or a commercial hard-surface disinfectant. Remove your gloves, and wash your hands thoroughly.

When the tools have completed their cycle (usually about 45 minutes), allow them to cool inside the autoclave to maintain sterility while the packages are still moist. When fully cool and dry, don fresh gloves and place the packages carefully in their storage drawers. If the seal is ever broken, or the tool inside tears the bag, it should be rebagged and sterilized before being used.

All trays, containers, and dishes used in the piercing area should be made of stainless steel. This will allow them to be autoclaved or disinfected daily and whenever contamination occurs. There

is a special setting on most autoclaves for these large items (unwrapped). Remove the autoclave trays, place the dishes and trays directly inside, and run them on the proper setting. They will be extremely hot when they come out of the autoclave, so be aware not to drop them on the floor and recontaminate them! And be sure to wear clean gloves when handling them. Items too large to fit inside the autoclave can be cleaned with hard-surface disinfectant.

SUMMARY —
1. Reusable tools are used on only ONE PERSON then cleaned, packaged, and autoclaved.
2. An autoclave is the only truly reliable method of sterilization.
3. Clean accumulated matter off tools by placing them into the ultrasonic machine for 20 minutes.
4. When tools are dry, seal them in individual autoclave bags and run them through the autoclave on the proper cycle.
5. Consider everything in the sterilization area contaminated.
6. Handle sterilized tools only with freshly washed hands inside of a fresh pair of latex gloves.

The container holding your supply of jewelry disinfectant (i.e. Madacide) must be watched carefully. If contaminated jewelry is accidentally dropped into the container, not only is the disinfectant fluid itself contaminated, but so is the dish. It must be rinsed and autoclaved before it is used again. Once again, err on the side of caution. Any jewelry that has not just come out of your own stock of clean, unworn jewelry should be sterilized in a separate dish. Use disposable plastic relish cups with enough Madacide to cover the jewelry.

Tools such as pliers, nail clippers, scissors, gauge wheels, and ring expanders must also be autoclaved after any contact with broken skin, direct or indirect. Tools used on uncontaminated jewelry or unbroken skin may be thoroughly wiped down with bleach solution, or hard-surface disinfectant. Seek out stainless steel tools whenever possible; everything else will quickly rust.

Many pliers have serrated jaws which can scratch and mar jewelry. You may not be able to see them, but scratches can irritate delicate tissue and harbor germs. To avoid this, wrap the rough surfaces of tools with surgical tape. Remove the tape and sterilize the tool between uses.

Nonmetal tools, such as calipers, must also be sterilized between uses. Wipe them down thoroughly with 70% alcohol after contact with unbroken skin. If you have been handling them with contaminated gloves, or if they have come into contact with contaminated jewelry or broken skin, clean them with bleach solution for five to 10 minutes, or hard-surface disinfectant for one to five minutes. Consult the product label.

Many supplies are used only once and then discardedf. Rubber bands, used to adjust the tension of forceps, should be soaked in 70% rubbing alcohol, diluted bleach solution, or other hard-surface disinfectant prior to storage. Corks, toothpicks, and some types of cotton swabs are autoclavable, and should be sterilized in this way before storage.

Store these items in stainless steel, glass, or disposable containers with lids to protect the contents from airborne contaminants. If a piercee or unthinking piercer should happen to reach into one of these containers with bare hands, both container and contents are contaminated. Discard or resterilize all contaminated materials, and sterilize the container before they are used again. Autoclave stainless steel or pyrex, use bleach or hard-surface disinfectant for regular glass.

TABLE FOR DISINFECTION AND STERILIZATION

MICROORGANISMS:	METHOD:	PROCESS:	TYPE OF ITEM:
All forms of microbial life are killed. All bacterial spores. All bacteria. All fungi. All viruses.	Sterilization	Saturated Steam: Autoclave 220-270 kP pressure,140° C, 284° F for 15-40 minutes depending on cycle. Pressure cooker at maximum pressure for 45 minutes. Dry Heat (Dry-Clave) 177° C, 350° F. for 1 hour. Gas Plasma (ETO gas). Not practical for piercers.	CRITICAL (Dark Red): Likely presence of bloodborne pathogens. Contact with normally sterile tissue or direct blood contact. Forceps, needles, used jewelry, contaminated trays, jewelry disinfectant dishes
Some bacterial spores. All bacteria. Most non-lipid viruses. Fungal spores.	Hospital level disinfection.	Pasteurization. Chemical exposure for 10-20 minutes: Gluteraldehyde 2% solution* for 10 minutes; Synergistic compounds (Madacide) for 10 minutes; Sodium Hypochlorite (bleach) 10% solution for 10 minutes; Phenolics (Lysol) 10% solution for 20 minutes; Alcohol, 70% solution for 20+ minutes; Iodophores (iodine) for 20+ minutes; Formalins (formaldehyde)* 20+ minutes. *classified as nonbiodegradable biohazard.	SEMI-CRITICAL (Red): Possible presence of bloodborne pathogens, direct or indirect contact with mucous membranes or broken skin. Calipers and other non-autoclavable items.
Vegetative bacteria. Lipid viruses. Some Fungal Spores. HIV. Gram positive bacteria.	Low-level disinfection.	Chemical exposure for 10 minutes or less: Quaternary ammonium compounds, Phenolics (Lysol), Alcohol (70%).	NON-CRITICAL (Pink): Contact with unbroken skin only, no bloodborne pathogens. Surfaces, doorknobs, faucets, uncontaminated calipers, pens, etc.

SUMMARY —

1. All trays, dishes, and containers must be made of stainless steel or pyrex to allow them to be autoclaved and/or disinfected regularly, and whenever contamination occurs.
2. Tools such as pliers also need to be autoclaved after each use.
3. Wrap rough edges of tools with surgical tape. Remove this tape before autoclaving.
4. When nonmetal, nondisposable tools become contaminated, wipe them down thoroughly with bleach or hard-surface disinfectant.
5. Some disposable items should be autoclaved before they are stored. Others can be soaked in disinfectant.
6. Avoid contaminating cleaned, stored equipment. Handle freshly cleaned and autoclaved items only with a fresh pair of gloves.

• NEEDLES—Special Tools

Needles present unique safety concerns. They must be inspected for sharpness, sterilized before use, used at most two or three times ON ONE PERSON ONLY, and then must be immediately disposed of in a sharps container.

You may choose to presterilize your own needles. If so, inspect each needle carefully for gauge, sharpness, and to weed out any defects. They are then carefully inserted into a length of sterilization tube, sealed with autoclave tape, and labeled clearly and accurately with the appropriate gauge. Needles are available from Gauntlet presterilized and ready to use. Examine the packets and their contents through the clear plastic film before use. Make sure the needles look sharp and the packets unopened and untorn. If the needle inside is dull, discard it or return it. If the packet is open or torn, simply rebag and sterilize it.

Needles need to remain in their individual, sterile packages right up until the moment of piercing to minimize any risk of airborne contamination and accidental needle sticks.

Store packaged needles in a cool, dark, dry place to prevent accidental contact. Touch them only with fresh gloves or a clean tissue.

When you set up to do a piercing, be sure to select the proper gauge needle for the piercing you are about to perform. Since many piercees are needle-phobic you might want to lay the package needle side down on the tray.

Piercing needles are very sharp, so never be careless when handling them. The risk of a needle stick must be always in your mind.

Be aware of the location of the needle at all times. And don't mix insertion tapers and needles together on the tray.

Have only one needle out of its package at any one time, even if multiple piercings are taking place.

Don't leave a piercee unattended with an uncorked needle sticking out of their piercing.

If more than one piercing will be performed ON ONE PERSON with the same needle, cork the needle between piercings to reduce the risk of needle sticks.

If possible, recork the needle right after removing the forceps.

Dispose of the needle IMMEDIATELY after use; if possible, don't even return it to the tray. The proper receptacle for piercing needles is a sharps container. These are available at hospitals, clinics, and pharmacies, which charge little or nothing for the revolving service. Store this container in the contaminated area of your piercing room, marked clearly as a biohazard (most sharps containers come with a biohazard sticker). Keep it away from piercees, and remember that the entire container is considered to be contaminated.

When the container is nearly full, but not so full as to present a hazard, seal it well and autoclave it. Then return it to the hospital, clinic, or pharmacy to receive a new, empty container. It is wise to have several empty containers on hand to prevent accidents and overstuffing. NEVER THROW A NEEDLE IN THE TRASH. Dirty or clean, new or used, needles can threaten your health, as well as that of your clients and your trash collector.

Finally, don't forget to run a spore test at least once a month to assure your autoclave is working properly.

SUMMARY —

1. Piercing needles are designed to be used on ONE PERSON ONLY in a single piercing session. Do not resterilize needles.
2. Inspect even prepackaged needles carefully. Store needles in a safe, cool, dark, dry place.
3. Remove needles from the sterile package only when you are ready to use them.
4. Be extremely cautious with needles; know where an exposed needle is at all times. Whenever possible, cork the needle.
5. Dispose of the needle immediately in a sharps container. When container is nearly full, autoclave it and return it for another.
6. Run a spore test monthly.

ATTENTION! THIS DOCUMENT IS FOR HISTORIC REFERENCE ONLY!

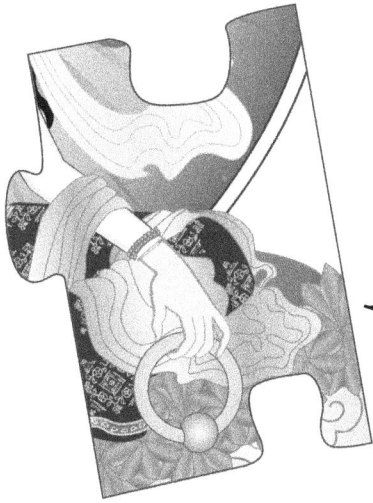

CHAPTER 4 —
SELECTING APPROPRIATE JEWELRY

One of the most important duties of every responsible piercer is to guide his/her clients in making their jewelry choices. You will soon discover that most people are clueless. Most will appreciate your assistance and willingness to answer their questions. There will be some who come to you with very definite ideas and strong opinions, but who, with patience and finesse, can be steered into accepting the right option. Invariably you will encounter a few immovable individuals who think they know more than you. And for them you must learn how to politely say, "No."

Let us begin by making it clear that every client is unique. About the time you think that a certain jewelry style and/or size is the standard for everyone, someone will walk through your door who, assuming you take the time to look, will require something completely different. Never become complacent; always be prepared for surprises.

The criteria by which good body jewelry is judged will remain the same as long as there are no major evolutionary changes in the human form. Body jewelry should almost always be fitted to the piercing, not the other way round. It is common for people to want a piece of jewelry that is too small in diameter or thickness. They seem to think if the ring is thinner the piercing will hurt less. With gold jewelry the motivation is usually price. If you take the time to present the alternatives and explain their pros and cons, the majority of people will accept your suggestions.

For those who insist they must have a too-small diameter try to persuade them to at least start with a larger one through the complete healing period. There is a chance, not necessarily a good one, they may be able to wear the smaller one later.

Sometimes an interim piece of jewelry or retainer is required while the piercing heals, after which time appropriate jewelry can be installed. For example, most surface-to-surface piercings have a very low success rate, but the chances improve if a piece of flexible monofilament nylon is worn for several months.

With the exception of tongues, frenums, ampallangs, and apadravyas, barbells don't allow many piercings (particularly nipples or navels) to be cleaned well. A ring would be worn for the first several months, and then the barbell can be safely worn.

The ideal piece of jewelry is safe in material, style, diameter and gauge. It is a source of decorative and functional pleasure for the wearer, and free from any scratches, nicks, or other damaging flaws. A responsible piercer tries to have an ideal piece of jewelry available for every piercee.

> SUMMARY—
> 1. Every piercee and every piercing is unique, and requires unique jewelry solutions.
> 2. There are standards for selecting appropriate jewelry based upon years of collective experience. If you follow them you can avoid many problems.

• METALS

In much of the current press coverage of piercings, there is often a passing reference to a "silver" ring dangling off of some scandalous part. While many people do wear silver in their piercings, it is neither a safe or professional offering. The human body contains a significant amount of the element sulfur which has an affinity for silver, even "sterling," an alloy of silver and copper. The sulfur attacks silver, turning it black and corroding it. Consequently, many people have reactions to silver jewelry. It should only be worn in well-healed piercings.

The metal that piercers use most frequently is a surgical grade of low-carbon stainless steel, preferably 316L. Parts, such as balls, which do not go through tissue can be made of other 300 series stainless steels. Highly polished and annealed, stainless has a look similar to silver or platinum (though cooler in color), is reasonably inexpensive, and nonreactive. Surgical stainless steel has, in the past, been used for implants and bone replacements, but has largely been replaced by titanium.

All stainless steels contain a small percentage of nickel, a metal to which some people, depending upon their sensitivity, may react. This is something of which you should be aware. If a client's piercing shows signs of an allergic reaction, it may be to the nickel in the jewelry.

Nothing looks quite so wonderful against skin tones as gold, but solid gold jewelry is expensive, and many people are unwilling to pay the price. What they opt for instead is a cheap imitation: "gold-plated," a microscopic coating of gold coating a mass of inferior metal (nickel, copper, steel, etc.) or "gold-filled," a layer of low-carat gold (less than 1%) over base metal. Plating gradually, or not so gradually, wears through or flakes off, exposing the inferior metal beneath. Infection, and allergic reaction, or constant irritation can be the result.

Some people spring for solid gold, but only 10 or 12 karat (9 in Great Britain). These grades of gold are heavily diluted with alloys, copper and/or nickel among them, and are not suitable for body jewelry.

In contrast some people go so far as to insist on only 24 karat gold. Certainly it is hypoallergenic, but it is also so soft that the many scratches and nicks it is sure to collect can irritate the piercing and create a welcome environment for infection. In thin gauges the jewelry will not hold its shape. This is even a problem with 18 karat.

Never sell or install jewelry you know or suspect to be anything lower than solid 14k or 18k gold. White gold is beautiful, but is likely to contain nickel. There are nickel-free white golds, but they are more expensive, and most manufacturers don't even know about them.

All metals become stiff and springy if they are bent frequently. A heat process called annealing will make them malleable again, however, from a technological standpoint the process is practical only for gold jewelry.

The most colorful metals being used for piercing jewelry are niobium and titanium. In their raw state both elemental metals are pewter colored. When dipped into an electrified, oxygen-rich bath, a microscopic oxide layer forms on the metal. This process is called anodization. The thickness of the layer is determined by the voltage of the bath, and the color is determined by the thickness of the layer. What you perceive as color is the result of light refracted through the oxide layer.

Since the oxide layer is extremely thin, it can wear off, especially if the jewelry rubs constantly against clothing. Fortunately, it does not flake. The darker colors are generally more durable than the lighter ones, and charcoal wears the best.

Unlike anodized aluminum, no dyes or pigments are used on titanium and niobium. Because of its exceptional hypoallergenic qualities, titanium has largely replaced stainless steel in the manufacture of surgical implants. There are very, very few people who have problems wearing niobium or titanium. Though both are lighter than steel, titanium is the metal of choice where heavy jewelry would be undesirable.

If money is no object, the piercee may want their jewelry made of platinum. It is inert, heavy, tough, and very hypoallergenic. Since it is expensive, most people choose surgical stainless steel or white gold.

Some piercing jewelry these days is being made of high density, low porosity plastics such as Lucite, monofilament nylon, or acrylic. They have the advantage of being very lightweight, sometimes flexible (as with nylon monofilament), generally nonreactive, and inexpensive.

Plastics are ideal to wear for X-rays, mammograms, or surgical procedures where metal jewelry would need to be removed. They must only be worn by one person, however, as they cannot generally be autoclaved. Plastics tend to be more delicate and breakable than metal jewelry, and are usually considered to be temporary alternatives to metal.

Organic materials, such as bone, quills, leather, or polished wood, have been worn in piercings for many thousands of years. But the *National Geographic* magazine articles and *Africa Adorned*-type coffee table books rarely tell of the severe infections that many tribal people suffer and even die from as a result of wearing such things. Organic jewelry should be worn only in very well-healed piercings and only for limited periods of time. Move them frequently to avoid their tendency to adhere to your own tissue.

SUMMARY —
1. When selecting metal for use in piercings, choose materials that will not corrode or react with the body.
2. Nickel, a metal to which human tissue is highly sensitive, is frequently used in many alloys, including stainless steels and white gold.
3. Jewelry of low-carbon, 300 series stainless steels, particularly 316L, is suitable for most people.
4. People who choose gold jewelry should wear nothing less than 14 or 18 karat gold and never gold-plated or gold-filled.
5. Annealing is a heat treatment which renders metals more malleable. Outside of industry, it is practical only for gold jewelry.
6. Niobium and titanium are elemental metals that are extremely inert (nonreactive), and can be anodized.
7. Anodization is a process of passing electrical current through an oxygen-rich solution to oxidize the surface of a piece of metal.
8. Platinum is an expensive but pure metal for use in body piercings.
9. Dense plastics such as nylon, acrylic, and lucite can be inserted in piercings, but are best used temporarily and worn by one person as they are not suitable for autoclaving.
10. Jewelry made of organic materials such as bone, quills, or leather should be highly polished, and worn only for short periods of time in well-healed piercings.

• STYLES

Lots of people complain that the jewelry available for piercings is too plain, too unimaginative. They say they want something different, unique. Unfortunately, piercers, like all craftspeople, are limited in their creativity by the boundaries of the medium, in this case human tissue.

As we have discussed, only nonreactive, highly polished, round wire jewelry should be worn in piercings, especially new ones. The part of the jewelry which passes through the piercing shouldn't have any carvings, indentations, or other surface irregularities that could irritate delicate tissue and encourage infection. Jewelry is almost always the same thickness all the way around, to allow for thorough cleaning and even weight distribution.

When piercings are new, it is especially important that the jewelry be as lightweight, simple, and practical as possible. But once healed, piercings can easily be customized with dangling charms or beads, or by changing the style of the threaded balls, or adding weights.

Ear jewelry is just that, jewelry intended to be worn in the lobe of the ear. Most of what is available as ear jewelry, especially if it is gold, is frequently unsuitable even for that purpose. Wires are dangerously thin and there are often rough, unfinished edges.

Ear rings or studs, no matter what the material, simply were not designed for use in body piercings. Cleaning would be difficult if not impossible, the aesthetics would be awkward if not ugly, and the thin gauges and generally cheap construction are simply not durable enough for body use.

A very frequent mistake made by wannabe piercers is to assume that the plastic gun used to pierce young ears in malls across America and around the world would make a fine body piercing tool. Thus armed they set about busily damaging and contaminating hundreds of equally naive piercees.

A professional piercer does not even use this gun to pierce ears. Since it is plastic it cannot be autoclaved. What metal parts there are would rust or corrode if sterilized with disinfectants. There is just no way to adequately sterilize it between customers.

The piercing itself is accomplished, not by a sterile, sharp, accurate piercing needle, but by the blunt end of the jewelry itself. And, finally, the studs designed for sole use in these guns is absolutely wrong for any part of the body. Period. The posts are too short to allow adequate cleaning of the piercing. And the studs are made of gold-plated stainless steel. The plating will eventually wear through, and, because stainless is difficult to gold plate, some manufacturers apply copper or nickel under the gold, two metals which are seriously incompatible with human tissue.

• COMMON JEWELRY STYLES

Over 20 years ago Gauntlet's founder Jim Ward was one of a handful of modern piercing enthusiasts. He and his friends put all kinds of things in the little holes they had made in their bodies: ear jewelry, paperclips, hand-twisted bits of wire, whatever they could find. Some of these experiments proved somewhat successful, if less than beautiful, while others tore, infected, or irritated the piercings they were intended to decorate. Being a jeweler, Jim set about creating a line of jewelry that would be both functional and beautiful, jewelry designed just for body piercings.

Since it would be passing through very delicate tissue, the jewelry could have no rough edges or rough textures. The jewelry had to be secure enough to withstand friction, play, and body pressure. It had to be made of nonreactive metal, and it had to be thick enough not to tear tissue. The original designs that Jim produced are more or less the same designs that hundreds of thousands of people around the world now wear in their piercings. Virtually every design is a variation on one of two basic designs: the ring and the stud. One is round, the other straight. The variations are endless.

SUMMARY —
1. Jewelry style are limited by the safety and comfort requirements of the human body.
2. The surface of jewelry that will pass through piercings must be completely smooth and free of carvings, markings, indentations or other irregularities.
3. Jewelry worn in new piercings should be lightweight and practical, with nothing dangling from it.
4. Jewelry intended to be worn in ear lobes is not only inappropriate for body piercings, but usually inappropriate for earlobe piercings as well.
5. Plastic ear piercing guns are unsanitary, unnecessarily painful, and install inappropriate jewelry. Professional piercers do not use these guns for any purpose.

• RING VARIATIONS

Bead Ring

The bead ring is a continuous circle (or other body-friendly shape) of non-reactive metal. On one end of the circle is a permanently attached bead which can be whatever shape the designer desires. The free end fits snugly into a hole drilled into the side of the bead. When closed the ring will not come out of the piercing, and the bead keeps any rough joint from getting inside.

Bead rings come in diameters from ¼" to 2" or more and gauges from 20 to 10. Anything thicker would be difficult or impossible to bend especially in a small diameter.

The bead ring is opened by twisting the free half away from the bead slightly. Depending on the gauge, use either fingers or pliers.

Captive Bead Ring

To the casual observer the captive bead ring looks just like a standard bead ring. The difference is that the bead is not attached to the ring but instead held "captive." The two ends of the ring snap into indentations on opposite sides of the bead. Captive bead rings present more design options, as the bead can be made of many different materials. Captive bead rings also have an advantage in the larger gauges; the ring usually needn't be bent to be inserted. Just pop out the bead while spreading the ring with ring-expanding pliers. Captive bead rings aren't so practical in thinner gauges; the bead can easily be lost.

Captive bead rings are available from 18 gauge to 2 gauge. Beyond that the metal is too thick to open even with ring-expanding pliers. This style is available in many diameters.

Circular Barbell

Combining the attractive design of a ring with the convenience of a barbell, the circular barbell is just that: a threaded post curved into a ring shape. Piercees who need to remove their jewelry frequently will appreciate the ease of removability. Because the ring need not be bent to be inserted, circular barbells make excellent choices where thick-gauge, small-diameter rings are desired.

Too Small!

The smaller diameters make ideal septum jewelry as the space between the beads allows one to flip the ends up into the nostrils during the day, then flip them down at night. The circular barbell comes in all gauges 14 and thicker, and in diameters from ⅜″ up.

When buying circular barbells make certain the ring is internally threaded. Expect to pay a little more for this comfort feature, but what responsible piercer would want to insert rough male threads through a sensitive piercing?

• STUD VARIATIONS

Barbell

Some piercings would be very uncomfortable or even dangerous if a ring were worn in them. For these the barbell, a straight bar with balls at each end, at least one of which is threaded. Like the circular barbell make sure the post is internally threaded. It is important to note that many inferior barbells are manufactured with the male threading on the post itself. This short-cut saves time and labor but represents a lack of concern for the well-being of the delicate tissue inside the piercing which can be easily abraded by the rough threads.

The barbell is available in all gauges 14 and thicker in ¹/₁₆″ increments starting at ¼″.

Minibar

Also known as dydoe studs, these scaled down barbells are the only piece of jewelry that is not internally threaded. Its very thin gauge (17 ga.) makes external threading the only option. Because the threads can abrade fragile tissue, coat them with wax before insertion. Minibars are popular for clit, dydoe, and eyebrow piercings.

Labret Stud

Lip and labret piercings sometimes do just fine with a small barbell, but for many people, the friction and pressure of the inside ball against teeth and/or gums is quite uncomfortable. For the majority, a a two or three part labret stud is the answer. The internally threaded, three-part stud consists of a short barbell post, a flat, smooth disc, and a ball or decorative end for the outside. The interchangeable parts make it easily sized or customized.

L-Bar or PA Bar

Rings in the larger gauges often add a tremendous weight to the piercing, and in the genital regions particularly this effect is not always desirable. An L-bar can maintain a larger-gauge piercing without unnecessary bulk or weight. It looks just like a barbell but with a very slight curve to follow the lines of the body more comfortably.

Sometimes an L-bar in a smaller gauge is preferable to a straight bar, as an aid in healing a stubborn piercing such as a navel.

• NOT QUITE RING OR STUD

Nostril Screw

For many thousands of years East Indian women have had nostril piercings to signify their marital status and religion and for the sake of adornment. What do most of these women wear in their piercings? A nostril screw, a little coil of wire bent to fit the individual wearer. The head of the screw can be decorated with a shape or a stone, or be a simple small bead.

This is one piercing most people want to keep small. Consequently, they are usually offered only in 20 gauge. Gauntlet supplies its stores with unbent nostril screws. This way the piercer can

bend each one to fit the wearer, minimizing discomfort and possible loss of the jewelry.

Septum Retainer

There are many social situations which unfortunately make it inappropriate to wear septum jewelry at all times. For those occasions when subtlety is desired, a septum retainer is just the ticket. Retainers are also ideal for piercees who may need a little time to adjust to the idea of having a ring in the middle of their face. Retainers look like little horseshoes or staples, and are made of niobium, titanium, or surgical stainless steel. They are designed to fit comfortably and securely up inside the nostrils, and can be installed in a new piercing. It is important to adjust the retainer's size and gap to the individual's nose. If it is too loose there is a risk that the retainer could be lost or even swallowed. Retainers are available in several different proportions and in gauges 14 and thicker.

SUMMARY —
1. Bead rings are circular wires permanently attached at one end to a metal bead. The other end fits securely into a hole drilled into the bead.
2. Captive bead rings have unattached, indented beads held "captive" by the ends of the ring.
3. Barbells are internally threaded straight posts with a countersunk bead at either end.
4. Circular barbells are barbells that have been formed into a circular form.
5. Minibars are miniature barbells designed for use in dydoes, clits, and eyebrow piercings. Due to their thinness, they cannot be internally threaded. A small amount of wax on the threads helps ease insertion.
6. Labret studs are internally threaded posts with a flat, smooth disc on the inside and a decorative bead on the outside. They are the most comfortable lip and labret jewelry for many people.
7. Nostril screws are thin wires with a decorative bead attached to one end, bent into a comfortable shape to fit snugly against the nostril wall.

• WHEN ONLY THE WORST WILL DO

Selling Difficult & Opinionated Clients

You will have many piercees insisting upon a much smaller, thinner ring. They may have even seen a friend wearing some tiny little earring in a body piercing. This is a situation which can be frustrating and demanding of your patience and most skillful powers of pursuasion and salesmanship. An important part of your job is to help your clients select jewelry which will not only please them aesthetically but be safe and comfortable as well. Try some of these approaches:

1. A common reason why piercees insist they want a thin ring is an often unspoken fear which perceives thickness as an indication of painfulness. It is important from the start to put this fallacy in perspective. As discussed in chapter one, pain is determined more by the skill of the piercer than the size of the jewelry.

2. Next ask the perspective piercee if their intended piercing will be purely ornamental or if they anticipate play once healed. If for play, ask if they like it light, moderate, or heavy. Depending on body part, for a strictly decorative piercing the absolute minimum gauge for piercings below the neck is 16. For light to moderate play piercees should choose nothing thinner than 14 gauge, and for heavy play nothing thinner than 12 gauge.

3. If the piercee still has it in his/her mind that these are too thick, explain the "cheese-cutter" principle: the thinner a piece of wire is, the sharper a cutting edge it becomes. At very least a thin piece of jewelry can irritate delicate tissue, and at worst easily slice through a piercing. Using a thinner gauge can also encourage keloids, tearing, or accelerated rejection.

4. It is sometimes helpful for the piercee to actually see what a particular size ring will look like. Have them hold the jewelry in place in front of a mirror. Rings tend to look much larger in a showcase than in a piercing, and seeing often helps put things in proportion.

5. Usually by the time you have presented all this information the piercee will have been pursuaded to accept your advice. If not, you will be wise to kindly but firmly refuse to do the piercing. Should you give in and something go wrong, as is all too likely, rest assured you will be blamed for whatever it is.

While we have been dealing with gauge issues, be prepared to also deal with the matter of ring diameter as well. Rings (and barbells, too, for that matter) should always be at least ⅛″ more in diameter (length) than the width of the piercing. If a ring is too small it will probably never lie flat and, in addition, can create painful, unsightly ulcerations at the bottom edge of the openings of the piercing. These may completely refuse to heal.

Make piercees aware of all these facts. In most cases they will concede to your suggestions.

8. L-bars are slightly curved barbells. They are most frequently worn in large gauge PAs, but creative piercers can find many uses for this versatile piece.

9. Septum retainers are staple-like wires which keep the septum piercing open when it is not possible to wear visible jewelry

• JEWELRY SIZING

Frequently, the very smallest and very largest of these guidelines is not the most commonly appropriate size. For example, while a 16 gauge ⅜″ ring is the absolute minimum size for a male nipple, and then only in the rarest of cases, almost everyone needs to wear at least a 14 gauge, ½″ ring to avoid problems. These situations will be discussed at length later in this chapter.

Nervous piercees often make the erroneous assumption that a smaller or thinner ring makes for a "less painful" piercing. It is important to explain that this is not so, and help the piercee select a piece of jewelry that is not going to create problems for them. Find out if the piercing is to serve some function, i.e. is it going to be played with, or if it's purely decorative. Look at how the individual is built. And, of course, find out their aesthetic preferences. Ultimately, the issue of safety overrides all other considerations. You are not required, and should never allow yourself to be coerced into installing jewelry that is likely to cause problems. Not everyone will end up with the jewelry they had envisioned, but most of them will accept your guidance, and usually become comfortable, even happy, with the choice.

Very occasionally, a piercee's requirements will genuinely fall out of the standard range. While you are still a novice, it is not suggested that you take it upon yourself to reach such a conclusion on your own. The standards were not decided lightly. Piercings with

Too Large!

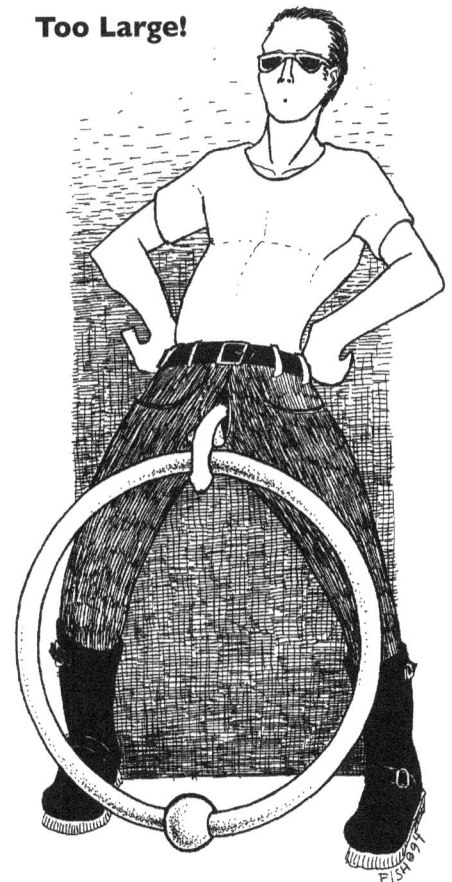

• CONVERSION TABLE
Inch Fractions to Millimeters

¼″	6.35mm
⁵⁄₁₆″	7.94
⅜″	9.53
⁷⁄₁₆″	11.11
½″	12.70
⁹⁄₁₆″	14.29
⅝″	15.88
¹¹⁄₁₆″	17.46
¾″	19.05
¹³⁄₁₆″	20.64
⅞″	22.23
¹⁵⁄₁₆″	23.81
1″	25.40
1¹⁄₁₆″	26.92
1⅛″	28.58
1³⁄₁₆″	30.16
1¼″	31.75
1⁵⁄₁₆″	33.34
1⅜″	34.93
1⁷⁄₁₆″	36.51
1½″	38.10
1⅝″	41.28
1¾″	44.45

unusual size requirements are generally very technically advanced operations anyway, and should not be attempted by other than a very skilled piercer.

Diameter/Length

If the diameter (or length in case of a barbell) is too small, the jewelry can pinch and inhibit growing tissue, encouraging keloiding, swelling, irritation, and/or infection. Sometimes undersized jewelry can even pull into the piercing, requiring a difficult and painful removal.

No piece of jewelry should be the same size as or smaller than the piercing itself. A minimum of ⅛″ to ¼″ is required to allow for adequate movement through the hole.

Don't assume that larger diameter is always better, though. Jewelry that is too large is prone to being snagged and twisted by clothing, towels, and bedding. Oral piercings in particular could be endangered by excessively oversized jewelry which can rip the healing tissue.

Diameter/length is usually measured with a pair of dial calipers.

Gauge

Gauge is the thickness of the jewelry wire. This is measured with a gauge wheel. For safety, the gauge of a piece of jewelry needs to be thick enough neither to bend easily nor cut through tissue if there is any weight or pressure put upon it. Ornamental piercings have different jewelry requirements than functional ones. And some tissue, such as the inner labia and ear lobe, is soft and more vulnerable to tearing than tougher, thicker tissue such as the outer labia. We've all seen women, old and young, with slit ear lobes. These are usually the result of wearing heavy earrings which have very thin wires. Had they worn thicker jewelry this likely could have been avoided.

If the gauge is too thin, tearing can occur gradually or suddenly. Sometimes a piercing will seem alright, but the tearing will become apparent when a thicker piece of jewelry slides easily through without need of an insertion taper.

Jewelry that is too thick can also create problems. If the area to be pierced is small, a larger gauge needle will literally overwhelm it. If thicker jewelry is desired, pierce and heal with a thinner gauge, then later slowly stretch the piercing to the desired size. Large gauge jewelry can inhibit oxygen supply to the cells in the piercing, impose painful weight on the area and/or prevent the escape of pus and matter and encourage truly dramatic infections. Don't take chances with gauge on either extreme of the scale.

A related and important issue is the gauge of the piercing needle. Skilled piercers usually use the same gauge needle as jewelry. An exception is sometimes made for cartilage piercings. As this tissue is rigid and sees limited blood flow, many piercers like to use a needle one gauge larger to make the jewelry more comfortable and help healing. Some piercers, however, feel that this larger opening may encourage more airborne particles to enter the piercing. Either choice is valid.

Piercing needles are currently being sold in gauges ranging from 19 ga all the

way through 6 ga. Dermal punches are also available, to make holes 4 ga and even larger. There are some serious health and safety concerns to be considered when choosing which needles to pierce with.

Needles smaller than 18 ga aren't really practical, and can lead to mishaps during jewelry transfer. Use of piercing needles larger than 12 ga, especially larger than 10 ga, requires absolute skill, experience, and judgement. Therefore, we strongly suggest that readers of this manual steer clear of needles larger than 10 ga until they acquire sufficient experience to choose otherwise. There are many reasons for this precaution.

A well-developed piercer's eye is required to discern the appropriateness of a larger gauge piercing. There is always the risk of obliterating the very area you were intending to enhance. Very few nipples, for example, could withstand a 10 ga piercing. The added amount of tissue that the body must regenerate after a 10 ga or larger piercing will add weeks or months to any healing time. The piercee could easily heal a 12 ga and have stretched it twice in the time it takes to heal a 10 ga piercing, so why not do it that way?

Most larger gauge jewelry is both large and heavy, creating unwanted weight and movement related irritation of the delicate growing cells. These can lead to problems in the form of irritation, prolonged healing, infections, and abscesses. Larger is not always better. Lighter jewelry of materials such as titanium can sometimes be found, but the design should keep movement to a minimum. Jewelry made of acrylic can also be found but is unsuitable for healing.

• APPROPRIATE JEWELRY SIZES FOR DIFFERENT PIERCINGS

The information that follows is intended only to provide guidelines. These are not figures etched in stone. It requires more than just knowing these numbers to qualify as a skilled piercer. It takes time and experience to gain the knowledge required to deviate from the norms listed here. Piercing is a skilled craft that takes years to learn, longer to master. Some

34

ATTENTION! THIS DOCUMENT IS FOR HISTORIC REFERENCE ONLY!

of the sizes listed below are designated *rare*. If you are wise you will refrain from attempting to use them until you have had enough experience to know that they are appropriate. Until then stick (no pun intended) with the standards.

Ampallang—The jewelry best suited for this piercing is a barbell. To find the correct size, clean and mark the penis where the piercing will be done. Ask the piercee to get an erection—if he is nervous this isn't always possible—and measure with calipers the distance between the two dots. He may be less nervous with a bit of privacy, so send him to the bathroom or leave the piercing room until he is ready for you. Sometimes the measurement will be off by a few sixteenths of an inch. If necessary the piercee should return two or three days later for a more precise adjustment.

This is a very advanced piercing, and should be attempted only by a very skilled piercer.
Length: varies from 1″ to 2″, average 1⅜″.
Gauge: 14, but 12 not uncommon.

Apadravya—Ideal jewelry for this piercing is a barbell. To find the correct size follow the same procedure as for the ampallang. Apadravyas pass through the urethra and so tend to heal a bit faster than ampallangs.

This is a very advanced piercing, and should be attempted only by a very skilled piercer.
Length: varies from 1″ to 2″, average 1¼″.
Gauge: 14, but 12 not uncommon.

Cartilage—The jewelry best suited for this piercing is usually a ring; ear studs are not recommended until the piercing is well healed. Barbells have a tendency to snag on hair, etc. Many sizes are worn in the ear cartilage; try to scale the size to other jewelry in the ear and to the piercee's proportions.

This piercing is suitable for a moderately skilled novice under observation by a more experienced piercer.
Diameter: varies from ⅜″ to ⅝″, average ⅜″.
Gauge: 20 minimum, 18 and 16 are more comfortable and considered standard. 14 is generally acceptable, and 12 gauge rare.

Clit Hood—For this piercing choose a closed ring. The tissue stretches easily, so circular barbells and barbells can actually slip right through. Size varies according to piercee's aesthetic and functional needs.

This is an intermediate level piercing; piercers attempting this piercing should have plenty of experience before attempting it, and should be observed by a more experienced piercer.
Diameter: varies from ⅜″ to ⅝″, average ½″
Gauge: 16 minimum; 14 is much more comfortable. No larger than 12 gauge for a new piercing and then only if there is sufficient tissue to hold it.

Clitoris—Jewelry of choice for this piercing is a small ring or minibar.

Most women are not developed sufficiently for a clit piercing; of the few who are, the majority require the smallest possible ring.

As this is one of the most difficult piercings to perform, it should only be attempted by highly skilled, experienced piercers, who have reached an advanced stage of capability.
Diameter for this piercing is almost always ⅜″.
Gauge: usually 16; rarely 14.

Conch—The most suitable jewelry for the conch, or inner cartilage shell of the outer ear, is a barbell, but rings are not uncommon. When sizing for this piercing, allow an extra ¼″ on a barbell, or make sure the ring will be able to move easily up and down, rather than fitting tightly against the cartilage.
Keloiding can occur when the conch is irritated during healing; hot soaks are recommended.

This is an intermediate level piercing; piercers should have plenty of experience before attempting it, and should be observed by a more experienced piercer.
Length: varies from ⅜″ to ⁹⁄₁₆″, average ⁷⁄₁₆″.
Diameter: varies from ½″ to ¾″, average ⅝″.
Gauge: 14 standard; 12ga not uncommon.

Dydoe—The jewelry best suited for this piercing is a minibar or a barbell.

When sizing, assume that at least ⅛″ of tissue will be lost during the course of healing. Use a longer bar and pierce ⅛″ deeper to compensate. Dydoes are best attempted only on very well-flared corona; their success rate is only fair.

This is a very advanced piercing, and should be attempted only by a very skilled piercer.
Length: varies from ⁷⁄₁₆″ to ⁹⁄₁₆″, average ½″.
Gauge: 17 (minibar), 14ga barbells are very common.

Earl—For the Earl, a piercing located between the eyebrows, choose a barbell. Remember to allow at least ⅛″ extra room for cleaning.

This is an intermediate level piercing; piercers should have plenty of experience before attempting it, and should be observed by a more experienced piercer.
Length: varies from ⁷⁄₁₆″ to ⅝″, average ½″ or ⁹⁄₁₆″.
Gauge: usually 14; 12 also common.

Earlobe—As with many piercings, the piercee will find a ring much easier to

BROWN & SHARPE GAUGES		
•	•	•
20 ga .032″ 0.813mm	18 ga .040″ 1.024mm	16 ga .051″ 1.290mm
•	•	•
14 ga .064″ 1.629mm	12 ga .081″ 2.052mm	10 ga .102″ 2.588mm
●	●	●
8 ga .128″ 3.264mm	6 ga .162″ 4.111mm	4 ga .204″ 5.189mm
●	●	●
2 ga .257″ 6.543mm	0 ga .324″ 8.230mm	00 ga .364″ 9.246mm

clean. Appropriately made ear studs (solid nonreactive metal, at least 20 gauge, no threading, not excessively heavy in weight, and with sufficiently long post) are acceptable but less ideal.

People have many different ideas as to the perfect size of ear ring. Make sure that any jewelry is not so small that it creates pressure against the healing tissue, and not so large that it gets a lot of movement or snags on passing objects. Scale the size to other jewelry on the ears, and to the piercee's proportions. This piercing is suitable for a novice under observation by a more experienced piercer.
Diameter: varies from 5/16″ to 3/4″, average 3/8″ to 1/2″
Gauge: 20 minimum; 18 is safer and more comfortable. No larger than 12 gauge in a new piercing unless the lobe is quite large and fleshy and then no larger than 10.

Eyebrow—The preferable jewelry for this piercing is a ring. Minibars or small barbells are not uncommon but should be at least 1/8″ longer than the piercing to allow for cleaning. After healing many like to wear a D-ring designed just for eyebrows.

People frequently imagine eyebrow jewelry much smaller than is possible in a new piercing, often even smaller than exists. They also tend to have a mental picture of the placement that is too centered along the eyebrow. When selecting jewelry for the eyebrow, or any other facial piercing, it is especially important to take the time to show piercees how the different rings will look up against their skin. Most people will prefer the smallest possible piece of jewelry. If they select a ring that is smaller or thinner than 18ga 3/8″, let them know that the chance for rejection is a bit higher with that ring.

This is an intermediate piercing, suitable for an experienced novice under observation by a more experienced piercer.
Diameter: varies from 5/16″ to 7/16″, average 3/8″
Length: varies from 1/4″ to 3/8″, average 5/16″
Gauge: 20 minimum; 18 a better choice. 16 or 14ga occasionally used.

Fourchette—The jewelry best suited for this piercing, the female equivalent of the guiche piercing, is a ring. Barbells can be worn in this piercing, healed or new, and can often feel more comfortable to wear than a ring. However, barbells have the undesirable tendency to be easily and rather uncomfortably pulled into or through the very stretchy tissue. Wearing a ring insures that the jewelry will not come out.

This is an intermediate level piercing. Get plenty of experience before you try your hand at it, and make sure you are supervised by a more experienced piercer.
Diameter: varies from 3/8″ to 1/2″, according to body proportions.
Length: varies from 5/16″ to 9/16″, according to body proportions.
Gauge: 14 minimum, but 12ga is more practical and comfortable.

Frenum—The most comfortable jewelry for this piercing, at least while it is healing, is a barbell. When the penis is fully erect, the jewelry should be just snug against the piercing. Once healed, a large ring that encircles the penis head can be worn if the corona is well flared. A small ring that dangles can also be worn but may get in the way during intercourse or oral sex.

Amateur piercers often place this piercing too shallow to be comfortable for the wearer. Such a piercing also has a tendency to heal out.

This is an intermediate level piercing; piercers attempting it should have plenty of experience first and should be observed by a more experienced piercer.
Length: varies from 9/16″ to 3/4″, but standard length is 5/8″.
Gauge: 14 minimum, 12 or 10ga much more comfortable.

Guiche—The jewelry best suited for this piercing, located horizontally near the perineum muscle between scrotum and anus, is a ring. Barbells are a poor option but can be tried if the piercee is having a friction-related problem. Rings allow for optimal ease of cleaning and are less likely to be pulled into the piercing. Be careful not to undersize or oversize the ring! For really problematic guiche piercings try a guiche retainer made of monofilament nylon until tenderness abates.

This is an intermediate level piercing; piercers should have plenty of experience before attempting it, and should be observed by a more experienced piercer.
Diameter: is pretty standard at 5/8″
Gauge: 12 minimum; 10 is not uncommon.

Hand web—For this very rare, usually unsuccessful piercing, the jewelry choice can be either a ring or a barbell, depending on the piercee's proportions, anticipated amount of handling, and aesthetics. Rings may get snagged a bit more than barbells, but are much easier to clean, a valuable feature for hand web jewelry. Either way, be prepared to switch to a piece of monofilament nylon if necessary a few weeks into the healing. Add at least 1/4″ to the length or diameter; these piercings are known to swell quite a lot.
Length: varies from 3/8″ to 9/16″, average 1/2″.
Diameter: varies from 3/8″ to 5/8″, average 1/2″.
Gauge: 16 minimum, and 14 or 12 have a better chance of success.

Labia, Inner—Choose a ring that is a complete circle for this piercing. The tissue stretches readily and open style jewelry (circular barbells, barbells) have been known to pop out at inopportune times. As the tissue is very light and thin, choose a piece that corresponds in gauge to the anticipated amount of handling. If medium to heavy play may occur, larger gauges are strongly suggested. Make certain that the jewelry is large enough in diameter to place it deeply enough that it won't be torn out. Most women require at least 1/2″ diameter rings.

This is an intermediate level piercing, suitable for an experienced novice under observation by a more experienced piercer.
Diameter: varies from 3/8″ to 5/8″, average 1/2″.
Gauge: 16 if the labia are very petite, but 14 or 12 strongly suggested.

Labia, Outer—For this piercing the jewelry of choice is usually a closed ring (circular barbells can catch on clothing and on each other). Since women with large thighs may experience severe irritation caused by walking, barbells could dramatically improve this situation.

Choose a ring large enough to move freely, but not so large that it will snag easily. After you have made the marks for the piercing, check to be sure the size is correct.

Mistakes are frequently made with the placement of and jewelry for this piercing, increasing the likelihood of problems. Consequently, this should be considered an intermediate level piercing and piercers should have lots of experience before attempting it. They should be supervised by a more experienced piercer.
Diameter: varies from ½" to ¾", average ⅝".
Gauge: 14 minimum, 12 suggested for more comfort.

Labret/cheek—For this piercing choose a labret stud or a barbell. Many people like the look of a ring, but unfortunately the ring creates a lot of irritation, and keloiding can result. Save the ring for later.

If placed too low on the inside, labret piercings can and often do cause severe gum erosion and tooth enamel damage, not to mention severe keloiding. Save your piercee from this unpleasantry by inspecting their mouth carefully, noting where the frenulum ends on the inside. It looks like a little white line. Don't pierce any lower than the very top of the frenulum. Even properly placed, many piercees have some difficulty with the labret backing. Experiment with balls versus disc backings. Labrets, like all oral piercings, swell during the healing process. Allow at least ¼" extra length, and downsize slowly to avoid problems. When doing a cheek or upper labret piercing, remember that these piercings swell instantly and dramatically. It would not be unwise to add a whole ½" to the length.

This is an intermediate level piercing; piercers attempting it should have plenty of experience and should be observed by a more experienced piercer.
Initial length: varies from ⅜" to ⅝", average: ⅜" female, ⁷⁄₁₆" male.
Finished length: varies from ³⁄₁₆" to ½", average: ¼" female, ⁵⁄₁₆" male.
Gauge: 16 minimum, 14 is better.

Lip—The jewelry best suited for this piercing can be either a ring, labret stud, or barbell, depending on location and aesthetic preference. Rings work well along the sides of the lip, but as you approach the center, they can cause too much irritation for the healing tissue. If a ring is desired in or near the center of the lip, put it in after the piercing has completely healed. Like all oral piercings, the lip swells during healing. Allow at least ¼" extra length or diameter. A common mistake is to pierce directly into the lip; the jewelry won't have any secure tissue in which to anchor and usually will reject. The lip line ends a bit farther down than is immediately visible.   This is an intermediate level piercing; piercers should not attempt it without plenty of experience, and should be supervised by a more experienced piercer.
Initial length: varies from ⁵⁄₁₆" to ½", average ⅜".
Finished length: varies from ³⁄₁₆" to ⁷⁄₁₆", average: ¼" female, ⁵⁄₁₆" male.
Diameter: varies from ⁵⁄₁₆" to ½", average: ⁵⁄₁₆" female, ⅜" male.
Gauge: 18 minimum, occasionally 16 or 14 is desired.

Navel—For this piercing the most popular jewelry choice is a ring. Once healed, barbells or L-bars are very attractive in the navel. It is unfortunately all too common to see a ⅜" or ½" ring struggling in an angry ⅝" or ¾" deep navel piercing. This kind of irritation leads to infection and sometimes quite severe scarring. Avoid the deep piercing syndrome by measuring for the chosen jewelry, then remeasuring with the piercee lying down. Often the two measurements will be dramatically different.

Many piercees want the smallest, thinnest possible ring in their navel, a big mistake. Be aware that all navel piercings tend to reject at least ⅛" of tissue. If a ⅜" ring is installed in a navel that is deep enough to take ½", the frequent result is even greater rejection. Too much irritation and tearing of the tissue occurs when jewelry is not chosen carefully. Only people with very small, nearly unpierceable navels should select ⅜" rings.

Although the navel is considered to be an intermediate to advanced piercing due to the toughness of the tissue and placement difficulties, its extraordinary popularity induces us to teach it to novices in hopes of averting hundreds of poorly done piercings. Novice piercers attempting the navel piercing are urged to remain aware of the potential difficulty of every navel piercing. Know your limits!
Diameter: varies from ⅜" to ¾", average ½".
Gauge: 16 minimum; 14 strongly suggested; 12 for deep navels (rare).

Female Nipple—The jewelry best suited for this piercing is usually a ring. This allows for easy cleaning and maximum comfort for most women. However, larger-breasted women, or women with poor circulation in their breasts (i.e. women who have had breast surgery) often have problems with rings, up to and including rapid rejection. These women are urged to try barbells, with ⅛" minimum allowance for cleaning. If a woman has had breast surgery any time in the last three or four years, or if she has a family history of breast conditions, she should consult with a physician prior to being pierced. Women who anticipate breast feeding in the next year should wait until the child is weaned. Although well-healed nipple piercings do not present any problems for breast feeding, the constant oral contact, milk passing through the ducts, pressure, and irritation could make for a difficult healing period.

When choosing a diameter, remember that an erect nipple appears much smaller, the nipple spends most of its time in a flaccid state. The difference between erect and flaccid nipples can be quite dramatic. For this reason, even smaller nipples usually require at least ⅝" ring diameter to heal properly. The ring should be able to be moved freely up and down. If it refuses to lie flat after a few weeks healing time, the diameter is probably too small.

Women who anticipate moderate to heavy play should be pierced with 12 gauge. Women who will be using a barbell due to having larger breasts or poor circulation should select a 12 gauge barbell. Although the nipple, particularly the female nipple, is considered an intermediate level piercing, its popularity induces us to teach it to novices. Marking for this piercing should always be done carefully and slowly, as misplaced nipple piercings can be uncomfortable, unattractive, and possibly dangerous. Never perform this or any piercing if you feel unsure of the results. Know your limits!

Diameter: varies from ½″ (rare) to ⅞″, ⅝″ to ¾″ fairly standard.

Length: varies from ½″ to 1¹⁄₁₆″, ⅝″ most common.

Gauge: 16 (rare) if the piercings are purely ornamental. 14 common, 12 for heavy play.

Male nipples—The jewelry best suited for this piercing is a ring. Male nipples vary greatly in size and proportions. As a general rule when selecting jewelry, keep in mind that, even when very small, the relaxed nipple usually requires at least ½″ ring diameter to heal comfortably. If the piercing will be purely decorative, 16 gauge may be used. 14 gauge is considered the standard, at least for light to moderate play. For heavy play use 12 gauge assuming there is sufficient nipple development to handle it. It is not a good idea to do an initial nipple piercing larger than 12 gauge. If 10 gauge is desired, it is by far better to heal with 12ga and stretch up, unless the nipple is truly gargantuan. Starting with 10 gauge can overwhelm the nipple tissue and lead to possible rejection.

Although the nipple should be considered an intermediate level piercing, its popularity induces us to introduce it to novices in an effort to avert poorly done piercings. Remain aware of the uniqueness of every nipple, and make your marks slowly and carefully to avoid a misplaced piercing.

Diameter: varies from ⅜″ to ¾″ (rare), most common ½″ and ⅝″.

Gauge: 16 minimum, 14 fairly standard, up to 12 gauge.

Nostril—The jewelry best suited for this piercing is a ring or a nostril screw. Consider that although screws are smaller, more subtle, and less easily snagged, they are somewhat difficult to clean. With either choice, leave at least ⅛″ extra room to allow for the swelling which often occurs in the first week. The sizing may be adjusted after about a month, if the piercing is doing well.

To choose proper ring diameter mark where the piercing will go, and measure with dial calipers, allowing at least ¹⁄₁₆″ extra for clearance. A ring can be a little snug to the nostril, but not so tight that it pinches.   This piercing is suitable for a novice under observation by a more experienced piercer.

Diameter: varies from ⁵⁄₁₆″ to ⁷⁄₁₆″, average ⅜″.

Gauge: 20 minimum, 18 more common, 16 maximum.

Prince Albert—The most common jewelry choice for this piercing is a ring, occasionally an L-bar. Rings generally are preferred for healing. Bead rings and captive bead rings are continuous, and will not snag on clothing as easily as circular barbells, but the latter allow for easier removal after the first 6 weeks. Discuss the pros and cons of each design before deciding on jewelry. Piercees with foreskins should be made aware of the small chance of irritation or rejection of a PA. Occasionally the ring prevents the foreskin from fully retracting. If a piercee has foreskin, select the smallest diameter which will allow the ring to move freely without pinching. Remember that the tissue changes dramatically when the penis becomes erect, and always stretch the tissue to simulate erection when marking and selecting jewelry. A diameter that is too large in this area will often develop a tender redness around the ring, and discharge plasma. The body is attempting to prevent the irritation of the moving ring. Avoid this uncomfortable situation by choosing a ring that fits well the first time. Although 12 gauge is acceptable, the vast majority of men will find 10ga to be much, much more comfortable, and, as most men eventually stretch the PA to a larger gauge, this will give them a good head start.

Men with a smallish urethra located high on the head usually require a larger ring, while men with a larger urethra located lower down need a smaller ring.

This is a slightly advanced piercing; piercers should have plenty of experience before attempting it, and should be observed by a more experienced piercer.

Diameter: varies from ½″ (rare) to ⅞″, average ⅝″ to ¾″.

Gauge: 12 minimum, 10 most common.

Scrotum—Depending on the location, the jewelry best suited for this piercing may either be a ring or a barbell. Along the sides of the scrotum, rings generally fare better, as barbells tend to snag on underwear. Along the seam that runs down the center of the sac, either barbells or rings are fine. Never pierce more than the surface tissue of the scrotum. While certain nomadic North African people are said to perform a piercing at puberty which passes between the testicles, it is not within the scope of even a skilled modern piercer to attempt this delicate surgical procedure.

This tissue moves about annoyingly, changing what appeared to be symmetrical marks into shapeless, embarrassingly crooked blobs. Mark, wait, and mark again. Never pierce using the first marks; they will almost always be much deeper than the diameter of the jewelry.

This is an intermediate level piercing; piercers should have plenty of experience before attempting it and should be supervised by a more experienced piercer.

Diameter: varies from ½″ to ¾″, average ⅝″.

Gauge: 14 minimum, 12 much more comfortable.

Septum—These fare best with a ring, circular barbell, or septum retainer. Most piercees, unfortunately, are unable to wear visible septum jewelry during the daytime. A septum retainer is therefore the most popular choice for new septum piercings. Circular barbells can function in much the same way as retainers, as the opening between the beads can be adjusted slightly to allow the ends to be flipped up into the nostrils.

Choose a retainer that is broad enough to fit without pinching, yet snug enough to resist being lost. If necessary tighten or spread the ends for proper fit.

This is an intermediate level piercing; piercers attempting this piercing should have plenty of experience before attempting it, and should be observed by a more experienced piercer.

Diameter (ring or circular barbell): varies from ⅜″ to ⅝″, average ⅜″ or ½″.

Gauge: 16 minimum, 14 more comfortable, can go up to 10 gauge.

Surface-to-Surface piercings—There really is no jewelry suitable for these piercings, as the high surface tension and frequent pressure almost always forces them to reject within weeks or even days. The piercee usually ends up not with a piercing but with a scar. For this reason, surface piercings are generally discouraged. If a skilled, experienced piercer and a determined, experienced, informed piercee decide to attempt a surface piercing, the best bet is usually a length of nylon monofilament to start. After several months, when the piercing has shown some indication of possible success, appropriate jewelry may be selected and installed. As surface piercings are practically guaranteed to lose at least ¼″ of tissue, pierce deeper than the intended diameter.

Again, these piercings are not recommended. Only a very experienced piercer possesses the judgment to decide under which circumstances they feel comfortable attempting such piercings, and the skill to give them even a minor chance of success.

Diameter/length: varies according to individual circumstances, allowing minimum ¼″ extra for rejection.

Gauge: usually 14 to 12.

Tragus—This piercing heals best with a ring. It can be a tricky healer, swelling, keloiding, and otherwise making a general nuisance of itself. A bar, ear stud, or nostril screw would make a fresh tragus piercing quite unmanageable. Save mini-bars or screws for later, and don't ever put ear studs in tragus piercings. Because swelling is so common, allow for an extra 1⁄16″ diameter initially, and be sure the ring moves freely.

This is an intermediate level piercing; get plenty of experience before attempting it and be supervised by a more experienced piercer.

Diameter: varies from 5⁄16″ to 7⁄16″, ⅜″ most common.

Gauge: although 20 gauge rings are acceptable, they may increase the risk of tearing, keloiding, etc. 18 gauge is suggested.

Triangle—The jewelry best suited for this difficult piercing is a ring. This piercing, located in a very precise place along the triangle of connective tissue that anchors the clitoris to the base of the pubic muscles, should only be attempted by very skilled, experienced piercers. The shaft of the clitoris, as well as the muscular tissue, nerves and blood vessels in the area make it an extremely advanced piercing. Approximately ⅓ of women abandon this piercing at some point because of difficult healing. The other ⅔ have no problems and love their triangles. Only women possessing appropriate anatomy should be considered as candidates for a triangle.

Ideally the clit hood and inner labia are very pronounced, seeming to be almost separate from the pubic area, with very small outer labia. Again, this piercing is only done by very experienced piercers.

Diameter: varies from ½″ to ⅝″, ⅝″ average.

Gauge: 12 gauge.

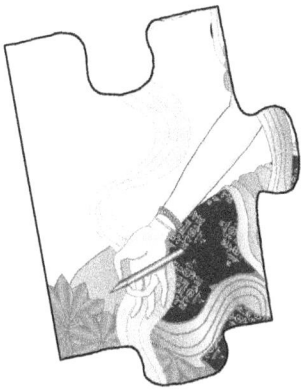

CHAPTER 5—
HANDLING THE TOOLS—PRACTICE MAKES PERFECT

• THE PRACTICE BOARD

Anyone who has studied a musical instrument well remembers the teacher's insistence upon correct hand position and the seemingly endless hours spent practicing exercises. While becoming a skilled piercer may not take as many years as becoming an accomplished musician, for both developing a solid technique results from using the instruments correctly and practicing the basic movements until they become second nature.

Before your hands ever touch a body to do an actual piercing, they should begin to get the feel by working on a practice board. With the help of this simple device, you can learn the techniques for doing both a clamped and freehand piercing, and get the feel for smooth jewelry insertion.

There may be some who will view these exercises as time-consuming busy work, but rest assured there is no faster, safer way to develop your basic skills, and the practice board is much more forgiving of fumbles than any human

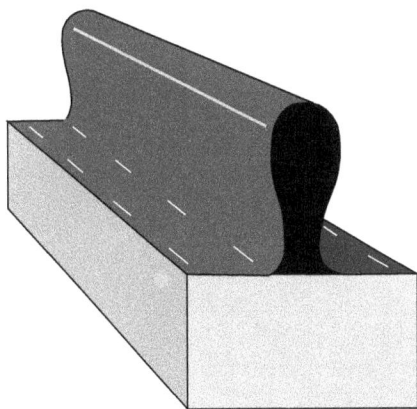

The Practice Board

subject. If you have done some piercings but have never used a practice board, you will find it an excellent way to unlearn any bad habits you may have developed and to retrain your hands to pierce even the toughest tissue with smoothness and ease.

• PREPARATIONS

Before we start, make sure you have all of the things you need:

1. A practice board. If you need to build one, just staple one long side of a 6 inch x 12 inch rectangle of light, garment-weight leather along the edge of the broad face of a foot-long 2″ x 4″; then staple the opposite edge. Add a second row of staples about an inch from the first row. That's it.
2. A small rubber band ½″ to 1″ in diameter.
3. A pair of Pennington forceps. Before preparing your forceps, examine them near the finger holes and you will notice a series of locking teeth. Some piercers assume that since they're there they are meant to clamp the forceps in place. Yes, were you doing surgery that would be exactly what they would be used for, but just try this on the web of tissue between your thumb and forefinger. Ouch! Not only is it painful, but locking the forceps on some delicate tissue can cause bruising. Besides, for our purposes locking isn't necessary. All we are trying to do is hold the tissue securely.

   Making the grip of the forceps less painful and adjustable is easy. Wrap the rubber band around the forceps handles several times. Check out the grip on your hand web. If you need

more tension, roll the rubber band further down the handles. If you need less, roll it up. Once you are satisfied with the grip, you are ready to proceed.
4. A small thimble.
5. A small cork. Select a cork that will fit snugly into the thimble, or obtain a thimble that will snugly fit the cork.
6. A clean piercing needle, preferably 14 gauge.
7. A needle holder.
8. An open ring the same gauge as the needle, ⅝″ to ¾″ diameter.
9. A small needle receiving tube.

You are now ready to begin. Start by learning the proper way to hold your tools.

The illustrations that follow show the piercing technique used by a right-handed piercer. If you are left-handed, you might find it helpful to study the illustrations in a mirror.

• HOLDING THE CORK

Hold the thimble securely between your thumb and forefinger. Notice that the axis of the thimble runs parallel to the forefinger. Your fingers are never in the path of the needle! Instead of bracing the backside of the cork, tightly grip it on either side.

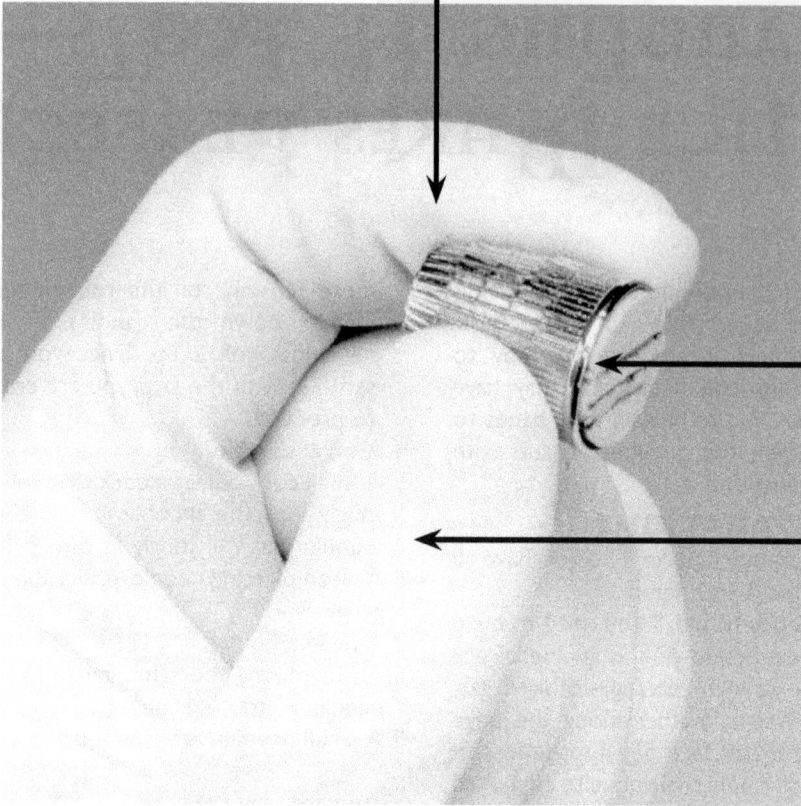

Prevent needle sticks. Place the cork into a metal thimble. For safety it should fit snugly.

Press the tip of your thumb firmly against the thimble. Notice that the line of the thumb is at a 90° angle to the axis of the thimble.

• TWO WAYS TO HOLD A NEEDLE

I. *A needle pusher gives you greater control and greatly facilitates the handling of a piercing needle, particularly when you anticipate going through tough tissue. Holding your needle pusher as shown here will give you the greatest control. It is also the best grip for piercing really tough tissue, commonly: nipples that have seen a lot of heavy play, navels, ampallangs, and apadravyas.*

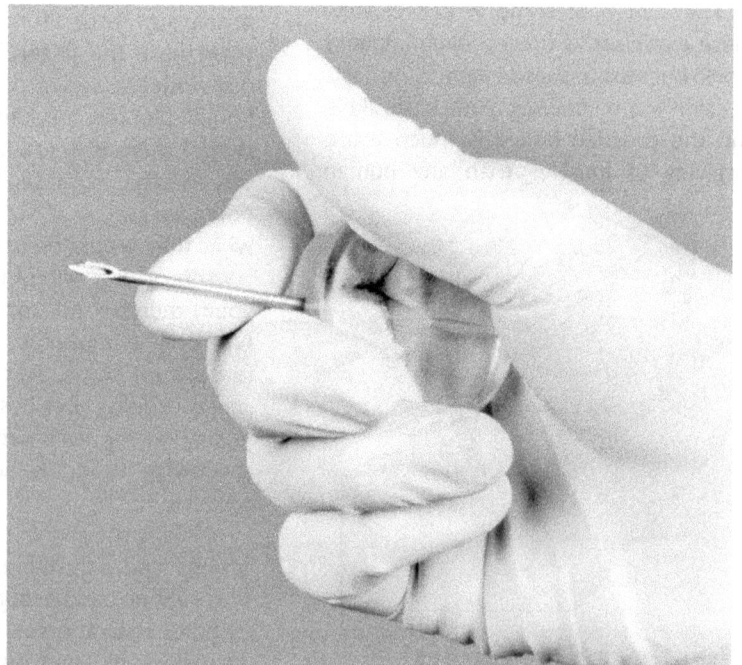

42

• HOLDING THE FORCEPS & CORK

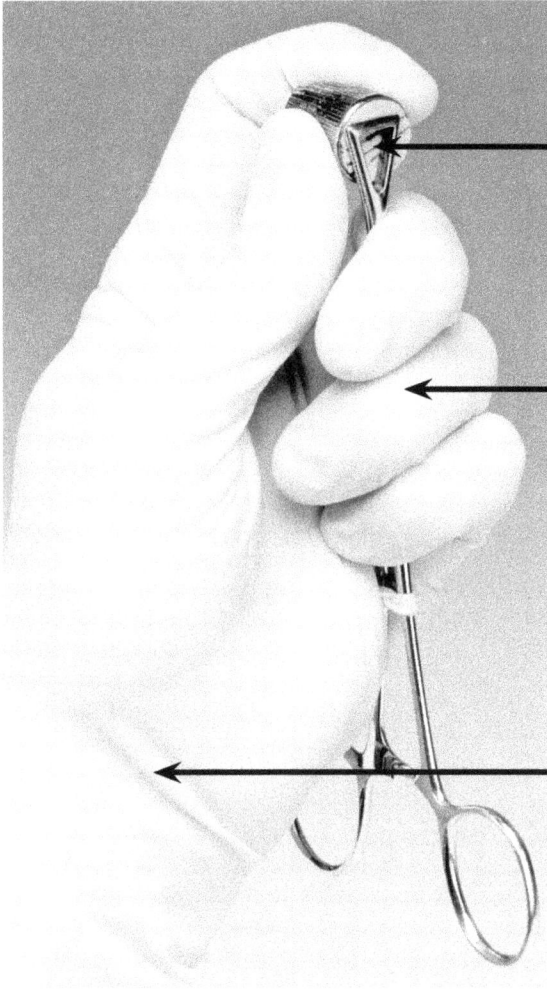

With the cork and thimble held securely between thumb and forefinger, press them firmly against the openings of the forceps. This is very important to keep the forceps from twisting during the piercing process. Center the cork just below the top of the opening.

Use your middle, ring, and little fingers to press the forceps firmly against the side of your palm and flat against the end of the cork.

The wrist is slightly bent but not enough to cause pain. When you first begin practicing the positions may seem uncomfortable, but persist. Soon enough they will become second nature. If the discomfort persists consult an experienced professional for tips on adjusting your hand position.

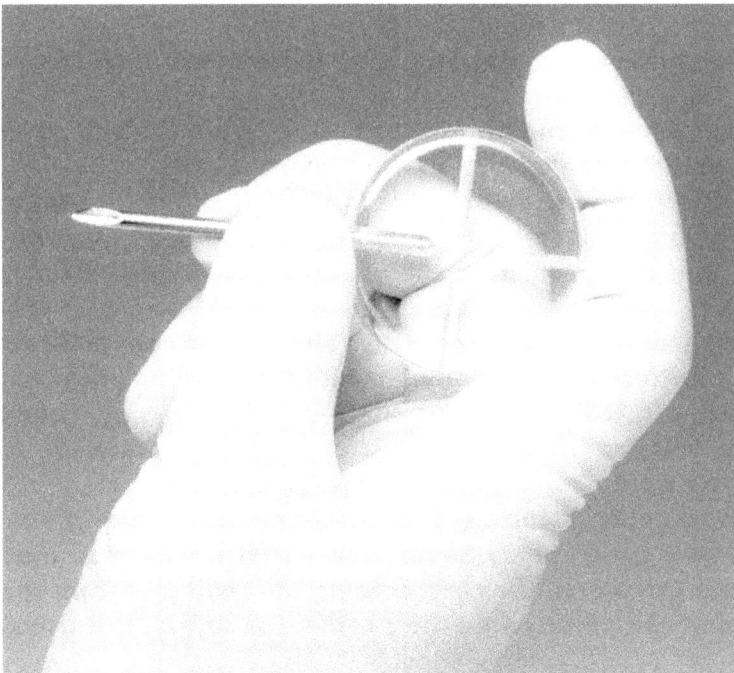

2. You may find trying to pierce in some areas too tight to comfortably use the other grip. Holding the needle and pusher as shown here works best in those situations and where the tissue is soft and offers little resistance.

• PUTTING IT TOGETHER

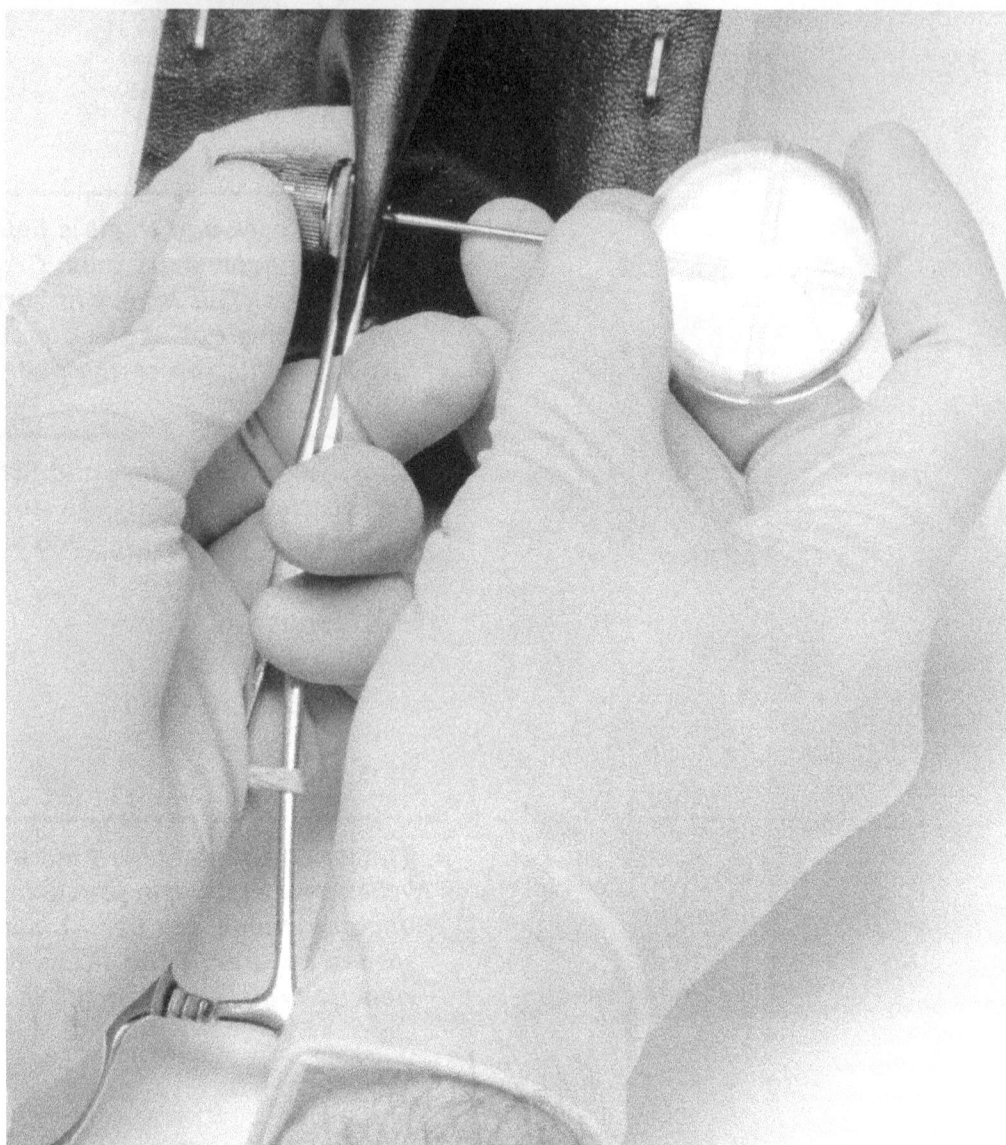

Start by clamping the forceps onto the fold of leather with the openings about a half inch from the fold.

Align the needle directly perpendicular to the openings and in a spot about ⅛″ from the end of the opening. If the needle is too close to any edge you risk snagging the point where it exits.

Do NOT jab the needle through the leather. Use firm, steady pressure instead. It should not take more than a second or two to get through. And do not attempt to embed the needle deep into the cork. Only the point needs to go into the cork, and once it is, push the needle through until about ¼″ protrudes from the entry side.

Removing the forceps can be painful and dangerous if done incorrectly. The utmost care and focus is needed at all times. First, change your hand position so that your right hand is grasping both the forceps and needle. Hold the needle tightly, and, with your left hand, use a careful, twisting, coaxing motion to remove the cork. Done carelessly, you can incur a needle stick, so remain focused. When the needle point is exposed, be even more aware. Don't move recklessly.

You may now remove the forceps. The goal is to avoid disturbing the needle or tissue more than necessary. If the tension of the rubber band is very tight, it may be necessary to decrease it so that the forceps open freely. Then, carefully slide the forceps to the right freeing the right jaw from the short end of the needle. Now slide to the left and completely free the needle. For safety, it is usually wise to recork the needle.

• OPENING A RING BY HAND & WITH PLIERS

To open a ring, gently pull it apart at the closure just enough for the ends to clear each other. Now bend the right half of the ring away from you until the ends are about ⅜″ apart.

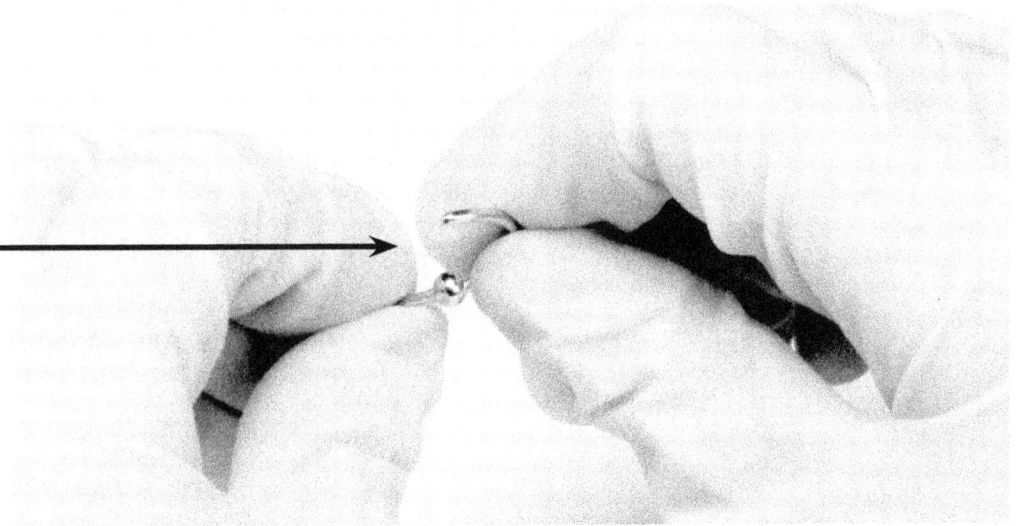

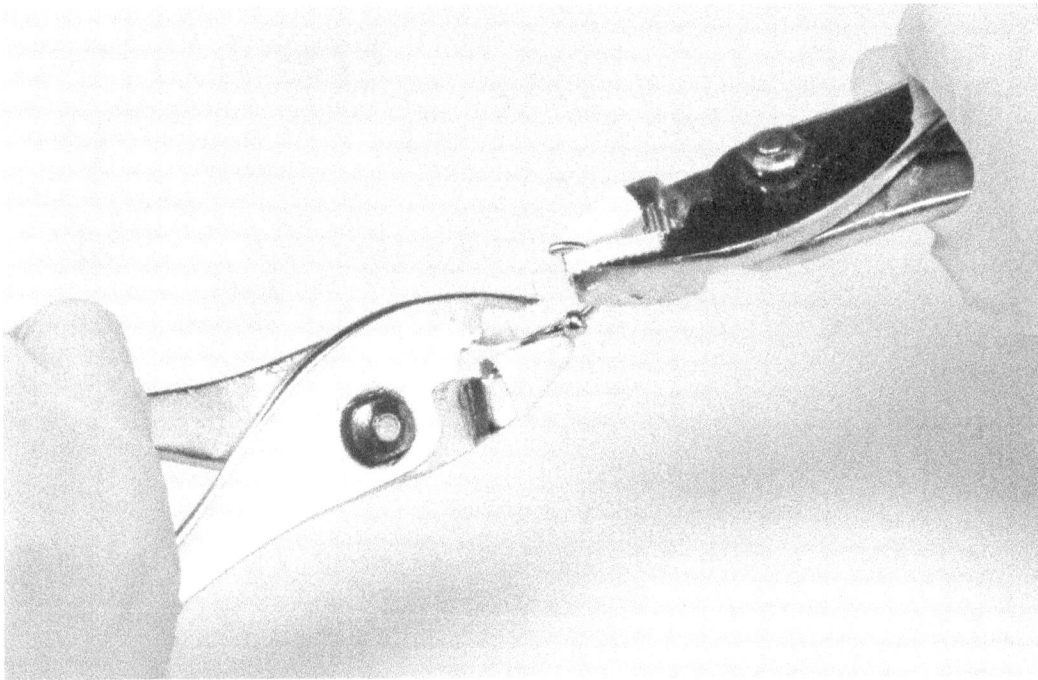

Opening and closing jewelry with pliers: The practice board is an excellent way to practice painless tool use. The goal in opening and closing jewelry is always to avoid slipping, catching, pinching, tearing, or twisting the tissue. Focus, patience, and skill should be developed and utilized for every situation.

Before starting, wrap the jaws of two pair of pliers with two or three layers of surgical tape.

To get a feel for using pliers to open and close jewelry practice on a 12 gauge, ⅝″ ring. Practice opening it as described on the previous page. To close it, first make sure the ends of the ring overlap slightly. Use hog ring pliers if necessary. Then twist the ring closed, and gently make sure the plain end snaps into the ball closure. Once you have the feeling, practice closing the ring while its through the leather.

• JEWELRY INSERTION

Grasp the needle firmly from above between your left thumb and your middle and ring fingers. Apply steady pressure to the tissue where the needle exits with the side of your index finger. Hold the jewelry between your right thumb and middle finger, using your index finger as a guide. Be sure that your fingers leave enough of the ring to pass completely through the piercing. Butt the end of the ring tightly against the end of the needle, and adjust the angle so they are in a smooth continuous line.

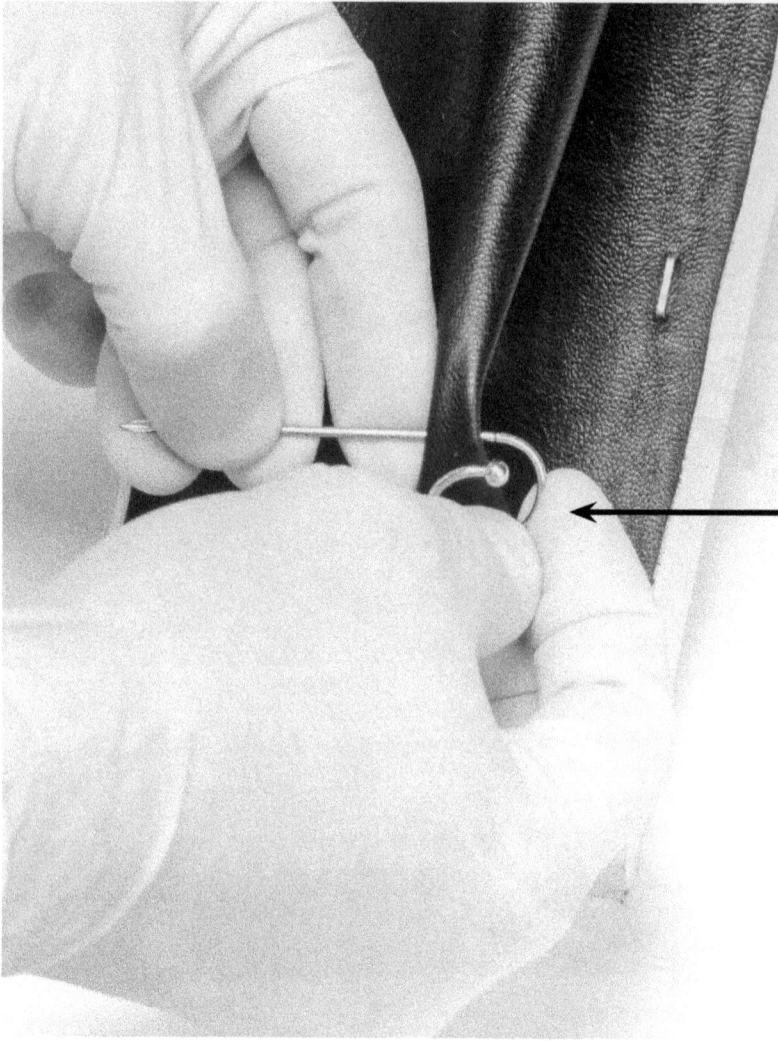

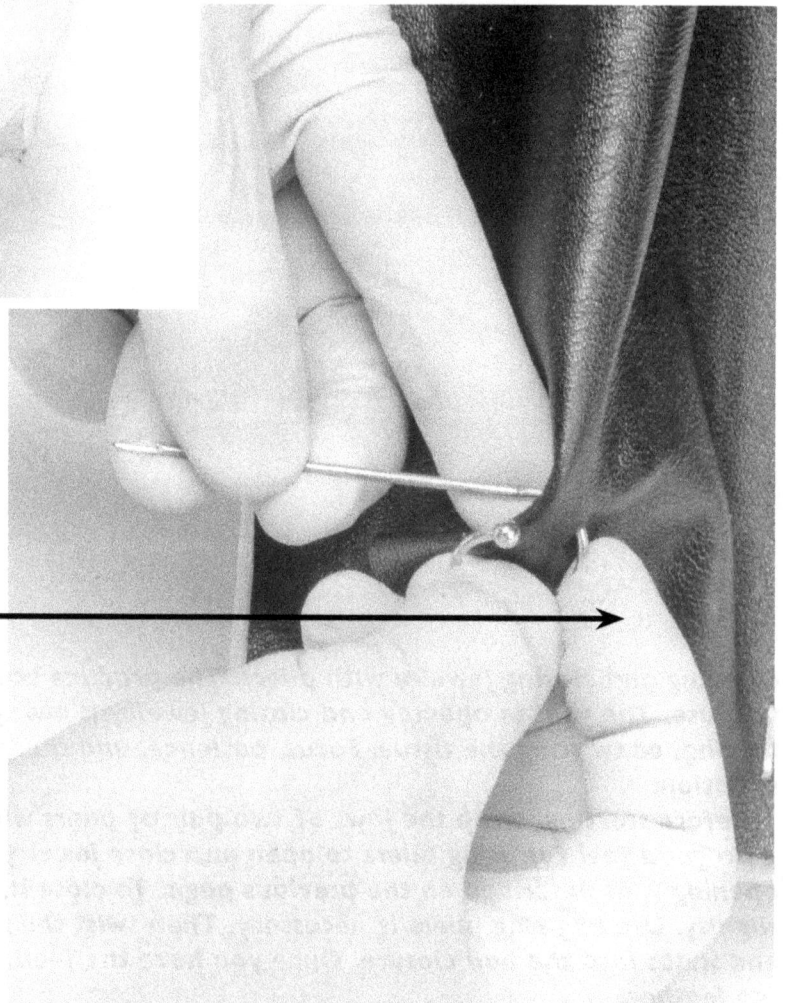

Maintaining a tight connection, push the needle out of the piercing with the jewelry. Do not let go of the needle with our left hand and do not attempt to pull the jewelry through with the needle.

• FREEHAND PIERCING PRACTICE

Freehand piercings: The practice board is also an excellent tool to develop freehand piercing skills, the leather acting very much like human tissue. The technique shown here is that used for doing a Prince Albert piercing. Insert an NRT under the fold of leather. Hold the tube firmly with the middle, ring, and little finger of the left hand. Stretch the leather tightly over the end of the tube with the left thumb and forefinger and the ring finger of the right hand. You should be able to see the outline of the end of the tube through the leather. Hold the needle securely between the right thumb and middle finger and place the point in the center of the tube outline. Firmly push the needle through the leather and well into the tube until about ¼" remains.

There are several freehand variations for other piercings. Get the feel of working on a nostril by piercing into a nostril tube, then try your hand piercing into an NRT placed opposite the needle on the outside of the folded leather. This is the way septum piercings are usually done.

With each variation practice jewelry insertion.

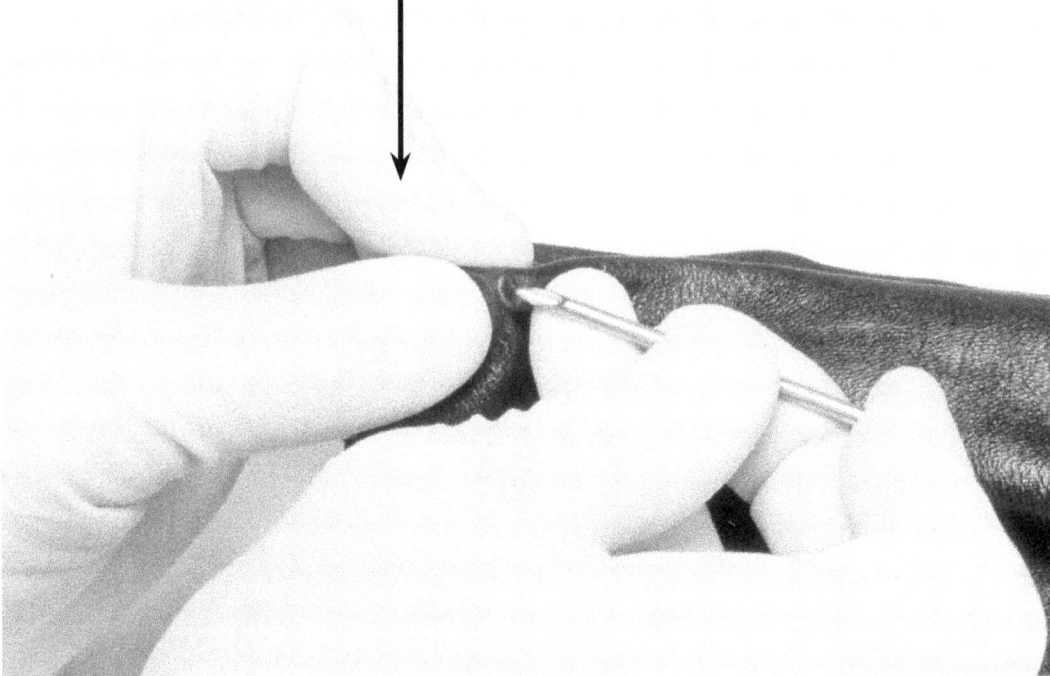

CHAPTER 6—

An Introduction to Basic Technique

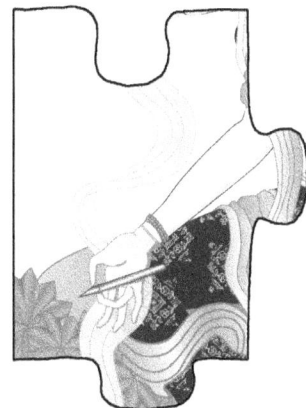

Whether you will be piercing an earlobe or labia, nostril or navel, frenum or fourchette, there are certain procedural and technical commonalities which all piercings share. This is the core of the piercing process, and it is essential that you be thoroughly familiar with it. From there it is simply a matter of learning the slight additions to or variations of this basic procedure required for each individual type of piercing.

There are two essential techniques used by piercers. The most common we call the "clamp-and-pierce" technique. This is used for probably three out of four piercings. Since there are some parts of the anatomy which do not lend themselves to clamping, we must rely on "freehand," our second technique.

Regardless of which technique is used, the piercing process always follows the same basic procedure. This we will detail in the next few pages. We begin with:

• STANDARD SETUP

Although the equipment, jewelry, and piercee will vary from piercing to piercing, there is one standard method for setting up your piercing tray. Develop the habit of doing it the same way every time and and save yourself the embarrassment of rummaging around looking for that implement you forgot. Things will go faster and smoother. Let's go through a setup, step by step:

1. Invite the piercee to use the bathroom, or have them go through any necessary prep cleansing techniques for the piercing. More on this later.
2. Drop the jewelry into the jewelry disinfectant. This will give it time to sterilize while you're getting ready. Remember that contaminated jewelry previously worn by the individual you will now be piercing is sterilized in a disposable plastic cup. If the jewelry needs to be opened up with pliers or ring expanders, do that now. If a wire connector snip is needed to join the jewelry to the needle during transfer, drop that in the disinfectant with the jewelry.
3. Prepare the room. Ideally you have already picked up any remainders from the last piercing; if not, do it now, with gloves if necessary. Change the lighting to be most effective for the piercing. If genital piercing will be performed, tear off a layer of hospital exam paper and lay it horizontally across the width of the table, giving you a double-layered square underneath the piercee. If the piercee will be laying or reclining, set up the pillow, cushion, or "husband" in the

proper place. If the piercing will be performed in a chair, position it for greatest convenience. Do now anything you won't be able to do after you've washed up.
4. Wash and scrub your hands. Use a vigorous manual scrubbing and a strong but mild antibacterial soap. If the sink is not available, scrub for one full minute with 70% alcohol gel. Dry hands with clean paper towels and return to the piercing room without touching anything.
5. Place a plastic-backed dental bib or few tissues on the steel tray. If you are not sure the tray is clean, wipe it down first with disinfectant first. If using tissues use three or four to reduce the chance of soaking through.
6. Place a small dab of antibiotic ointment on one corner of the paper.
7. Using clean hemostats or needle holders, remove a sturdy cork and rubber band from their containers. Select a packet each of povidone-iodine and benzalkonium chloride. Place each item in the upper area of the tray, being sure that nothing touches.
8. If cotton swabs, tissues, toothpicks or other items will be needed or anticipated, use the hemostats to remove these from their containers. Place them in the upper area of the tray, without allowing them to touch other items.
9. Using a fresh pair of gloves, a clean tissue, or a pair of hemostats or a needle holder, select from the drawer the appropriate packaged forceps. Inspect the bag for any tears or punctures. Set the bag down in the lower right hand corner of the tray.
10. Using the same pair of gloves, clean tissue, pair of hemostats or needle holder, carefully select the appropriate sterile piercing needle. Inspect the package carefully to be sure it is sterile and is the proper gauge. Set the needle face down in the lower left hand corner of the tray.
11. Prepare any inks, Gentian Violet, alcohol or other liquids now. Pour a small amount into a disposable plastic relish cup, being careful not to spill anything on the sterile field. If there is room without crowding, set the cup or cups directly onto the very top area of the tray. There may not be adequate room; if not, take a few tissues, fold them neatly, place the cups on the tissues, and place them on an accessible area near the tray where they won't be accidentally spilled. Don't set anything onto the sterile field without a protective tissue underneath.

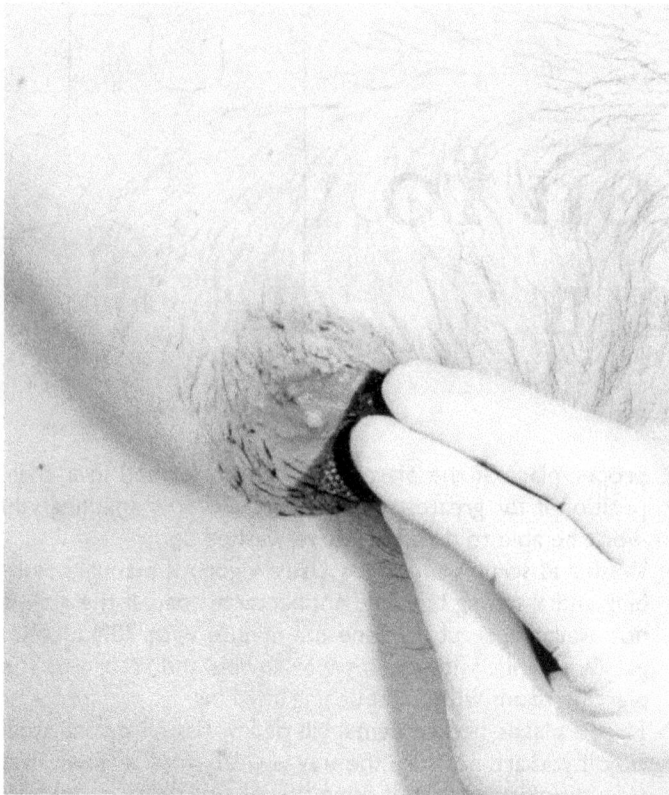

Step 1. Every piercing is prepared with an anti-septic scrub.

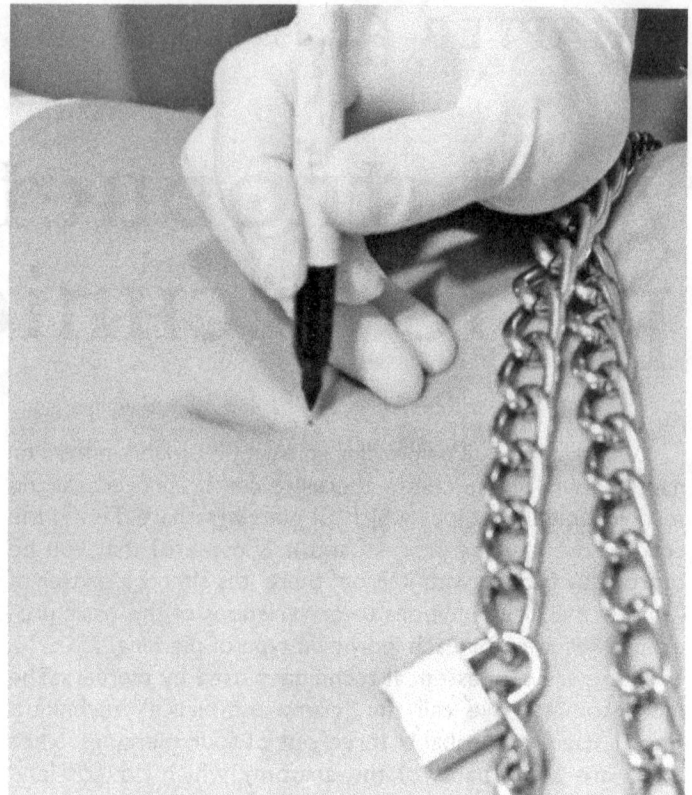

Step 2. Once cleaned, marks are drawn on the skin where the openings of the piercing should be.

12. Prepare any calipers, marking pens or other tools that may be used. Disinfect if necessary, and lay them on a tissue to one side of the tray.

13. If five minutes have elapsed, remove the jewelry from the Madacide with a pair of hemostats and dry it thoroughly with several layers of tissue. Set the jewelry down closest to the Bacitracin on the tray.

14. If you have touched anything other than what is on the sterile field (i.e. curtains, doorknobs, any part of yourself or any light fixture or other furnishing), go wash your hands again.

Your piercing setup is complete. Invite the piercee into the room and proceed to the next step.

• STEP 1: PREPARATION

While you were setting up the room, presumably the piercee has used the bathroom and taken care of any necessary preparation.

Before any oral piercings (tongue, lip, labret, cheek), piercees must thoroughly rinse their mouths, using full-strength Listerine, Biotene, or similar antibacterial mouthwash for one full minute. They may wish to rinse with water after doing so; it can produce a burning sensation.

Before any genital piercings, particularly guiche piercings, you may wish to ask the piercee to clean him/herself in the bathroom using a benzalkonium chloride swab. This will hopefully remove any unpleasant aromas that may be lurking in some people's crotches.

Any person, be they coworker, friend of the piercee, or the piercee him/herself, who anticipates handling or assisting with the piercing, needs to thoroughly wash their hands with antibacterial prep scrub. They will also need to wear gloves for the procedure.

By now your piercing room should be set up. If necessary, once again wash your hands. Invite the piercee and any companions into the room. Ask the piercee to remove whatever clothing is necessary. Guard your sterile field; explain why nothing should be placed on it, and direct those in attendance where to place their belongings and themselves. Make sure you will have a clear path between the "sterile" field, contaminated area, piercing area, and doorway.

The piercee should now be ready. Some piercings, such as nipples, need to be marked while the piercee is standing, and others, such as the nostril or earlobe, require that the piercee be seated.

Occasionally, before proceeding, you will need to include a minor pre-preparation step. This step is the removal of hair (should such be necessary) around male nipples, navels, and the guiche area, and around female genitals.

Our constant step one is *cleaning*. Put on your first pair of gloves, open the package (or packages for multiple piercings) of povidone-iodine and remove the saturated wipe. Swab the area to be pierced in a firm circular motion where possible. Fold the wipe so a fresh surface is exposed and repeat a second time. When the povidone-iodine has completely cleaned the area, remove any excess with a clean tissue or a benzalkonium chloride wipe. This will minimize the risk of a future allergic reaction.

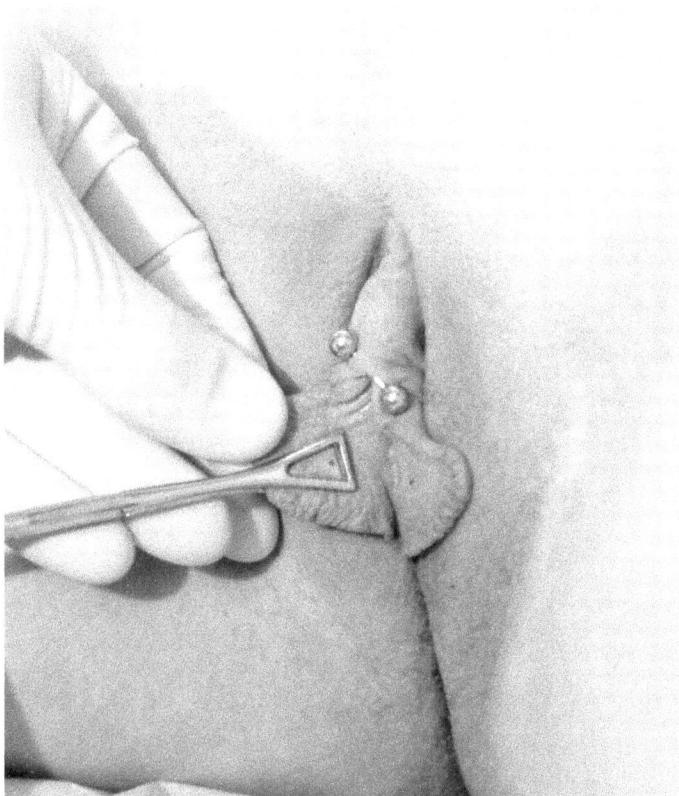

Step 3a (*clamp-and-pierce*). The tissue is now clamped into the jaws of the forceps, or

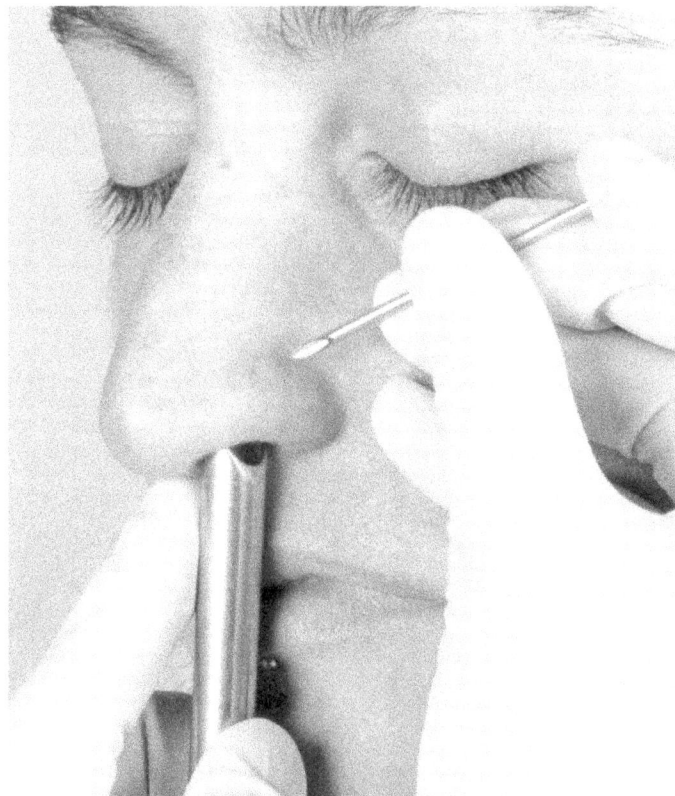

Step 3b (*freehand*). The necessary tools are placed in position.

For those persons allergic to povidone-iodine, use 70% alcohol for no less than one full minute, followed by a benzalkonium chloride wipe. This method is only for persons who react to povidone-iodine.

• STEP 2: MARKING

Make your marks, using a Sharpie marking pen, or a toothpick dipped in India ink or Gentian Violet. If the piercee is dark skinned, making it difficult to see the marks, dip a toothpick in a small dab of opaque titanium white water color or the moistened point broken from a white pencil kept only for this use. Care must be taken not to rub the marks off during the clamping procedure. If you are working in good light, white pigment may be unnecessary anyway, since India and Sharpie ink have a bluish sheen visible even on the darkest skin.

Your marking process will go much easier if you can see clearly. Use as much light as you need. If matching piercings were requested, use the calipers to measure distance and a folded tissue to measure angle. This will be discussed later.

Remember that skin moves. This is especially true of nipples and genital tissue! Make what you think are the right marks, wait a few minutes, and see how much the marks change.

Occasionally during the marking process it becomes apparent that the jewelry that was originally selected is no longer appropriate. The area might be much smaller or larger than it was thought, or the jewelry might not be aesthetically pleasing. If this occurs, remove your gloves, fetch the appropriate piece of jewelry, drop it into the Madacide, wash your hands, put on a new pair of gloves, and continue from there.

Never rush the marking process. It's better to take a half hour to get it right the first time than to have to redo the piercing next week.

• THE PIERCING PROCESS

When the marks are right, prepare the piercee. Have him/her sit, stand, lie down, or assume whatever comfortable position will make it easiest for you to pierce. Bedside manner plays a strong role at this stage of the game. Check the piercee for any signs of trouble while soothing them and making them feel calm enough to accept the piercing. If there is ANY indication of trouble at this stage, STOP. Do not proceed until both you and the piercee feel sufficiently relaxed and ready for the piercing.

If topical anesthetic is used (only for Prince Alberts and apadravyas), apply it now and wait approximately five minutes before proceeding. If a coworker, friend, or the piercee will be assisting, give them a pair of gloves and any instructions and equipment now.

Remove the gloves that were used for marking. Visually check over your piercing setup one last time. Did you forget anything? Have conditions changed enough to require additional equipment? Do you have the right pair of forceps, the proper gauge of needle, and, most importantly, DOES THE JEWELRY SELECTED FIT THE MARKS YOU HAVE MADE? Check your paths through the room, making sure everything is clear.

Continue to soothe the piercee as you put on a fresh pair of gloves and prepare the jewelry. Bend it, thread it, or

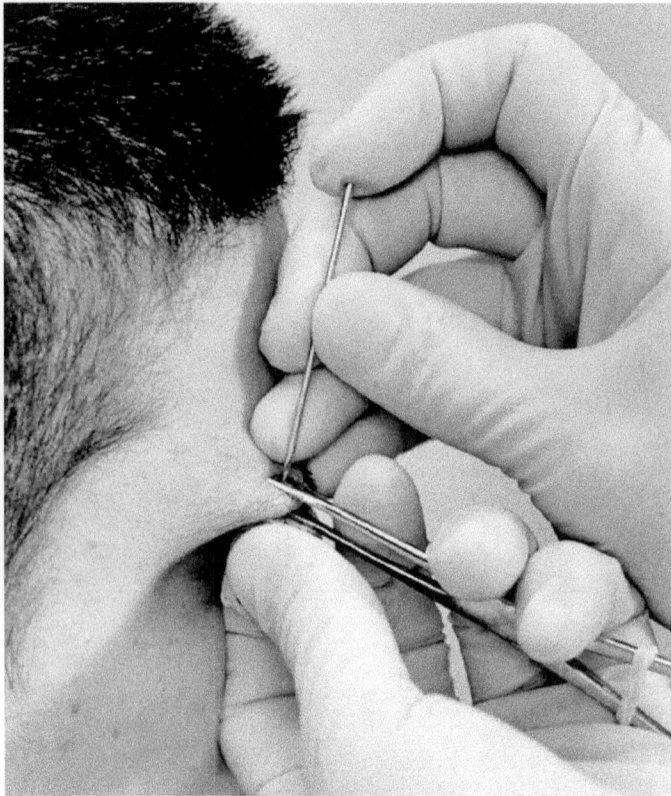

Step 4. With maximum control the piercing needle is pushed, not jabbed, through the tissue.

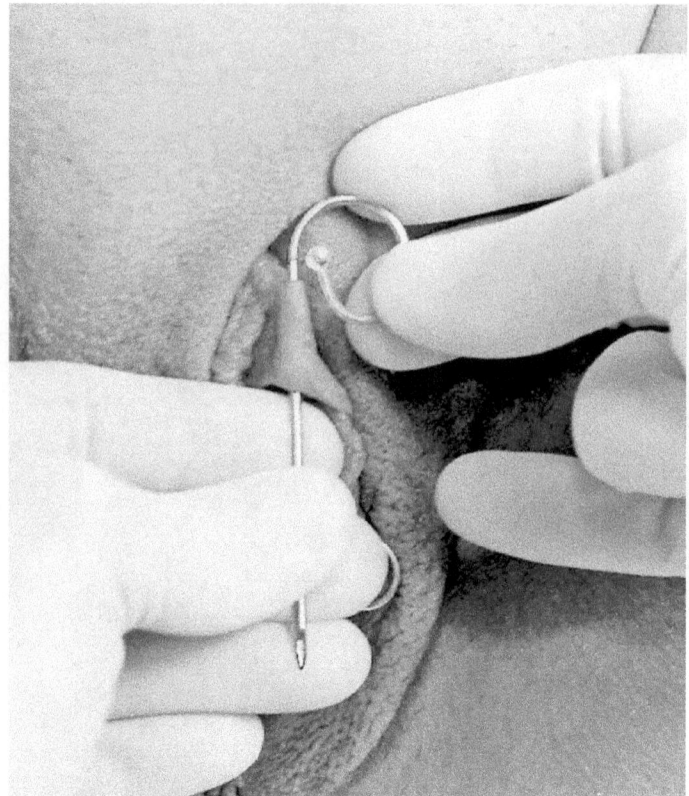

Step 5. The jewelry is inserted and closed.

unscrew it if you haven't already, and place a very small dab of Bacitracin on the end that will pass through the piercing first. Don't use too much. It can make you lose the jewelry in the piercing during transfer, which is embarrassing and can be painful.

Tear open the bags containing the needle and the forceps. Once the needle is out of its package, be extremely careful! Place just a very tiny dab of Bacitracin on the tip of the needle and hold it up to the jewelry for one last size check. Place the needle and jewelry in such a manner as to be easy to pick up together.

• STEP 3: CLAMPING OR POSITIONING

Wind the rubber band three or four times around the handles of the forceps, checking on your gloved hand web for a moderately firm grip (different piercings require different tensions; more on this later). Give your tray one last visual check, noting the location and preparedness of every item, and head for the piercee with your forceps.

Continue to soothe the piercee. People usually like to know what you're about to do, and a little information about how it's going to feel, so you might say something like, "I'm about to put the forceps on; it's only a slight pressure".

If this were to be a freehand piercing such as a nostril, septum, or Prince Albert, step three would be placing the nostril tube or needle receiving tube into position.

Ideally, your tray is close enough so that once the forceps are applied or the tube is in place you can simply hold onto them with one hand while carefully reaching for your needle (and cork, if it is needed) with the other. If this isn't

possible, have a gloved assistant, or the piercee, hold the forceps for you.

The next few seconds are generally very exciting and a little scary for the piercee. Be very sensitive to any changes in breathing or energy that might signify the need to stop and care for them. Mentally recheck everything out. Will the needle fit through the forceps or into the NRT? Is it the same size as the jewelry? Is the cork strong and firm? Where are your fingers? Are you calm, secure, and able to complete the piercing? Leave nothing to chance during this final, crucial inspection.

Urge the piercee to breathe deeply, slow breaths in through the nose, and out through the mouth. This will help calm them, steady their pulse and heart rate, and prevent them from hyperventilating. Whenever possible, try to pierce at the moment that the piercee exhales. This will greatly decrease the discomfort of piercing. Generally, even if a piercee states that they "don't want to know" when you're going to pierce them, it is much, much safer and less scary if you do let them know. It can be as simple a matter as saying, "Okay, now take a big deep breathe in, and here we go", or as complex as a roomful of chanting friends bringing their rhythm to a climax at the moment of piercing. The method is less important than having any surprises. The last thing you want is for the person to jerk or jump.

• STEP 4: PIERCING

When the piercee is totally ready, and is beginning that big exhale, firmly and smoothly push the needle completely through the tissue into the cork. This should take no more than a fraction of a second for most piercings, but it is important that you be absolutely focused during that time. Never jab! Piercees may move suddenly, moan or shout, scream for you to stop, or attempt to grab your hand or forceps, but while the needle is passing through the piercing, none of these can distract you. Your objective is to safely imbed the needle in the cork before anything else. Whatever you do don't stop halfway through the piercing. When the needle point is in the cork, press the needle on through until about ¼″ remains protruding from the entry side of the piercing.

Carefully remove the cork from the end of the needle, grasping the forceps and needle with one hand and GENTLY twisting/pulling the cork with the other. This procedure, done carelessly, can easily result in a needle stick, so remain focused and pay attention to the resistance and give of the cork and needle both.

When the cork is off, remove the forceps. Holding them with both hands, lift the one jaw away from the shortest end of the needle, then bring the entire pair of forceps away from the longer end. This will protect the tender area from unnecessary jostling. At this point, it is usually appropriate to recork the needle for safety. However, in some situations, recorking could actually increase danger of a needle stick. Always err on the side of caution.

Place the forceps on the tray or, if you are finished with them, directly into the contaminated tray. Don't touch the rim of the tray.

After the needle has been taken care of, check on the piercee. Are they faint? Do they look ill? If any symptoms of fainting or sickness are present, tend to them immediately. Jewelry insertion can wait.

• STEP 5: JEWELRY INSERTION

If piercees exhibit no more than the usual post-piercing grimaces, laughter, or gasps, go ahead with the insertion. Firmly insist that they not move during the transfer!

Retrieve the jewelry from the tray. Grasp the long end of the needle with the thumb, middle, and ring finger of your left hand. Use the index finger to apply pressure to the tissue. Place your right thumb, index and middle finger near the back of the jewelry to allow it to pass unobstructed through the piercing. When you are sure the transfer will be successful, in one swift, smooth motion push the needle out of the piercing with the jewelry. Never pull the needle out as you can lose that essential contact between jewelry and needle. Once the jewelry is safely through the tissue, set the needle back on the equipment tray if you will be using it to do another piercing; otherwise dispose of it immediately in the sharps container, being careful not to touch the rim.

Obviously, if you are left handed, use the opposite hand from that described above.

You can now return to close the jewelry. Depending upon its design, jewelry is closed a number of ways: with fingers, pliers, or by simply screwing on the ends. Any tool that is used during closure must have all rough surfaces taped with fresh surgical tape. Remember it is contaminated after use.

A great deal of damage can be done to a new piercing by a careless piercer during insertion. If the ring diameter is small, be very careful not to catch skin in the pliers. And pliers (fingers too) can slip, giving the jewelry a painful twist. Get a secure grip before you begin to apply pressure.

When the jewelry is securely fastened, center it attractively, if possible, and clean up any matter (blood, plasma, or antibiotic ointment) that may remain on the area. Some people get faint or queasy at the sight of blood. And remember, if you hand a piercee a mirror, either remove your contaminated gloves or use several tissues to protect the handle of the mirror.

It takes almost everyone a few minutes of resting to bring their body out of the light trance state which piercing induces. Don't let anyone leap up out of chairs or off tables too soon. Sometimes people look fine walking out of the piercing room, then crumple to the floor in the waiting room. This can cause real anxiety in any people waiting there. Always remain sensitive to the state of your piercees.

SUMMARY —
1. Prepare the piercee and any assistants by having them wash up.
2. Prepare the room by setting up the furniture, lighting, and piercing equipment.
3. A new pair of gloves is worn for each segment of the piercing process.
4. Clean the area to be pierced thoroughly with povidone-iodine.
5. Mark the area carefully and accurately with a Sharpie pen or toothpick and India Ink.
6. Have the piercee lie or sit comfortably as the particular piercing demands.
7. Prepare yourself and your equipment for piercing, making one final safety inspection.
8. Pierce with a smooth, controlled motion.
9. Secure the needle before attending to the piercee.
10. Insert and secure the jewelry.
11. Remain alert at every moment for signs of error or danger.

✦ THEME & VARIATIONS

On several occasions in this manual we have compared becoming a piercer to becoming a concert musician. Continuing with that metaphor, the previous chapter involved learning the required technique while in this one you learned to play a melody. In the following five chapters you will be introduced to many variations upon the basic theme, but before you can perform the variations, you must master that theme. Consequently, you should study this chapter in depth and refer to it often until its contents become second nature. In addition we encourage you to refer frequently to the drawings in the appendix and check out the anatomy books listed in the bibliography. These will help provide a foundation and a familiarity for what you will be dealing with as you perfect your profession.

The next five chapters contain detailed information on each of the traditional body piercings and many of the less common ones. As essential as it is for you to become totally familiar with the basic information presented in this chapter, for us to repeat it for every piercing would not only waste a lot of paper, but bore you to the point that important variations in technique or procedure could easily be overlooked. Consequently, the following five chapters have been streamlined and contain information specific to each individual piercing.

You will also note that while placement and marking of each piercing is discussed, all of the illustrations are of unpierced body parts. This is intentional. Working under the guidance and supervision of the seminar instructor, every student is expected to mark placement on the illustrations themselves as part of the learning process.

For each piercing you will find the following:

DIFFICULTY LEVEL
Every piercing will be designated with a difficulty rating from 3 to 10. There is no number 1 or 2 because as far as we are concerned to perform any piercing you should have a minimum of basic information and skills offered by this course. When you are finished you should be at least competent to perform a level 3 piercing and hopefully something higher. A number 10 piercing should only be undertaken by a highly skilled, very experienced piercer.

JEWELRY
While appropriate jewelry sizes were included in chapter 4, for easy reference this information will be repeated here in abbreviated form.

UNIQUE CONSIDERATIONS
What unique characteristics does this particular piercing have? There is information about many piercings which is pertinent to them alone. It is important that every piercer be well informed the better to practice their craft and to educate their clientele.

MARKING & PLACEMENT
Some of the most vital and essential information we can give you is how and where to mark each piercing. If you have developed good technique and can mark proper placement for a piercing, you are well on your way to becoming a competent professional.

TECHNICALITIES
Many piercings involve slight variations or additions to the basic procedure. And sometimes there are individual considerations or pointers which could be useful in perfecting your technique. These will be addressed under this heading.

Tray Setup for Each Piercing:

For each piercing you will find this representation of the stainless-steel setup tray with a list of the supplies and equipment needed for doing it.

CHAPTER 7—

THE THREE N'S

With this chapter we take a close look at the three most popular piercings being requested today. They provide an excellent introduction to both of our piercing techniques. Nipple and navel piercings are both performed using the clamp-and-pierce technique, while the nostril is done freehand.

✦ THE NOSTRIL PIERCING

DIFFICULTY LEVEL: 3 to 4

This is an appropriate piercing for an informed, conscientious novice to perform. The freehand technique and facial location require particular awareness on the part of the piercer who wishes to avoid accidents and/or needle sticks.

JEWELRY

A point must be made that no ear jewelry of any kind should ever be worn in the nostril. Not only is ear jewelry frequently made of inappropriate materials, but the design is often dangerous. Rings usually have thin wires and sharp edges. Studs have posts which can prick and lacerate the inside of the nostril. The back also makes cleaning difficult if not impossible. These design shortcomings provide an opportunity for infection which, in this particular area, could prove very serious, even fatal. Never put ear jewelry in any piercing but those of the ear lobe.

That said, you do have several options in selecting nostril jewelry. One popular choice is a ring, 20 gauge minimum, 16 gauge maximum. Regarding diameter, anywhere from ⁵⁄₁₆″ to ⁷⁄₁₆″ may be appropriate. Be sure the ring is not so small that it pinches or prevents cleaning. Some swelling usually occurs in the first week of healing.

The other choice of jewelry is the *nostril screw* based on an East Indian design over 2000 years old. It consists of a thin, solid wire that has been bent into a modified cork screw which lies flat and snug against the inside of the nostril and still permits easy cleaning. On the visible side of the piercing, some sort of decorative stone or shape is attached. Nostril screws made by Gauntlet are 20 gauge and can easily be worn by most piercees. Again, to allow for swelling, the screw should be a little bit loose for the first few weeks.

Although bleeding is fairly common with this process, many piercers like to pierce with a needle one gauge larger than the jewelry. This makes jewelry insertion easier and allows the jewelry a little room to move around in. It may be a little more comfortable for healing. One school of thought maintains that this allows more air into the piercing and would promote healing. Others feel the larger hole only provides a bigger entrance for bacteria. Either choice is yours.

UNIQUE CONSIDERATIONS

Piercings of the nostril have been practiced for thousands of years in Africa, India, Indonesia, and the Americas. The piercing traditionally has indicated the wearer's marital status, religious affiliation, tribal associations, and/or taste for decoration. Today the latter purpose is often cited by thousands of modern Americans and Europeans as their motive for having a nostril piercing.

This piercing is located in cartilage tissue and doesn't take kindly to being fiddled with. Since the area is exposed and vulnerable to accidental bumps, healing can be slow, sometimes taking up to a year. When removing clothing over the head or when toweling down after a bath or shower, care should be taken not to catch the jewelry. This is at least painful and at worst can tear the jewelry out of the piercing.

Nostril piercings do not do well if the jewelry is removed and left out. The tissue inside and out is very delicate and tends to close down almost immediately if jewelry is removed.

Nostrils are prone to dramatic keloids, which resemble red, oozing pimples. Still, in spite of all these factors, the extraordinary beauty of the piercing, and wide choice of jewelry with which to decorate it, keep people of all descriptions faithful to the style.

> **Tray Setup for Nostril Piercings:**
> • Povidone-iodine swabs
> • Benzalkonium chloride swabs
> • Marking pen or India ink and toothpicks
> • Nostril tube
> • Sterile piercing needle
> • Cork (to secure needle after piercing)

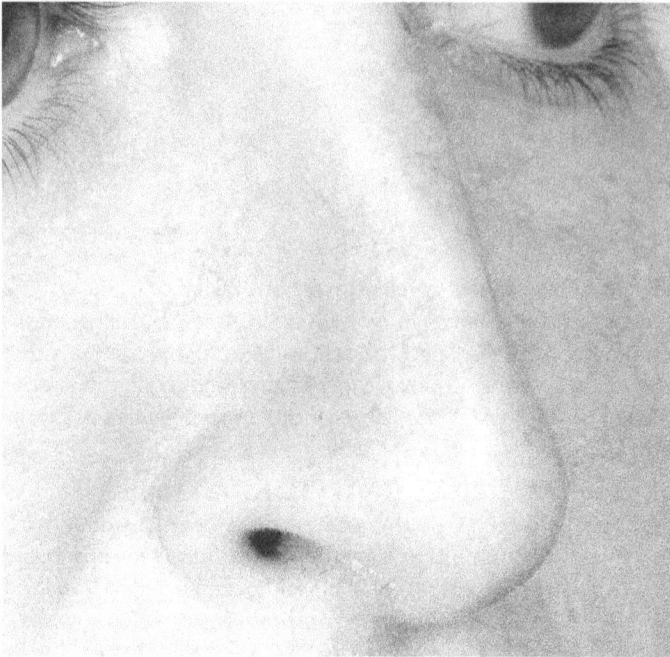

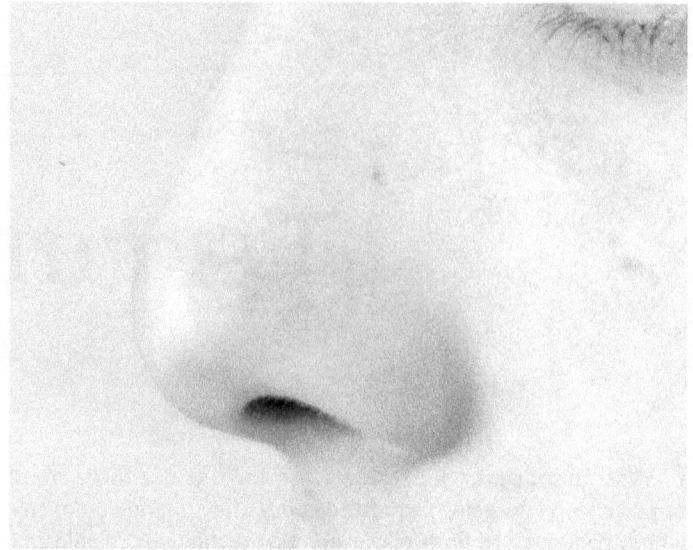

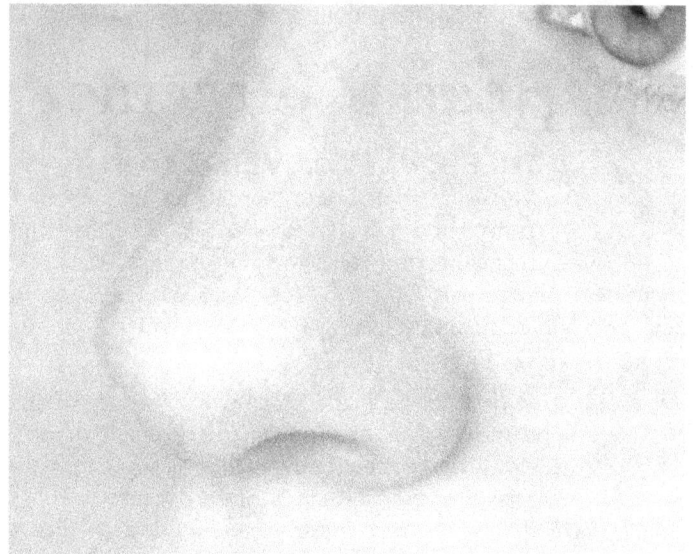

PLACEMENT & MARKING

While many people assume that any spot on the nostril is fair game for a piercing, this is not so. A piercing done too close to the edge of the nostril is very likely to be torn out, and looks unbalanced. A piercing done too deeply could interfere with the air-filtration process that our noses were set up to perform, become infected, or just plain look bad. There are limited options for nostril placement.

After the nostril has been cleaned, seek out the curved seam which all nostrils have. Some will be much more visible than others, but everyone has this curvature. At the apex of the seam, the nostril is thinnest, moves the least, and usually looks the best. This is where the mark goes. For further clarification, see the appendix.

Any bumps, growths, or freckles should be avoided. Scar tissue from former piercings does not pose a particular problem, however.

Angle is an important factor as you mark. Ask the piercee if they desire a standard, perpendicular placement, or if they would like the ring angled back slightly to appear more snug. Either way, you will have to compensate for the distortion caused by the nostril tube, which tends to push your angle slightly away from the face. When preparing to pierce the nostril, align the needle exactly, and then bring it slightly back towards the face to achieve the original angle.

When you have your mark, be sure that your jewelry will fit. If a ring is used, measure with calipers to check the diameter of the piercing in relation to diameter of the jewelry. Often, you will need a larger or smaller diameter ring.

TECHNICALITIES

When preparing to perform the nostril piercing, you will get a much more accurate angle if you overcompensate for the tissue distortion caused by the nostril tube. Tilt the needle about ¼″ more towards the face than the desired angle.

Some piercers use a needle that is one gauge larger than the jewelry in order to give the jewelry more room to move around inside cartilage. If you are using a 20 gauge or nostril screw, this is not a factor. If you are piercing for 18 ga or 16 gauge jewelry, however, take into account the fact that profuse bleeding is likely with a larger gauge needle. Also, the larger opening may allow more airborne particles into the piercing than if you had used a smaller gauge. The choice is yours either way, but piercing with larger than a 16 ga needle is not suggested.

Fainting is slightly more likely for nostril piercees, due to its facial location and the fact that it's usually one of the piercee's first. Remain alert.

After the piercing, be absolutely sure that the needle has cleared the tube before removing the tube. You wouldn't want to scrape the inside of the nasal cavity.

✦ ΠIPPLE PIERCIΠGS

DIFFICULTY LEVEL: 5

This is an intermediate level piercing. There are many variables when performing nipples and many different shapes and sizes of nipples, so the difficulty level fluctuates rather unpredictably. Don't ever assume that just because the last nipple came out fine, the next one is going to be a piece of cake.

JEWELRY

In the vast majority of cases, nipple piercings, both male and female, heal best with rings. The exceptions to this rule are women who have undergone breast augmentation or reduction surgery, or who just naturally have larger breasts. These women frequently find rings quite troublesome and uncomfortable. For them barbells seem to work much better, staying close to the nipple, reducing snags and the strain of gravity or the pressure of bras.

The ring sizes remain fairly standard 14 or 12 gauge, ½" or ⅝" diameter for men, ⅝" or ¾" for women. In the case of barbells, women generally prefer 12 gauge for comfort, and a length from ½" to ⅝", average ⁹⁄₁₆". It is very important for the stud to be at least ⅛" longer than the width of the nipple to allow for easy cleaning.

Refer to chapter 4 if you need to refresh your memory regarding appropriate jewelry selection.

UNIQUE CONSIDERATIONS

Almost without historical precedent, the popularity of the nipple piercing continues to increase. No longer the domain of the the young, the radical, and the kinky, nipple piercings are beginning to gain acceptance with otherwise conservative men and women. In a certain sense these could be considered unisex piercings, however, although the piercing procedure itself remains much the same regardless of gender, there are significant differences in the way each is marked and placed and in the choice of appropriate jewelry. One must also take into consideration the possibility that some women may someday wish to breast feed.

Gender Considerations

One common question asked by women is if nipple piercings will inhibit or prohibit their ability to breast feed at some later date. It might help answer this question if you refer to the anatomical drawing of the female breast in the appendix. There are many people with the erroneous impression that there is only a single duct through which milk flows during nursing. The fact is that the female nipple is a specialized sweat gland containing a network of milk ducts. Even if the piercing were to damage or block one of these ducts, there are many more which would continue to function normally.

A woman's primary consideration is not if, but when, she should have her nipples pierced. Ideally, there should be at least a year between the time of the piercing and the time of conception. This will allow nearly two years for the piercings to heal thoroughly before they will be called upon for nursing. If a nipple piercing is not well-healed when a piercee becomes pregnant, it might be best to consider letting the piercing go, and try it again at a less demanding time.

Once the baby arrives the jewelry can be removed. Some women leave their jewelry out until the child is weaned (an option which sometimes ends in a closed piercing). Others remove and reinsert jewelry regularly to assure that the piercing remains intact. We know of one woman who never removed her jewelry, merely inserting smaller diameter rings which would fit comfortably in the baby's mouth.

Men typically have a different consideration. Nature has not endowed most men with particularly large or well-developed nipples. In many cases they are scarcely larger than a match head. For this reason there are differences in the way a man's nipple is marked and pierced. We will discuss these at length shortly.

MARKING & PLACEMENT

Placement—Female

Have the piercee stand erect but comfortably in good light, with arms at her sides. The breasts should be free of any restrictive clothing. Wearing gloves, gently pinch the nipple, encouraging it to erect. Take note where it meets the plane of the areola. Usually there will be a crease where the two come together. If you can remember only to pierce in this crease, your piercings will never be too deep or too shallow, a common problem with nipple piercings done by amateurs.

Using your Sharpie marker or a toothpick dipped in India ink, place a small dot in the crease on either side of the nipple just slightly above horizontal center. Make the two dots as level a possible. As a visual aid it can be helpful to hold a folded facial tissue up to the nipple. Check your marks with your tissue level to be sure they are correct. If they are not, add new dots where they should be and check again.

Tray Setup for Nipple Piercings:
- Povidone-iodine swabs
- Benzalkonium chloride swabs
- Marking pen or India ink and toothpicks
- Regular or mini forceps
- Sterile piercing needle
- Needle pusher
- Rubber band
- Cork and thimble
- Optional: (barbell connecting wire)

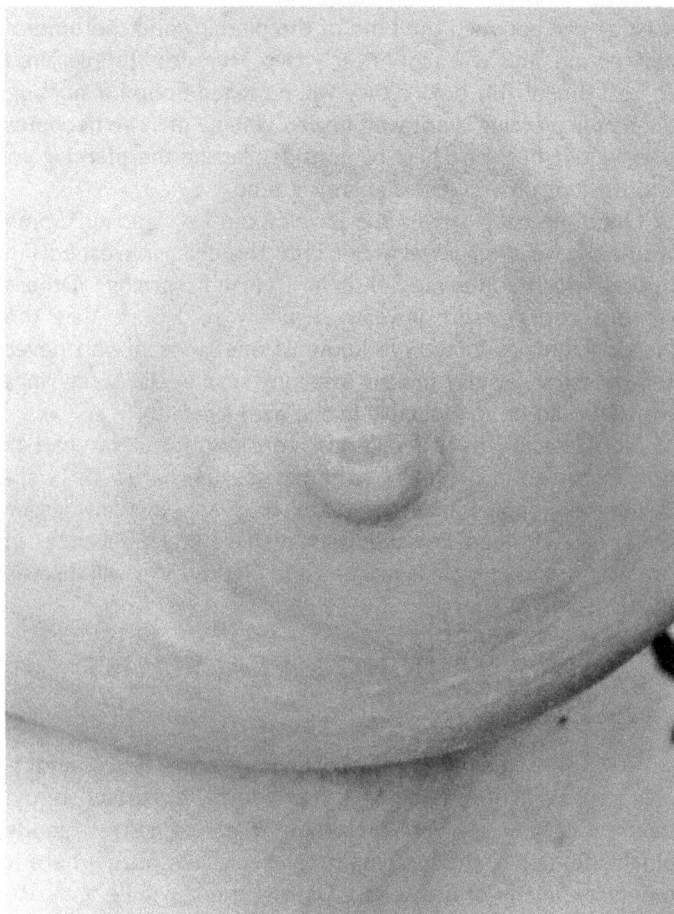

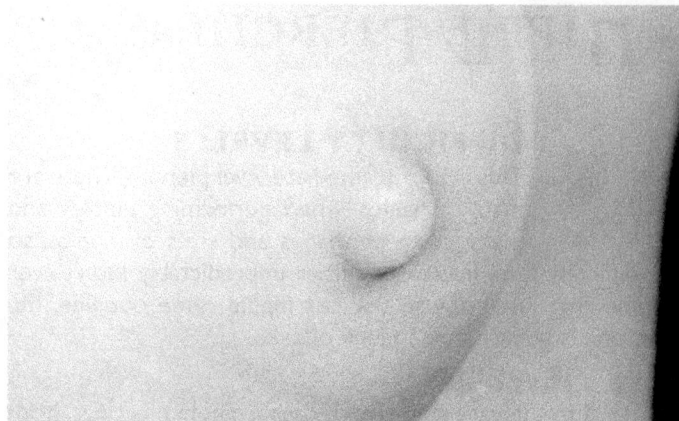

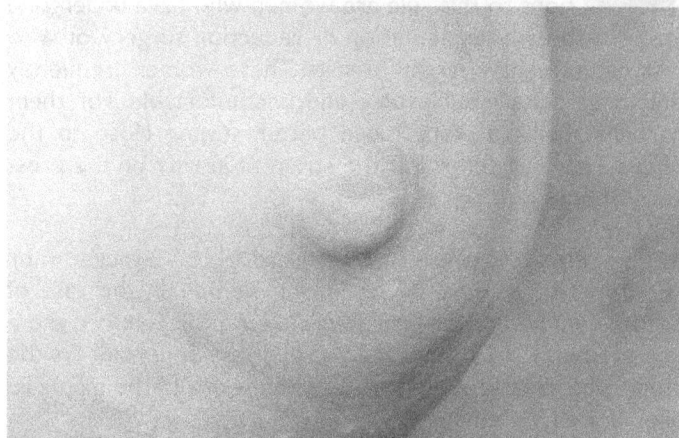

Three views of a typical, well-developed female nipple. At the left we see the nipple in a semi-relaxed state, on the right more erect.

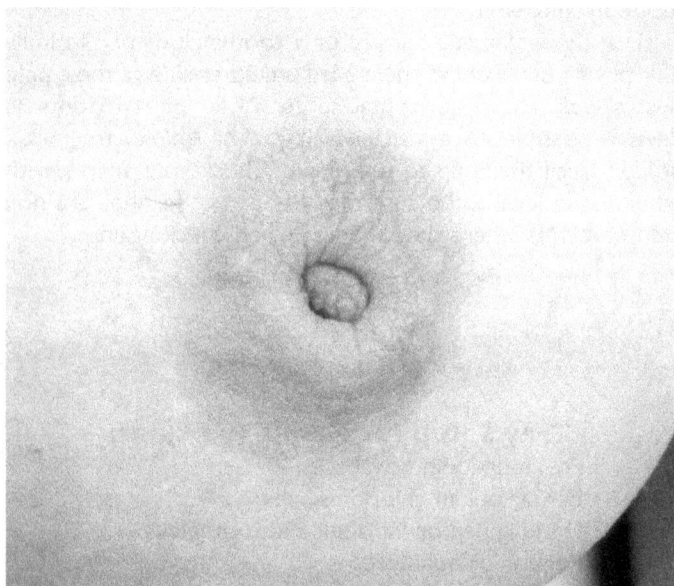

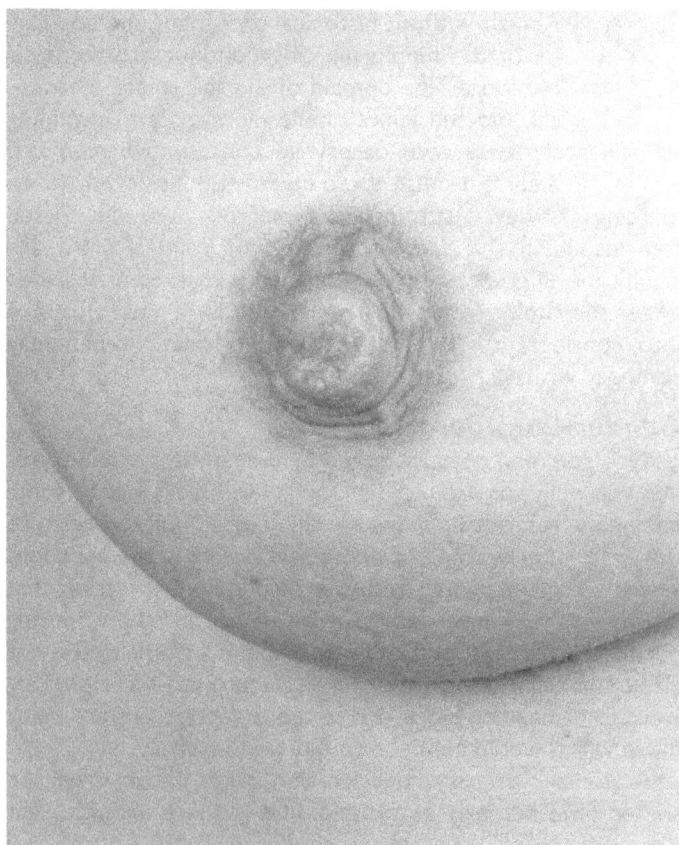

Something of a rarity is the concave or inverted nipple. At the left we see it in its relaxed state, on the right the nipple when erect. In some individuals the nipple never comes out of hiding, and in such cases is not pierceable.

Men can also have concave nipples.

Now, take a minute or two to observe how the nipple behaves. As it begins to relax from its erect state it is not uncommon for it to rotate slightly, your marks doing the same. Often, you'll find that your marks require some minor (or major) adjustments to bring them level. Keep the dots as small and precise as possible. Repeat this procedure as many times as you need: mark and wait; adjust, mark, and wait, until the marks are perfect.

By this time you may have a number of dots on each side of the nipple. To avoid any confusion erase the ones you don't need. Take a facial tissue folded in quarters and roll the edge into a tight, sharp point. As an alternative you can use a very small cotton swab. Moisten either one in your cup of rubbing alcohol and gently remove your unwanted dots. There is an important reason we wait to remove dots until this time. The cooling effect of the alcohol as it evaporates makes the nipple rotation more extreme, adding confusion to the marking process.

After the extra marks are erased, wait a minute and watch the nipple return to its normal position. Are your dots still symmetrical and level? If not, make whatever adjustments are necessary.

Some women have inverted nipples. Unless these can be coaxed to erect they cannot be pierced. If they can be drawn out, mark them at the base just like regular nipples. Be aware that once pierced and healed these nipples will not invert again.

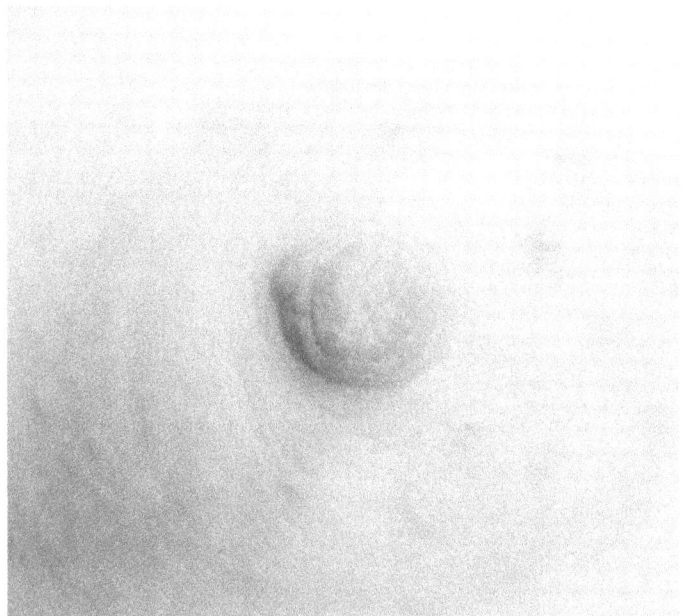

Piercers are often confronted with slightly misshapen nipples such as this one. Each presents a unique challenge to the piercer. Hint: treat the distortion as part of the nipple.

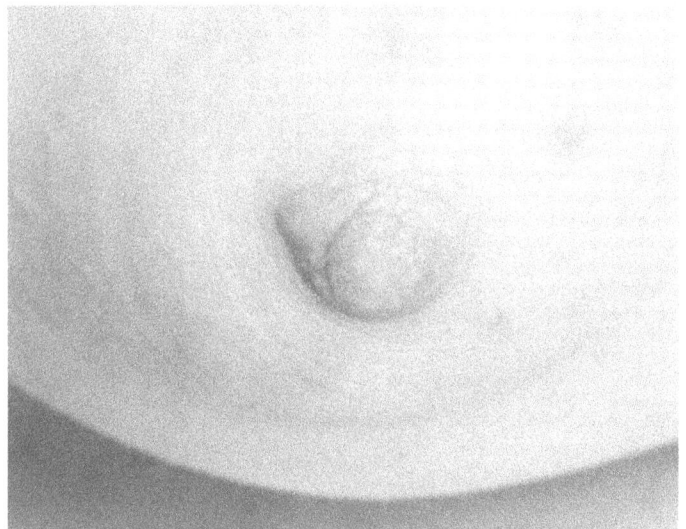

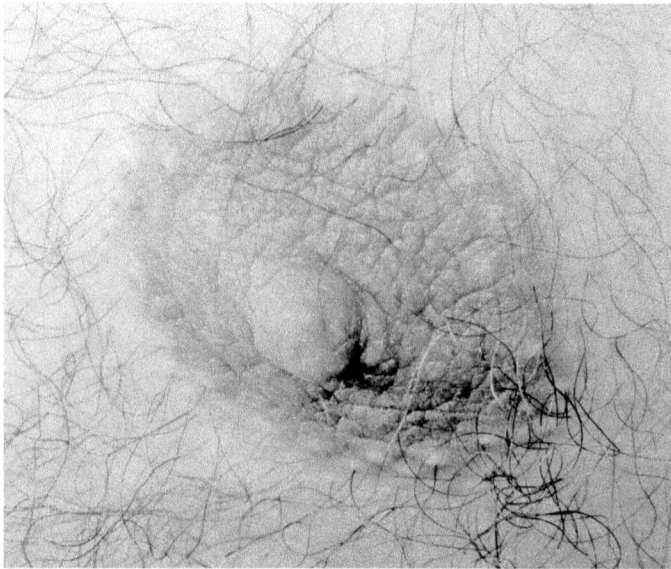

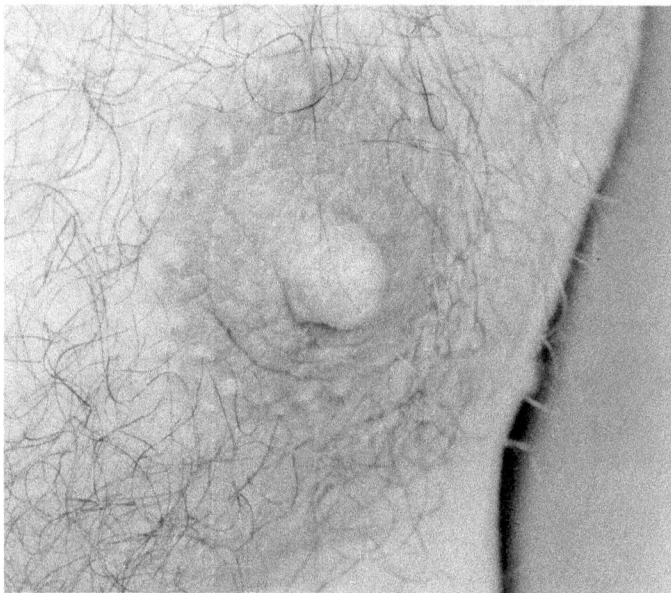

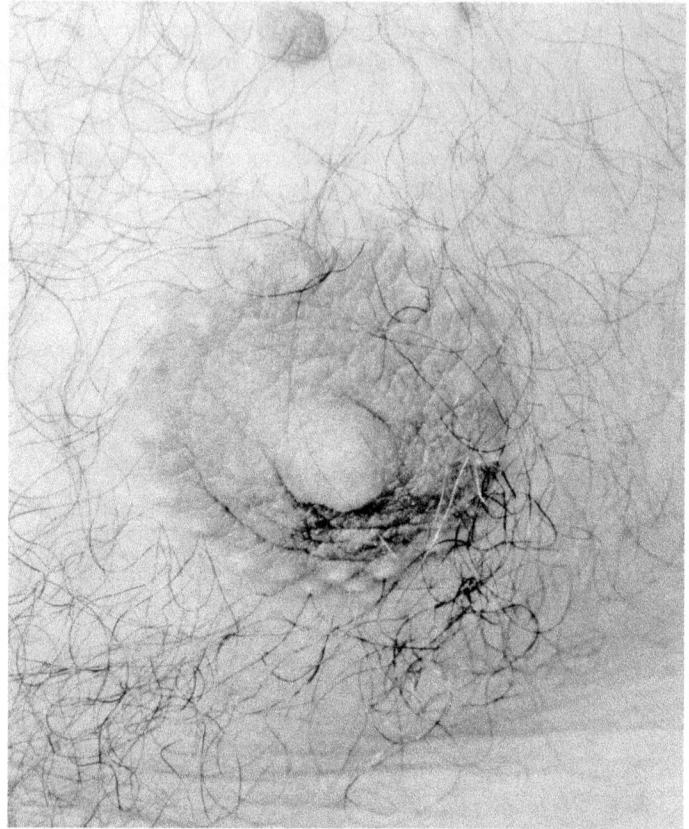

A typical well-developed, male nipple.

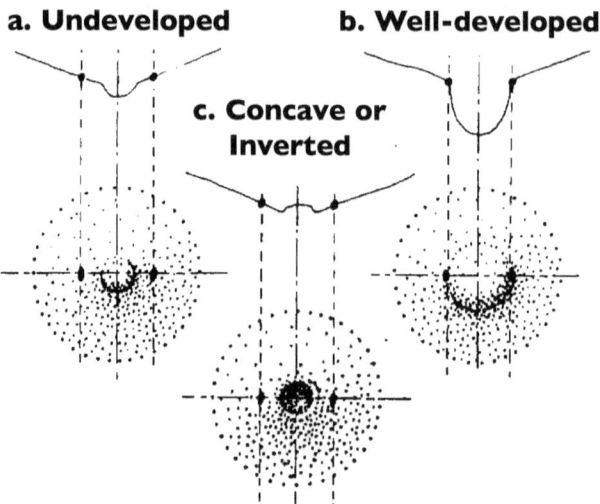

a. Undeveloped   **b. Well-developed**

c. Concave or Inverted

The three nipple types

Placement—Male

For men with large, well-developed nipples ⅜″ or larger in diameter, the marking process is exactly the same as that for women. However, the majority of men's nipples are considerably smaller, seldom larger than a match head. Were we to pierce these at their base like larger nipples there would be too little tissue for a successful piercing. The risk of tearing or rejection would be much greater, and such shallow piercings would be too fragile for any but the lightest nipple play.

Since the average male nipple is about ⅛″ in diameter, it is necessary for us to pierce slightly into the areola in order to have sufficient tissue to assure a safe, secure piercing.

Don clean gloves, open your calipers to between 5/16″ and 3/8″, and hold them above or below the cleaned nipple as a guide. Using your Sharpie marker or a toothpick moistened

60

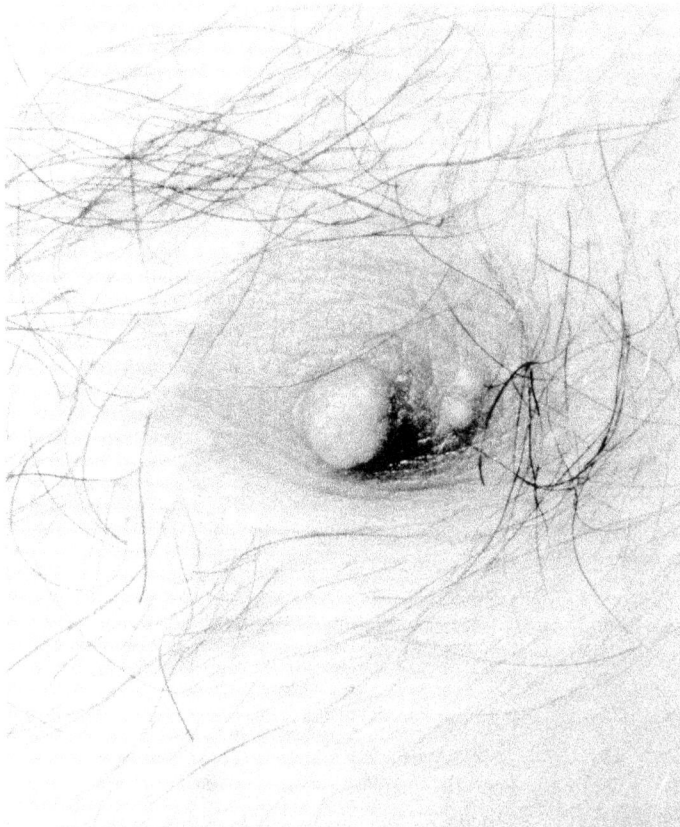

The most common type of male nipple: undeveloped.

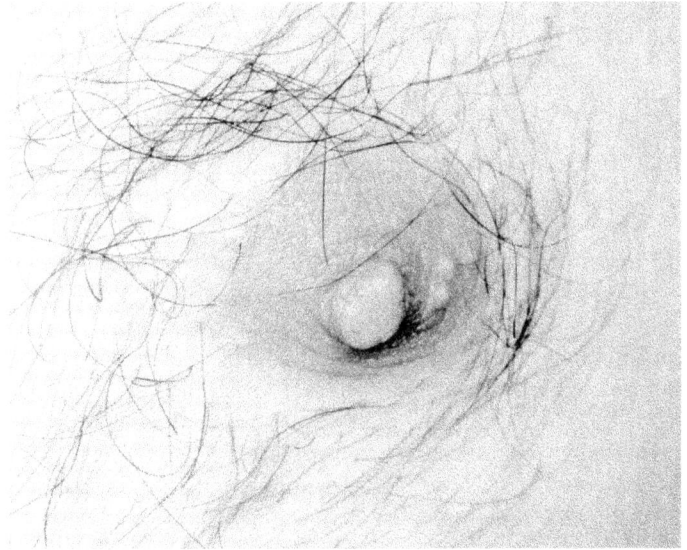

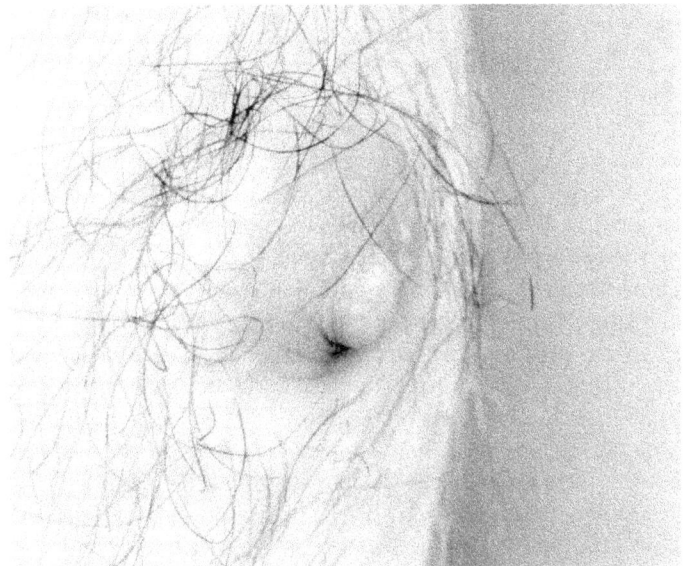

with India ink place a dot equidistant on either side of the nipple about 1/8″. The total distance from dot to dot should be between 5/16″ and 3/8″. A deeper piercing is unnecessary and would only prolong healing. Watch as the nipple relaxes, and see if there is any rotation or if the distance between the dots becomes significantly greater. Make adjustments as necessary, then erase unwanted dots. When you are satisfied with the marks, ask the piercee to lie down on the table so the nipple being pierced is closest to you.

TECHNICALITIES

Every nipple piercing is different. Although many of them are very easy to pierce, you will encounter the occasional unpleasant surprise. It is therefore a good practice to automatically select a needle pusher when setting up for every nipple piercing. This is particularly important if you know that the piercee engages in nipple play,

is repiercing over scar tissue, or has diabetes or other conditions that may toughen the skin.

The piercee may feel more comfortable reclining against a "husband," or may prefer to lie down. Consider which position, if any, is most comfortable for you and gives you best access to the nipple.

Forceps should be no tighter than necessary to hold the tissue securely.

THE NAVEL PIERCING

![puzzle piece icon] **DIFFICULTY LEVEL: 5**

This is an intermediate level piercing. Determining candidacy is not always a cut and dried matter. Marking and placement is fairly specific, and some navel tissue is tough enough to bend steel piercing needles. Piercing such a navel without serious accidents or needle sticks requires skill, confidence, and physical strength. Piercers should be familiar with nostrils, earlobes and nipples, at the very least, before attempting to perform a navel. Given the current popularity, it is likely that many piercers will perform navel piercings rather early on in their career. If you are a novice piercer who finds yourself in this position, remember to maintain focus and a strong awareness of limits.

![puzzle piece icon] **JEWELRY**

Navel piercings overwhelmingly heal best with rings as starting jewelry. A very few may need to be moved to barbells or L-bars, but that falls under troubleshooting. The size is fairly standard; most people require a 14 or 12 gauge, ½″ diameter ring. If the piercee is large, or has an exceptionally deep navel, ⅝″ or even larger may be necessary, but be sure with larger rings only to pierce superficial tissue. Measure with calipers at the jewelry counter to see if a larger ring really is needed.

Many piercees imagine a much smaller, thinner ring. They may have even seen a friend wearing a tiny little earring. Hold the ring you think best up to their navel and show them the proportions. Rings really appear much smaller next to the area they will be worn in than in your hand. A few people with smaller flaps may actually be able to wear a ⅜″ diameter ring, Try to suggest that they *still* pierce with 14 gauge, even though, if pressed, you could safely use 16 gauge (the very minimum). Using a thinner gauge and/or smaller diameter can result in keloids, tearing, or accelerated rejection. Make piercees aware of these facts should they insist on something smaller. NEVER allow yourself to be persuaded to insert anything smaller than a 16 gauge, ⅜″ diameter ring.

![puzzle piece icon] **UNIQUE CONSIDERATIONS**

Unfortunately, there are many people who are not good candidates for navel piercings. If the navel is shallow or flat, a piercing placed there will, of necessity, be so superficial that its likelihood of staying is poor. Likewise, never pierce an "outy." The scarred remains of the umbilical cord is connected to internal material, and if an infection developed, it could be deadly.

The ideal navel is deep and well formed with a pronounced fold of skin at the top, the preferred location for this piercing. To minimize irritation and maximize comfort, look and feel for a flap of tissue that will remain relatively still throughout the day. The more pronounced the flap, the better the chance for smooth healing.

Tray Setup for Navel Piercings:

- Povidone-iodine swabs
- Benzalkonium chloride swabs
- Marking pen or India ink and toothpicks
- Regular or mini forceps
- Sterile piercing needle
- Needle pusher
- Rubber band
- Cork (thimble optional)

Some piercees have shallow navels which, while still pierceable, are not ideal candidates. Offer them the option, but make it clear that they'll have extra work healing their piercing and success cannot be guaranteed.

Piercees often don't think about their wardrobe when considering this piercing, but navel piercings get very irritated if belts, tight pants, tights, or other constrictive clothing is worn frequently during the first six or seven months after the piercing. If the piercee wants a ring, and not a scar in their navel, they may have to dramatically alter the way they dress for a while.

This is a piercing perfectly situated for adornment. A colorful bead or charm looks so pretty dangling from a navel ring that many want to wear them right away. Be aware that any weight on the piercing can spell trouble. Start as simply as possible with navel piercings, coax them through their healing period, and then customize the look.

If your client desires a captive ring with a gemstone bead, avoid minerals such as malachite, lapis lazuli, and tiger's eye. These are soft, porous, and vulnerable to corrosion. When exposed to the moisture and sweat in the navel, irritating chemicals can be released which can cause ugly reactions in the piercing. And their porosity can provide a home for undesirable microorganisms. Choose instead hard, dense materials such as garnet, amethyst, onyx, agate, quartz, etc.

There isn't much blood flow to this area since navels largely completed their work once we were born. Even the best cared for tend to be fussy for up to a year, thus hot soaks are a must, and oils, lotions, or excessive friction can lead to failure.

Many women want to know what will happen to their navel piercing should they become pregnant. At about the eighth month of pregnancy, the navel pops inside out. Assuming that the piercing is well-healed at this point, it is a simple matter of installing either a barbell or length of monofilament nylon into the piercing. Unless the doctor strongly objects, these can be worn during the birth. If the doctor is piercing phobic and insists on removal, the jewelry or monofilament can be taken out just prior to delivery and reinserted just as soon after the birth as possible. If a navel piercing is not well-healed when a piercee becomes pregnant, it's best to let the piercing go, and try it again at a less demanding time.

Three navel configurations—*top:* the ideal navel, deep and well-formed; *center:* asymmetrical navel; not ideal, but could be pierced on the bottom or formed side; *bottom:* an "outy." There's nothing here to pierce.

PLACEMENT & MARKING

This is one of the few piercings where it is often appropriate to place the marks as deeply as the diameter of the jewelry. Appropriate placement, as we have discussed, is a very individual thing. Examine the area carefully. Is the navel more vertically oriented? Does it spread out horizontally? Diagonally? How much extra tissue do you have to work with? How much does it stretch out when the piercee lies down? All of the factors must be taken into consideration when determining how much tissue to pierce. For example, a person with a very well-defined, horizontally oriented flat flap can have quite a bit of tissue pierced, because when they lie down, the tissue isn't stretched at all. A vertical flap, on the other hand, will stretch out considerably, so much less tissue should be pierced. The final determining factor is the measurement taken with the piercee lying flat on the table.

For most people, however, an amount of tissue equal to the diameter of the chosen jewelry is appropriate. If a ½" ring will be used, make the piercing only a hair less than ½" deep. This is because the tissue is rarely stretched out to the full depth of the piercing, and to allow for the average ⅛" to ¼" of tissue that is lost during the healing period. Be sure to mark no deeper than the diameter of the jewelry!

Make your preliminary marks with the piercee standing. Start by marking the leading edge of the fold of skin. Then place your first dot above this line at about half the diameter of the ring. Exact placement will vary with each unique type of navel. Next, draw a thin vertical line down across the leading edge and into the navel. If the navel is fairly shallow, gently pull the tissue upward and end your line with a dot the same distance from the leading edge as the first one. Be sure that the inner mark is well clear of any scar tissue. If the piercee has a deep navel, complete your marking with them lying down. In some cases where the navel is exceptionally deep, it may not be possible to mark the inside dot, in which case the piercer must rely upon the leading edge line and the vertical line when placing the forceps.

Some piercees would like their navel jewelry to be placed off-center, or at an angle. Any placement is fine, provided the distance from the leading edge to the piercing does not exceed the diameter of the jewelry!

Occasionally piercees ask that the piercing be placed on the side or bottom of the navel. The success of this will depend upon the shape of the individual navel.

TECHNICALITIES

Always remember your needle pusher for this piercing! Navels can be amazingly tough and have even been known to bend 12 gauge needles.

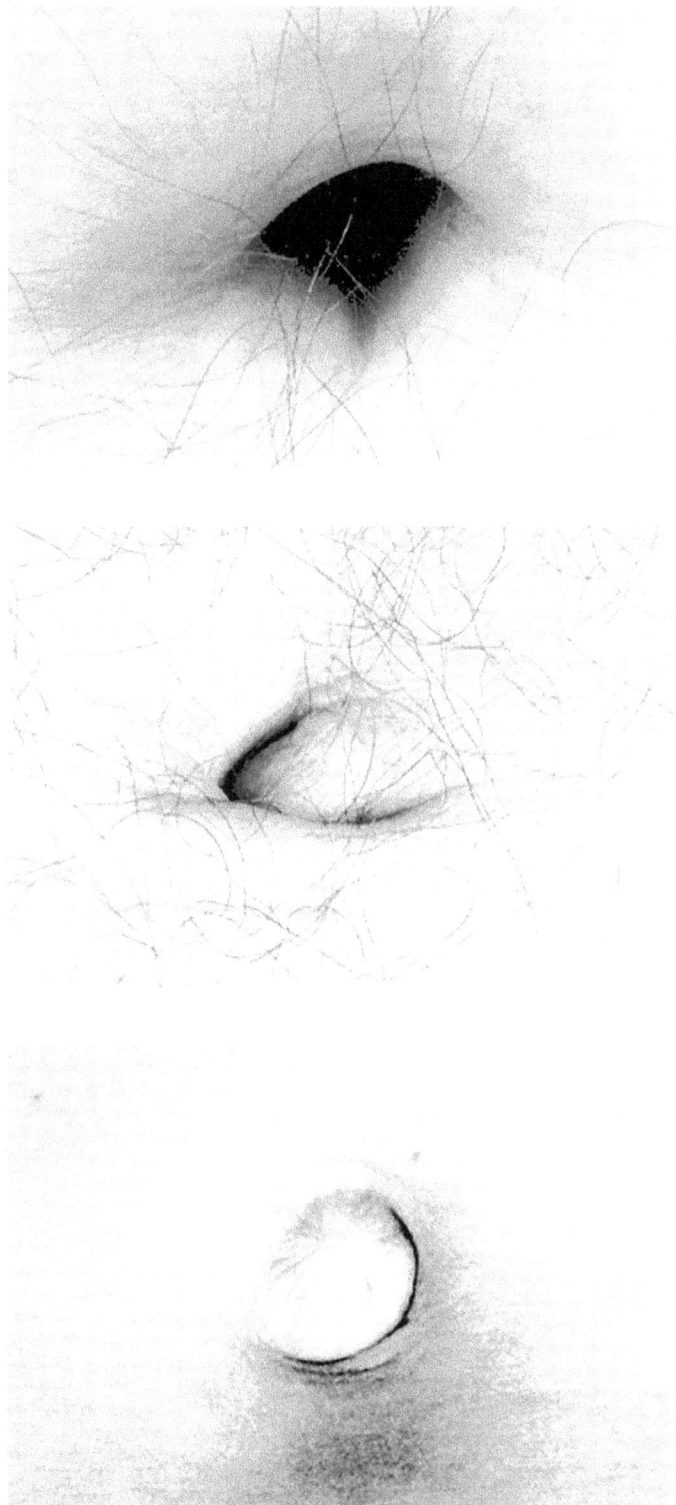

This piercing is easiest to perform with the piercee lying down. Although some piercers perform the navel from the outside in, you may find jewelry insertion easier if you perform it from the inside out. The direction you favor will determine whether the piercee should lie with their head to your left or right.

Be sure that piercees don't move or laugh during insertion. You could lose the contact between the jewelry and the needle, or the needle could accidentally be pulled out of the piercing. There is also the ever present risk of a needle stick.

CHAPTER 8—

ABOVE THE NECK PIERCINGS

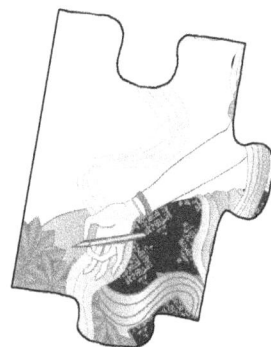

✦ THE EARLOBE

DIFFICULTY LEVEL: 3 TO 4

Carefully performed, this piercing is pretty straightforward, although marking and placement can continue to confound even a skilled piercer. Don't be lulled into complacency. Most needle sticks occur with earlobe and cartilage piercings.

JEWELRY

There are virtually unlimited choices when selecting jewelry for a new earlobe piercing. If an ear stud will be used, make sure that it meets the guidelines for acceptable jewelry:

- Solid surgical stainless steel, niobium, titanium, 14 or 18 karat gold
- Lightweight, without dangling or heavy parts
- Sufficient post length to avoid pinching and facilitate cleaning
- No threading or other textured surface passing through piercing
- Not worn by someone other than piercee unless autoclaved.

If the solidity of the metal is in question, but the piercee insists on it, make them aware of your concerns, and invite them to return for more appropriate jewelry should problems develop. If the jewelry does not meet the above guidelines, it is not appropriate jewelry for a new piercing, and it would be a great disservice to the piercee to install such a hazardous object.

Rings are far simpler to care for, and much less likely to be pulled out accidentally. Encourage your clients to purchase good quality, body jewelry. Avoid the shoddy ear jewelry commonly found in department stores and elsewhere. People will bring you all kinds of chintzy nonsense, because it's "only an ear." They will insist that the tiny, razor-sharp wire connector is "real gold." They may be able to wear these after the first six months to a year of healing when scar tissue will be strong enough to hopefully resist metal reactions and cutting. Many people, however, will not feel comfortable with this junk once they become accustomed to wearing quality product.

The choice of ring size will be influenced by many factors, so discuss all the elements carefully with each piercee. Do they have a job or other situation that requires subtlety? As the initial jewelry needs to stay in for a full six weeks, and something needs to be worn at all times for approximately

Tray Setup for Earlobe Piercings:
- Povidone-iodine swabs
- Benzalkonium chloride swabs
- Marking pen or India ink and toothpicks
- Regular or mini forceps
- Sterile piercing needle
- Rubber band
- Cork (thimble: optional)

the first four months, a very small piece might be the best choice for starters. Assuming the overall dimensions of the earlobe will allow it, nothing smaller than a 20 ga, 5/16" ring should be used. A larger lobe obviously requires a larger diameter to fit a properly centered piercing.

Does the piercee intend to stretch the hole once healed? If so, the largest possible gauge would be advantageous, as would a diameter large enough to place the piercing higher than usual. There is a trade off, however. As the hole size becomes larger, care must be taken to reduce weight as much as possible and keep the diameter/size reasonably small to minimize movement and irritation and the scarring and abscessing it can cause. For most people a 12 ga is sufficiently thick to start with, however, 10 is an option if the lobe is large and fleshy and appropriate jewelry can be found. If a thicker gauge is being used, keep ring diameters under 5/8". Most people's lobes are small enough that a 3/8" to 1/2" ring is perfect.

Will the piercing be one of a series already in the ear? Consider using rings in graduated sizes and gauges. Start with larger rings at the bottom, gradually decreasing the size as you go up the ear. While this is the more common and preferred choice, the reverse can also be attractive.

UNIQUE CONSIDERATIONS

It is by far the most popular of all piercings, worn singularly, in pairs, or multiple combinations by most women in the world, and increasingly by men.

The earlobe lends itself to highly individualized decoration and personalized placement. Perhaps it is its commonness which accounts for the multitude of poorly placed and performed piercings. The earlobe tends to be overlooked

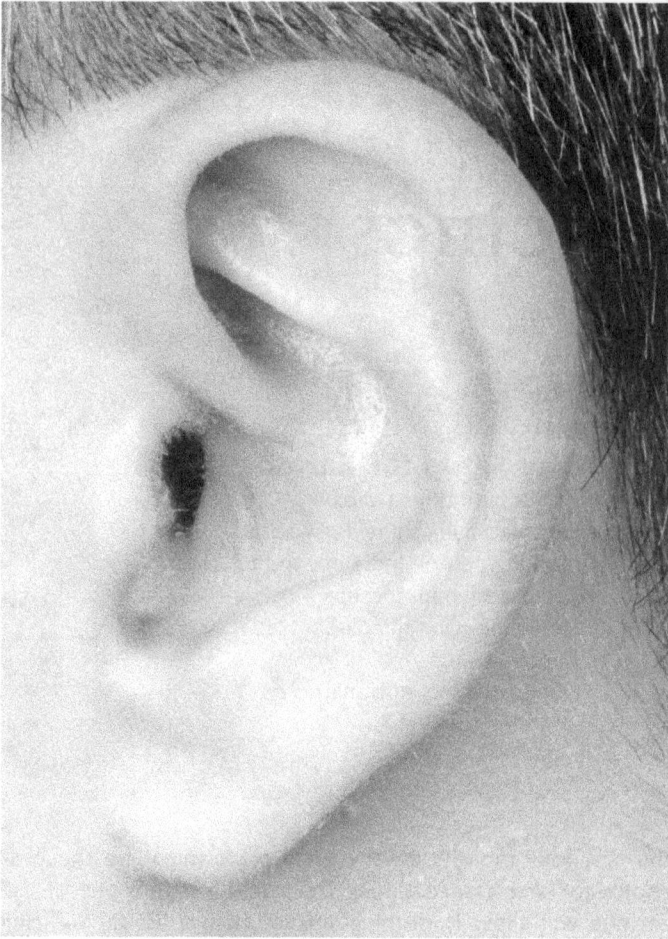

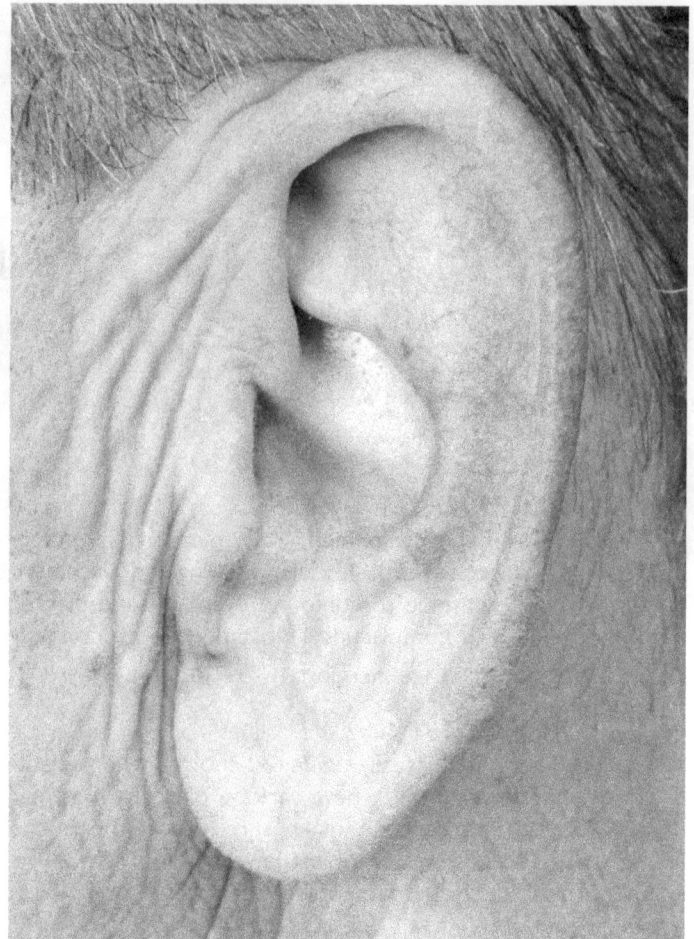

Two representative forms of the endless variety of ear shapes. *Left:* **a good example of an ear with a "horizontal wedge" lobe, reasonably uniform in width.** *Right:* **ear with a large pendulous lobe.**

as a "body" piercing, or a "real" piercing; even piercing-aware folks who should know better tend to suspend the rules of sterility and accuracy for earlobe piercings.

The earlobe is, in fact, one of the most difficult piercings to place, pierce, and heal. Sherlock Holmes observed that every earlobe is unique, different even from its mate. The spacing and angle of every ear piercing will present a new challenge. Earlobe piercees tend to faint more often than any other piercee, perhaps due to level of preparedness, proximity to the head, and vascularity. About one out of every three earlobe piercings will bleed profusely. Because it's "only my ear," piercees often neglect cleaning, remove the jewelry too soon, or constantly fiddle with it, often with dirty hands. One doctor who sees many pierced clients reports that the piercing which sends the most people to a doctor is the earlobe.

Consensuality sometimes gets suspended because of the perceived innocence of this piercing. People think their baby or dog would look "cute" with a little earring. After all, didn't Egyptian pharaohs pierce their cats' ears?

It is the opinion of these writers that piercing the ears of a baby, animal, or other being who cannot give clear notice of consent, is equal to the practice of circumcision: outmoded, barbaric, and inhuman. This does not even address the issue of liability, a very real threat which falls solely on the shoulders of the piercer. A professional piercer should pierce minors (above the neck and navels ONLY) only if old enough to give their consent. A record should be kept including the signature of the piercee PLUS that of any legally responsible guardian.

MARKING & PLACEMENT
Earlobes come in a great variety of shapes and sizes, and frequently one person possesses two very different lobes. Before marking, take a good look at the lobe or pair of lobes. They generally resemble one of a few main types.

If it is fairly large and fleshy, one can usually visualize the lobe as a circle or oval. The ideal placement is directly in the center of this imaginary shape. You will also encounter "lobes," which can best be described as horizontal wedges. Marks should fall on a line approximately centered between the two long sides of the wedge. The first dot should be equidistant from the face, the top and bottom edge of the ear "lobe."

If future stretching is planned, place the mark just slightly above the center, more if the lobe is smaller or if the desired final size is fairly large. It is not advised that you place a mark much lower than the center point as such a placement is not as visually pleasing, and there is a greater risk of the ring being torn out.

66

Some lobes are not clearly separate from the head, making a clear center point hard to find. You will often have to improvise as best you can, imagining placement slightly further from the head.

Avoid marking anywhere near the cartilage. Cartilage is located above the bottom center of the lobe, and is also present much lower on the rim than is readily apparent. To find the beginning of the cartilage, grasp the soft tissue near the juncture of tissue and cartilage and press up slightly. A small sliver of cartilage near the back of the ear usually makes itself known. A piercing in this area will "twist," resulting in a very crooked angle. It will heal like cartilage, and should be considered as such.

Avoid piercing any cysts, moles, freckles, or unidentified growths. This could encourage a cancerous condition in precancerous tissue, or cause an infection. Feel for any lumps carefully as you mark. A lump or tough area which is left over from a previous piercing, however, can be pierced, and will often heal faster the second time. Just be sure of what you're piercing.

This is also the time to consider the angle at which you will be piercing. Most people want the ring perpendicular to the lobe , but some prefer it to be angled a little closer to the face. Discuss this option with your piercee. If other jewelry is present, look at the angles they follow. Often each ring heads off in a different direction. If possible, try to avoid this sloppy look. Choose an angle for the new piercing that will disguise the imbalance as much as possible.

If this is a second or third piercing, be sure to maintain even spacing between each. Some people prefer their jewelry spaced close together. This can be done if they will only be wearing rings. If studs will be worn, it is best to leave about ¼″ of space between each piercing to provide room for the backs. A larger ear looks better with jewelry spaced farther apart.

Occasionally you will be asked to repierce an earlobe which has been torn. This tearing often results from years of wearing heavy jewelry with very thin wires. The hole may have been surgically repaired, but often it has not. The very first thing to consider in this case is the likelihood of reoccurrence. Urge the piercee to choose a thicker gauge (18, 16, or 14) and a smaller diameter (up to ½″) to minimize tearing. They should also be made aware of what is inappropriate jewelry for future wear.

Next, check to make sure that there is enough space remaining on the lobe to pierce well above the scar tissue or slit, or on either side of it.

When you have a good placement, draw a small, clear dot with the Sharpie marker or India ink and toothpick. Erase any mistakes or excess ink with a tissue or cotton swab moistened with alcohol. Show the marks to the piercee, explain your logic in arriving at the placement, and make minor adjustments if so desired.

TECHNICALITIES

Forceps pressure should be very light; ideally, so light that if you let go of them, they would practically fall to the ground.

Hair can ruin your prep scrub, so keep presterilized hair clips handy to clip hair out of your way. Remember that the rules of cross-contamination apply equally to innocent items like hair clips!

This piercing is usually performed with the piercee sitting on a table or chair, at a height comfortable for both piercer and piercee. If the piercee desires to lie down for the piercing, be sure to mark them before they lie down.

Remember that earlobe piercings can be surprisingly tough, particularly when repiercing.

Earlobe piercees are more likely to faint than any other group of piercees, possibly because they are sitting up, the ear is vascular and close to the brain, or the piercing may be their first.

Believe it or not, needle sticks are more common with ear piercings than any other, perhaps because of the great frequency with which they are performed, or because piercers become careless. In a word: DON'T!

Piercees do have a tendency to bleed when having their earlobe pierced. Tuck a tissue in the piercee's collar before you mark and pierce them, and have one handy when you come to insert the jewelry.

✦ CARTILAGE PIERCINGS

EAR RIM CARTILAGE —

DIFFICULTY: 3
Carefully performed, this piercing is pretty straightforward. Don't be lulled into complacency, though; most needle sticks occur with earlobe and cartilage piercings.

JEWELRY
The jewelry best suited to heal piercings of ear cartilage is almost always a ring. Ear studs, especially the department store variety, are much too short and can pinch off blood supply, make cleaning almost

Tray Setup for Cartilage Piercings:
- Povidone-iodine swabs
- Benzalkonium chloride swabs
- Marking pen or India ink and toothpicks
- Regular or mini forceps
- NRT or nostril tube
- Sterile piercing needle
- Rubber band
- Cork (thimble: optional)

impossible, and snag constantly in hair and clothing. Moreover, the sharp backing often pokes into the side of the piercee's head, or elsewhere, as they sleep. This is very uncomfortable. Please! don't insert ear studs in cartilage piercings.

Barbells or minibars are another option. But to allow room for cleaning and possible swelling, the barbell must be a bit long. This can look rather odd, and could cause discomfort if there is excessive motion or snagging. Study the area carefully to see if using a barbell might make healing problematic.

So what, then, does one suggest to a piercee who likes the look of a stud? Once the piercing is very well healed, a nostril screw can be bent and trimmed to fit. As long as there is neither too much or too little extra space, nostril screws are attractive and comfortable choices for a healed piercing. In a new piercing, however, cleaning could be less than thorough. A second option would be a labret stud. Just be sure the post is not too long, and the piercing is well healed.

So, this leaves rings as the best choice for new cartilage piercings. Nothing less than 20 gauge, or more than 12 gauge, should be installed in the new hole, but 18 gauge to 14 gauge is probably most comfortable.

Diameter is an individual issue. Be sure that any ring will be able to move freely up and down, and not hug the ear too tightly, or keloiding could result. Depending on placement, the very smallest diameter would be ⁵⁄₁₆″. the further from the edge the larger the ring required. New piercings are very sensitive to friction and snagging, so for them it's best to avoid jewelry larger than ½″ .

Try to proportion ring thickness and diameter to other jewelry in the ears. Generally, smaller jewelry or matching jewelry is more attractive in higher piercings, larger or matching jewelry in lower piercings.

UNIQUE CONSIDERATIONS

These piercings have become increasingly popular over the last few years as multiple piercings have made their way up the rim of the ear. Those who have them do not need to be told that they are much more difficult to heal than lobe piercings. They can ache for months, be slept on the wrong way, get snagged on shirts, hairbrushes, and helmets. They are also more prone to infections and keloiding, and can stay crusty for up to a year, or even longer.

The main reason for the longer healing time is the nature of cartilage tissue. The tissue is more dense, with far fewer blood vessels. Fewer blood vessels means less help from the body, and more chance of infections or irritations. In addition, the high, somewhat protruding location of the cartilage renders it susceptible to knocks and snags which considerably slow healing.

Placement is fairly arbitrary, although certain spots lend themselves more readily to piercing. Just be sure that you mark an area which is at least ¼″ away from other piercings, in a logical, even order.

PLACEMENT & MARKING

As we have discussed, there is generally quite a bit of leeway in marking for this piercing. But there are some placements that can look much more appropriate. Ear cartilage takes many forms and proportions. On some people, the fold is nearly invisible, and the tissue is very thin. Most people will have one or two slight bends in the shape of the cartilage. If the mark is made just inside the bend, the ring will hang in a more natural way.

Some people have very fleshy, thick cartilage tissue. On this type of ear, make sure that the diameter of the ring is adequate to allow it to move freely up and down. These people usually have pronounced folds or bends in the shape of the rim, and placement is practically predetermined. Always show the piercee, of course, and consult with them until you can agree on a placement.

Any bumps, moles, growths, or freckles should be avoided, but scar tissue from former piercings does not pose a particular problem.

A common mistake is to place the piercing too far from the edge of the ear. This is not only unattractive, but causes problems such as keloiding and tearing. In most cases, there is a clearly delineated groove running around the rim of the ear. Ideal placement is usually in this groove. A more experienced piercer and a well-prepared piercee may have something unusual in mind and set about to properly pierce and heal a deeper piercing; until a sufficient level of ability has been achieved, however, stick to the groove. If this is faint or indistinct, it should be easy to visualize its presence and mark there.

You may have seen shallow, non-cartilage piercings on the very edge of the ear. Perhaps the piercer or piercee thought it would heal faster. While possibly true, this unattractive, shallow placement is vulnerable to tearing or rejection. Sometimes the scar or tear caused by such a rejection is permanent. Avoid these problems. Either pierce through the cartilage or not at all.

Getting the angle just right can be tricky. When doing a cartilage piercing consider the angle of the needle in relation to that of adjoining piercings. In some parts of the cartilage, most notably where it meets the lobe, the tissue can "grab" or twist the needle as it passes through, resulting in an angle you may not have planned. Unfortunately, you'll have to learn how to compensate for this and deal with other idiosyncrasies by trial and error. It is wise to avoid such areas until you are more experienced.

TECHNICALITIES

For this piercing the piercee usually sits on a table or chair at a height comfortable for the piercer. If the piercee desires to lie down for the piercing, be sure to mark placement first.

Hair can ruin your prep scrub, so keep presterilized hair clips handy to clip hair out of your way. Remember that the rules of cross-contamination apply equally to innocent items like hair clips!

Ear cartilage is stiff and uneven, not suitable for the use of forceps. Consequently, cartilage piercings are almost always performed freehand. The likelihood of a needle stick is always greater when performing freehand piercings, and most needle sticks occur with ear piercings. Don't get careless about this "simple" piercing.

CONCH & OTHER CARTILAGE PIERCINGS

DIFFICULTY LEVEL: 6

An intermediate level piercing; it may look simple but can be very tricky, even dangerous. Inappropriate jewelry selection or placement can lead to severe infections, abscessing, and possible loss of hearing. Acquire sufficient experience with cartilage piercings before attempting the conch or other inner cartilage piercings (antihelix, helix, etc.)

JEWELRY

Either a ring or a barbell may be used; each has its own pros and cons. Barbells are less susceptible to snags, but can make cleaning more difficult. Rings are much easier to clean but are more prone to snag or catch.

This tissue requires at least 14 ga, but thicker than 12 ga. is ill advised. Although thicker jewelry has certainly been installed into new conch piercings, they present too much of a risk of serious problems to be considered an option for the safe piercer unless problems of weight and movement related irritation can be eliminated.

Barbells should be measured for length, with between $\frac{1}{8}''$ and $\frac{3}{16}''$ extra space to allow for swelling and facilitate cleaning.

Diameter is an individual issue. Be sure that any ring will be able to move freely up and down, and not hug the ear too tightly, or you could be dealing with a very persistent keloid before too long. Nothing smaller than $\frac{1}{2}''$ should even be considered. If the piercing is deeper, or the ear larger, choose $\frac{5}{8}''$ or larger. As these piercings are very sensitive to friction and snagging, it's best to avoid jewelry larger than $\frac{3}{4}''$ while the piercing is new.

UNIQUE CONSIDERATIONS

This piercing is performed in a very thick portion of cartilage which is close to the delicate workings inside the ear. Common problems encountered with a cranky or difficult ear cartilage piercing could be multiplied tenfold should this piercing go awry. It can ache for months, or be slept on the wrong way, or get snagged on shirts, hairbrushes, and helmets. This piercing is prone to keloiding, and can stay crusty for up to a year, or even longer. In the worst case scenario it could swell up and develop a nasty abscess which could threaten the piercee's hearing.

The main reason for the longer healing time is the nature of cartilage tissue. The tissue is more dense, with far fewer blood vessels, thus reduced circulation and greater risk of infections or irritations. Although the conch is protected somewhat better than the ear cartilage on the ear rim, it is so much denser that healing time is at least as slow.

PLACEMENT & MARKING

Care must be taken in marking the conch. You want to avoid any bumps or folds of cartilage, because these are especially dense and may contain things you'd really rather not pierce. You must be sure that your mark and angle will be matched by appropriately sized jewelry. And, of course, you want the piercing to look good.

An average conch is a well-formed, bowl-shaped area, the bottom of which (and most attractive place to pierce) is often adjacent to the narrow place on the ear rim between lobe and cartilage. Not only does piercing in this spot look most appropriate, it provides a convenient niche for the jewelry to rest against. You may adjust the placement slightly higher or lower, closer to or further from the head, but do stay in this general area.

Make a small, precise dot at the desired location, and then check several times to be sure that the placement will not conflict with anything happening on the back side of the ear.

TECHNICALITIES

You may be surprised by the extraordinary toughness of this cartilage. Always use a needle pusher.

The piercee may either sit or lie down depending on location, desire, and, as always, safety.

TRAGUS —

DIFFICULTY LEVEL: 6

This is an advanced intermediate level piercing. Technique varies widely, is almost always tricky, and can involve many stages and special equipment. Inappropriate jewelry selection or placement or aftercare negligence can lead to severe infections, abscessing, and possible loss of hearing. Acquire sufficient experience with cartilage piercings before attempting the tragus or other inner cartilage piercings (conch, antihelix, helix, etc.)

JEWELRY

Rings must be worn in this piercing while it heals. A year or so after piercing, a minibar or nostril screw may be worn. While 20 ga (the minimum) can be used, 18 ga is strongly suggested, as it facilitates cleaning and discourages tearing and keloiding. If the piercee's tragus is very prominent, a 16 ga (in a few rare cases 14) could be used. Don't use these thicker gauges until you have sufficient experience to judge their appropriateness.

Diameter is an individual issue. Just be sure the ring can move freely up and down and not hug the tragus too tightly, or you could be dealing with a keloid before too long. Depending upon anatomy, the very smallest diameter would be $\frac{5}{16}''$, although the "standard" size is $\frac{3}{8}''$.

UNIQUE CONSIDERATIONS

As lovely as this piercing looks when healed, many tragii go through some very ugly stages during the first few months of healing. Because there aren't many nerve endings in the area, problems can be elusive for several weeks. The tendency is to assume that the piercing has healed all on its own, and regular cleaning is no longer critical. That's when the infections or keloids can show up. Avoid this headache by sizing jewelry properly, and urging the piercee to be responsible with aftercare.

The main reason for the longer healing time is the nature of cartilage tissue. The tissue is more dense, with far fewer blood vessels. Fewer blood vessels means less help from the body, and more chance of infections or irritations. The tragus is protected somewhat better than the ear cartilage, and so if you make it through the first few months, the piercing tends to heal very smoothly.

PLACEMENT & MARKING

The tragus is a small, cartilaginous lobe which projects into the opening of the ear canal. Examine the tragus. Fold it gently, and stretch the tissue to see where it meets the head. Develop your piercer's eye by visualizing the tragus as one half of a diamond shape. Your dot should be placed in the center of this imaginary diamond.

Make a small, precise dot at the desired location, and then check several times to be sure that the placement is not too deep, too shallow, too low, or too high.

TECHNICALITIES

There are many ways to perform a tragus piercing. Some piercers have improvised special tools for the purpose. Others use a regular piercing needle and mini forceps in the usual manner, then a nostril tube or NRT to safely guide the needle past the conch and rim. You will need to experiment to see which methods are the safest and work best for you, but always remember your own limitations.

Piercees usually lie down for the tragus piercing, unless your method requires otherwise.

You may wish to let your piercees know that most tragus piercings have a few distinct stages: they will feel varying degrees of pressure at the time of setup, piercing, and insertion. Let them know the piercing will probably be more noisy than painful when the needle penetrates the cartilage.

✦ Ŧℋℰ EYEBROW

DIFFICULTY: 4

This is an intermediate level piercing. Less skilled piercers would be wise to pierce away from the eye to avoid accidental eye damage. Placement can be tricky, and the vertical nature of the piercings may increase the risk of a needle stick.

Tray Setup for Eyebrow Piercings:
- Povidone-iodine swabs
- Benzalkonium chloride swabs
- Marking pen or India ink and toothpicks
- Mini or regular forceps
- Sterile piercing needle
- Rubber band
- Cork (thimble: optional)

JEWELRY

Most people prefer the look and ease of a ring in their eyebrow piercing. The choice of ring size will be influenced by many factors, so discuss all the elements carefully with each piercee. Do they have a job or other situation that requires subtlety? As the initial jewelry needs to stay in for a full six weeks, and something needs to be worn at all times for approximately the first four months, a very small piece might be the best choice for starters. Nothing smaller than a 20 ga, 5/16″ ring should be inserted in a new eyebrow piercing, but consider the overall dimensions of the eyebrow. A larger or heavier brow, obviously, requires a larger diameter to properly center the piercing. Most piercees look and heal best with an 18 gauge, 3/8″ diameter ring.

Although the overwhelming majority of piercees prefer rings, a few desire the look of a barbell or minibar. If so, allow 1/8″ extra length for cleaning.

UNIQUE CONSIDERATIONS

Virtually unheard of until a few years ago, this piercing has become almost as common as the nostril piercing. Men and women of all ages find beauty in this new facial adornment.

Technically, the eyebrow is a surface to surface piercing, and eventually even the most successfully healed eyebrow piercings can begin to grow out. This needn't be traumatic as the area is so vascular that healing is rapid, and scarring is usually minimal to nonexistent.

MARKING & PLACEMENT

Examine the eyebrow in good light, from several angles. Look for a placement that will be balanced, and follow the line of the brow. The skulls of some people have a bump toward the outer edge of the eye socket. This is a particularly suitable placement. Although this may not be the spot most piercees had in mind when imagining the piercing, they tend to agree that it looks the most attractive.

Some people want a placement closer to the center of the brow, or angled differently. In any of these cases, discuss your marks thoroughly with the piercee, making any final adjustments before proceeding.

When you know the general location of the piercing, set your calipers to measure 1/8″ less than the diameter of the jewelry. As most eyebrow piercings grow out a bit during the first few weeks, it's a good idea to make the jewelry a little tight in the piercing for starters. The ring, as a result, may stick out a bit for a week. As the body rejects that 1/8″ of tissue, the jewelry will lay down.

With the calipers angled perpendicular to the brow line, make two small, precise marks. Generally it looks best if these marks fall just inside the edge of the brow, but this may not be possible if safety or aesthetics prevent. Hold the jewelry up for a quick visual check, to make sure the look will be pleasing to the piercee.

TECHNICALITIES

Tissue in this area is somewhat delicate, so a pair of forceps that is even a bit too tight can cause an ugly bruise that makes your piercee appear to have been in a domestic dispute. Avoid this embarrassment by using minimal pressure. The goal is to grasp the tissue enough to facilitate the piercing process.

Novice piercers should always pierce away from the eye, towards the hairline. This also very much applies to experienced piercers who, due to multiple piercings or other unusual circumstances, make the decision to perform an eyebrow piercing freehand.

This piercing may be performed with the piercee either sitting or lying down. The primary consideration, as always, is how can it be done most safely. Regardless, mark the piercing with the piercee sitting up.

This piercing is a well-known bleeder. It is an excellent idea to cultivate the habit of carrying a tissue with you as you make the jewelry transfer. Instant, dramatic bleeding often occurs at that time.

✦ Septum

DIFFICULTY LEVEL: 7

The difficulty is not so much in doing this piercing as it is in getting it symmetrical and parallel to the face. It may appear simple, but even in the hands of the most skilled piercer it can end up at an unattractive angle. Many people's septums twist to one side or the other or have tissue distortions which further challenge the piercer. The piercing cannot be marked or clamped, and the NRT can move the tissue sufficiently to misguide the needle. This requires a great deal of experience and precise overcompensation.

In addition every precaution must be taken to prevent an infection in this area. Because of its proximity to the brain and their shared blood supply, an infection could be quite serious, even fatal. Hence, we would consider the septum to be an advanced intermediate level piercing. It is suggested that the piercer acquire a great deal of skill with other freehand piercings, such as the nostril and Prince Albert, before tackling the septum.

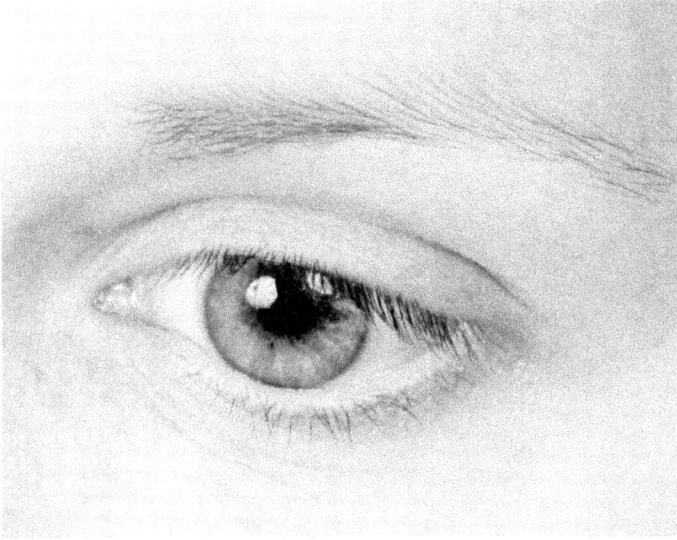

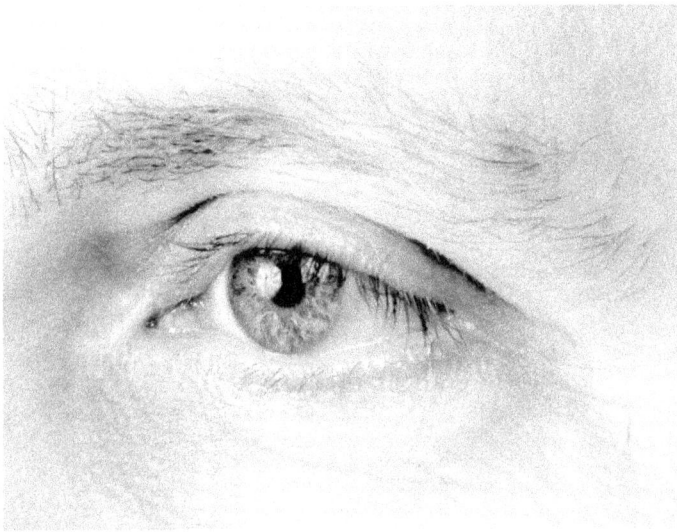

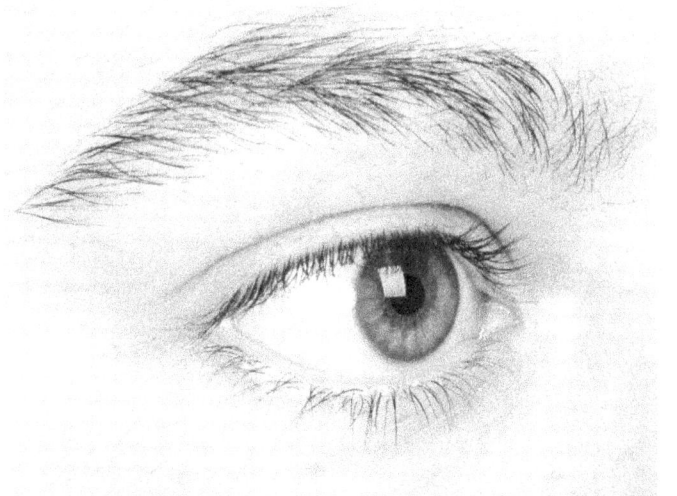

Several common brow types. *Top:* **nicely shaped, narrow, and continuous;** *middle:* **medium width with thinning hair;** *bottom:* **full brow.**

Tray Setup for Septum Piercings:
- Povidone-iodine swabs
- Benzalkonium chloride swabs
- Large blunt insertion taper (for placement)
- NRT (flared)
- Sterile piercing needle
- Cork(to secure needle after piercing)
- Optional: Needle holders

JEWELRY

Unfortunately, few people have the luxury of free self-expression in their workplaces or with their families, or they may simply need a little time to adjust to the visual effect of a septum piercing. Consequently, a septum retainer is the ideal insertable for most people. It can be hidden up inside the nostrils, but the ends can easily be exposed to facilitate cleaning. When selecting the appropriate retainer, examine the septum, and its surrounding anatomy. How broad is the septum? Are there any bumps or other obstructions that the retainer will need to clear? Find a retainer that will be comfortable, yet stay in place.

An alternative choice is the circular barbell. In the 14 or 12 ga, ⅜″ to ½″ sizes, this can function both as jewelry and retainer. Space between the balls must be adjusted to allow the ring to be flipped up inside the nose. Be aware that because of its shine this is not quite as inconspicuous as the retainer.

For those who don't have to worry about visibility, a captive ring is a fine choice. Start with at least ½″ diameter ring, then, if desired, downsize in a few months. Regardless of design choice, jewelry should not be completely removed for at least four weeks.

Although all manner of tusks and spikes are available to wear in healed septums, they are not practical for new piercings. Not only would the piercing be difficult to heal or clean, but they can easily fall out during sleep.

UNIQUE CONSIDERATIONS

The septum has been adorned for thousands of years, by people all around the world. The piercing gave the Nez Perce people their name and made the warriors of Papua New Guinea a well-known image. People in Africa, the Americas, and India have chosen ornaments ranging from rings to feathers to boar's tusks. As piercees search for new ways to decorate themselves, the septum presents itself as a great option for those desiring versatility. The piercing can sport a huge, flashing tusk at night, and be concealed with an invisible retainer at work the next day. This flexibility is one reason why many models are having their septums pierced.

PLACEMENT

Do what you can to help the piercee relax. To that end it is helpful if you describe what you will be doing through each step of the process. You will start by finding the piercing location. Use your little fingers to feel inside the nostrils and get a sense of what you will be dealing with. Also refer to the drawing in the appendix. Notice the thick, cord-like cartilage on the outer, bottom edge of the septum. Above it and just inside the nostrils you will feel a flat, semi-rigid cartilage with a fairly straight, horizontal edge. Between them you will find one small, thin spot toward the tip of the nose. Often referred to as the "sweet spot," this is where the piercing should go.

Some piercers find it helpful to use an insertion taper to zero in on the exact spot, to help visualize the correct angle of the needle, and to give the piercee some idea of what to

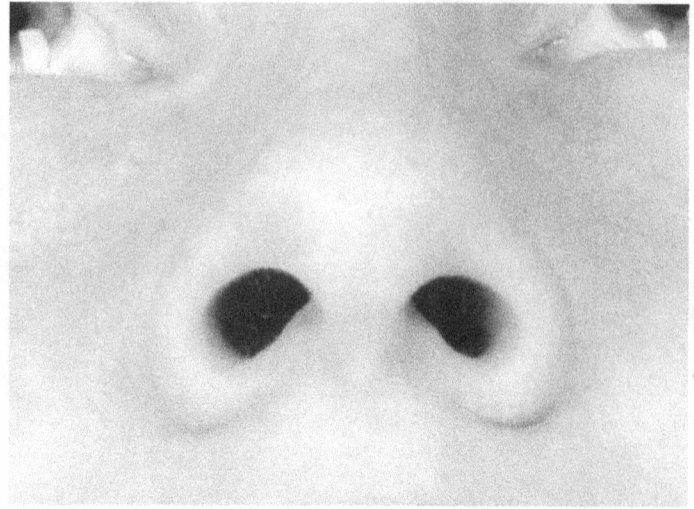

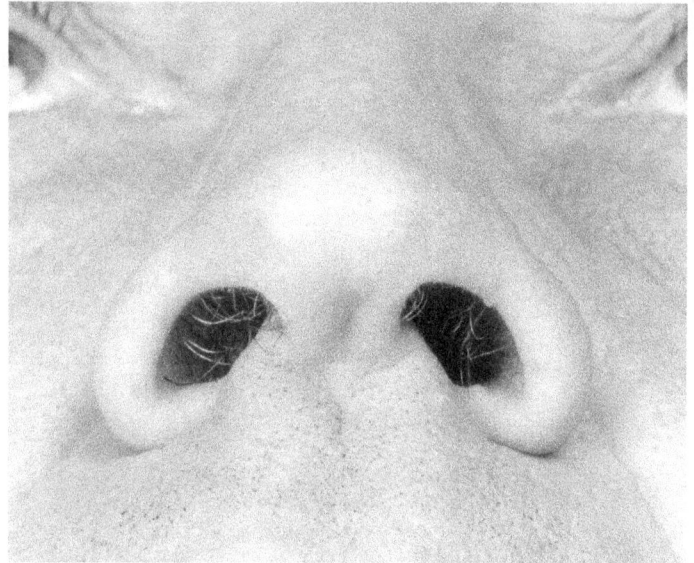

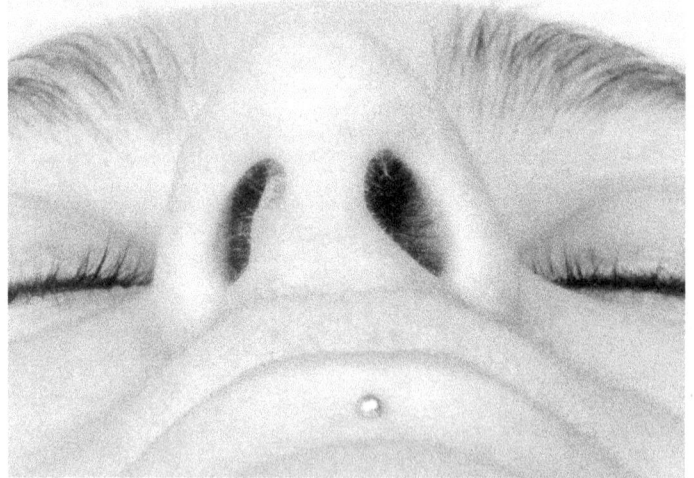

Three typical septums. *Top:* nicely symmetrical and narrow; *middle:* broad with minor irregularities; *bottom:* angled with thick tissue enlargement on the left.

expect in terms of sensation. The taper will be easy to feel on the other side.

Placement is so critical! It must not be too low or too high. The piercing should be high enough in the nose that it is not visible from the side, but not so high that it begins to intrude on cartilage, or make wearing jewelry difficult. Piercing through the cartilage can be very painful and lead to serious infections.

Angle is one of the most difficult things to get right when performing a septum piercing. Because the piercing is literally in the middle of the face, any slight error is glaringly obvious. Many septum piercings come out crooked, and need to be redone. Avoid most of these embarrassing episodes by using the taper to preview your angle. Then, when you are doing the actual piercing, correct the distortion caused by the NRT by bringing your needle slightly back towards the face. The angle will then be perfect, most of the time.

Deviated septums present unique problems. The fact that most piercees have some degree of deviation does not make your job any easier. Inform the piercee who has a deviation that their piercing may appear crooked when viewed from below. As long as you can align the piercing so it appears straight from the front and side, you may consider it a success.

TECHNICALITIES

Place the piercee in a position that works for you. Some piercers, particularly taller ones, like to put the massage table in the center of the room, with the piercee's head hanging slightly off the end. Shorter piercers may want to back a chair against the wall, with the piercee's head tilted back somewhat. What is important is for you to feel that the position will allow you the safest, most accurate approach.

This piercing may bleed, particularly if a larger gauge needle was used. Give the piercee a tissue and bring one with you when you approach for insertion.

For piercers with larger fingers, or very small jewelry/retainers, it may be easiest to perform the insertion using a pair of surgical-taped needle holders or hemostats clamped onto the jewelry.

Remember to overcompensate your needle angle towards the face. This helps correct the distortion caused by the NRT.

Although flared NRTs are preferable, non-flared NRTs may be used. If you must use one, be especially careful both with angle and with grip, as the non-flared end is not as stable and could slip.

If you don't get the right angle on the first try, STOP. Are you distressed? Is the piercee distressed? Think carefully before you decide to attempt the repiercing. Perhaps a coworker has a better chance at getting that angle. Perhaps the piercee wants a break. Or, perhaps you and the piercee both feel fine about a second try.

Whatever the case, don't pierce the septum more than twice at one time. After two attempts, the tissue will be slushy and bloody, and there's virtually no chance of getting the needle to go where you want it to go. Give it a week's rest, then try again, and don't feel incompetent! This can be one tough piercing.

CHAPTER 9—

⊙RAL PiERCiNGS

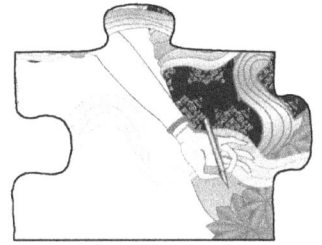

✦ LABRET & LIP

DIFFICULTY LEVELS

Labret: 5

This is an intermediate level piercing. Because of more precise placement requirements, piercings of the labret area (any oral area not immediately abutting the lip itself), particularly the center, are more difficult than a simple side of the lip piercing. Piercers should have sufficient experience with tongue and lip piercings before attempting a labret.

Lip: 4

This is an early, intermediate level piercing. After performing earlobe and nostril piercings, the lip is a natural progression for most. It is very important to remain focused at all times, and pay particular attention to placement. Less experienced piercers should make it a practice to pierce from the inside of the mouth out.

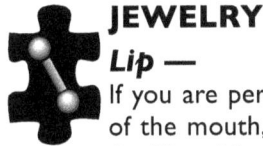

JEWELRY

Lip —

If you are performing a lip piercing along the side of the mouth, you have some options for jewelry. An 18 or 16 gauge ring, 5/16″ to 7/16″ in diameter may be chosen, if 1/8″ is allowed for swelling. A labret stud would be preferable if the piercee requires something more subtle. The dimensions would be 14 ga, 3/8″ to 9/16″ initial length, gradually downsizing to as small as 3/16″ in post length once the piercing has healed.

Labret/Cheek —

If you are performing a labret, cheek, or center of the lip piercing, a ring is not suggested. The risk of aggravated keloiding is very high due to the constant motion and play of the ring. Save rings until the piercing is several months old.

Labret studs will need a great deal of extra length if the piercing is far from the lip. Cheek piercings, on average, swell to about 5/8″, and sometimes even more. Think everything out, and check several times with the calipers before piercing. You don't want any shocking surprises.

Some people's gums won't tolerate the flat disks. If you find your piercee to be one of these, try a small threaded barbell ball. This will often solve the problem. If no changes in jewelry or cleanser are helping after a reasonable time has passed, perhaps the piercing was placed too low, or the angle is not compatible with the teeth and gums.

When a lip piercing is fully healed, a nostril screw may be specially bent to provide a subtle and very comfortable piece of stud-like jewelry.

UNIQUE CONSIDERATIONS

Piercings of the lip are well-documented among African, Alaskan, and South American peoples. Worn by both men and women for decorative purposes, to assist in drawing animal energy to the hunters and shamans, or as a symbol of marital submission, it has certainly proven versatile.

All piercings placed at or very near the lip line are called lip piercings. If the placement is moved further away, the tissue is thicker, and the piercing is called a labret. Labret could also describe piercings of the cheek, and the techniques and healing methods for cheek piercings are virtually identical.

Problems can arise for some people whose tooth enamel begins to wear away or actually chip. This can usually be prevented by avoiding the habit of constantly playing with the jewelry. Care must be taken during placement of the piercing, particularly if it is near the center of the lip; a low or improperly angled piercing can wear away at the gum line.

MARKING & PLACEMENT

Good placement is a very individual thing. When marking, let the lines and features of the lip guide your pen or gentian saturated toothpick. The lipline ends much lower than it appears. Piercings placed into actual lip tissue have little in which to anchor, and usually reject. So, carefully inspect the lip in question to find the actual lipline before making any marks.

One of the most popular placements for a labret piercing is the center of the lower lip. Here are some things to look for to assist in placement: Look for the frenulum, the

---

Tray Setup for Labret/Lip Piercings:
- Povidone-iodine swabs
- Benzalkonium chloride swabs
- Sterile gauze pads
- Antibacterial mouthwash in relish cup
- Marking pen or India ink and toothpicks
- Regular or new forceps
- Sterile piercing needle
- Rubber band
- Cork (thimble: optional)
- Barbell connecting wire
- Gentian Violet in relish cup
- Toothpick

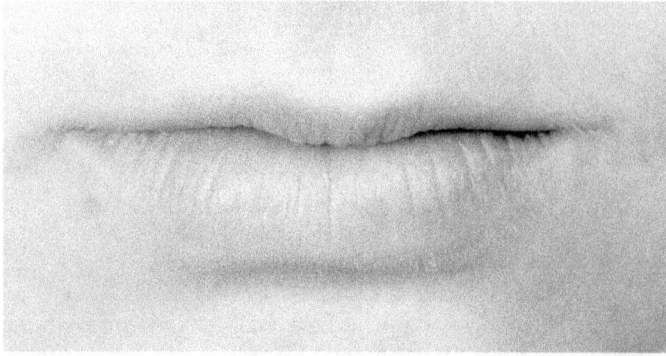

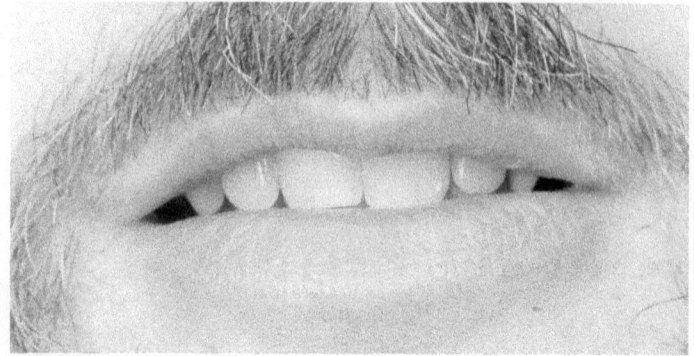

little web of tissue just inside the lower lip. Most people have a little crinkly seam in the center of the surface of their lip as well. These, along with gaps between the front teeth and position of the septum, will be of great assistance when finding a centered placement on a decidedly asymmetrical face. When in doubt, get several opinions.

You will find that many people have asymmetrical features which will present two or more placement options. For example, if the center of the mouth does not line up with the center of the nose (both important features that strongly define the center of the face), which would you choose as the guide for a central labret? Ultimately, leave the choice to the client. Explain the options, and let them make the final decision.

If you are performing a piercing in an unusual area, for example the upper labret, so-called "Madonna" placement, feel the inside carefully as you mark, to be sure that no invisible body part gets pierced by mistake.

Consider angle as you mark. For a central lip or labret piercing, you want to be sure that the jewelry will clear the gumline, as well as lie fairly flat. A slight upwards angle will accomplish these goals. If the jewelry for a lip piercing near the corner of the mouth is a ring, the piercing should be placed sufficiently deep, and angled so the ring will lie attractively.

TECHNICALITIES
At some point you will have to decide from which direction you prefer piercing the lip. Depending on whether it is on the left or right side of the body, what type of jewelry is being used, and what's easiest or safest for you, you can either pierce from the inside out, or from the outside in. Piercing from the inside out reduces the amount of time that the needle point is inside the piercee's mouth, and makes insertion much easier. The piercer must be very precise when applying the forceps with this style; as there's no inside mark to rely on, the forceps must not have disturbed any tissue as they were put on, or the piercing will be quite offset. Still, if the piercer is confident and careful, piercing from the inside out makes the piercing and insertion much faster and more comfortable for everyone. Sometimes, however, this is not practical, as with an upper labret (a "Madonna" piercing)—there's no way to maneuver the needle up into that kind of space.

Piercing from the outside in offers the advantage of greater control and precision. This is an equally valid option. Make your choice based on the individual situation, as well as your skill level and personal limits.

Don't be in too much of a hurry to size down the post. The lip swells less than the tongue, but remains swollen for considerably longer, up to two months.

✦ TONGUE

DIFFICULTY LEVEL: 4
This is an intermediate level piercing. Because of the location, there is always the risk of fainting, vomiting, or sudden movement for which to remain alert. Good bedside manner, keen trouble detection skills, and smooth, accurate speed are musts to perform a tongue piercing safely. Since it's a vertical piercing, take care to avoid a needle stick.

This piercing has traditionally been performed to demonstrate and enforce a religious vow of silence, both temporarily and permanently. Something akin to a skewer was worn in the piercing which prevented the wearer from drawing his/her tongue back into their mouth.

The modern tongue piercing could almost be considered a new piercing. Although there is some historical precedent for permanent tongue piercings, they have become popular only within the last several years. More and more people from all walks of life have come to appreciate this versatile piercing for its decorative statement and sensual functions. Numerous individuals have found the piercing provides sufficient oral satisfaction to help curb a craving for food or cigarettes.

Tray Setup for Tongue Piercings:
- Sterile gauze pads
- Antibacterial mouthwash in relish cup
- Sponge (tongue) forceps
- Sterile piercing needle
- Rubber band
- Cork (thimble: optional)
- Barbell connecting wire
- Gentian Violet in relish cup
- Toothpick

Problems can arise for some people whose tooth enamel begins to wear away or actually chip. This can usually be minimized or prevented by using plastic balls on the barbell stud or by overcoming the habit of constantly rattling the stud against the teeth.

JEWELRY

The jewelry that is comfortable for healing and daily wear is a barbell. Rings may, if desired, be worn for short periods in a well-healed piercing. However, this both impedes speech and is less comfortable, so few piercees ever take this option.

The minimum gauge is 14 ga, but some piercees like to use 12 ga. If they intend for the piercing to get a lot of use after healing, 12 ga may feel more secure.

Most tongues require a ¾″ barbell to start, but a few exceptionally large tongues will want up to ⅞″. To minimize discomfort, choose the shortest possible length that will still allow for quite a bit of swelling.

Once healed, the final jewelry may be anywhere from 9⁄16″ to ⅜″ in length, with 7⁄16″ being most common for females, and ½″ most common for males.

PLACEMENT & MARKING

The tongue is the second strongest muscle in the body, and it is a muscle over which most people have only minimal control. Consequently, marking and piercing the tongue can be something of a challenge. Despite its owners best efforts, the tongue may attempt to hide in the mouth, stretch way out, widen or swell. None of this should affect your marking process. Just remember:

The seam that marks the center of the tongue is connective tissue which holds the two pieces of the muscle together. As such, there are few blood vessels or nerve endings in that area. Looking underneath the tongue, you will see several very large blood vessels traversing the muscle, none of which intersect the center. Because of these blood vessels, many of which are not externally visible, piercing should only be done along this center line.

Also along the underside, you will find the lingual frenulum, a white webbing which anchors the tongue to the floor of the mouth. Try to avoid piercing that webbing as it could result in grossly exaggerated keloiding, and/or severe prolonged swelling and discomfort for the piercee. Tongue piercings should be placed far enough forward to avoid the lingual frenulum.

If you ask the piercee to make a "spoon" with their tongue, and make a small mark in the very bottom center of the spoon, you will have marked, by good coincidence, the very spot at which the lingual frenulum ends on the underside. If only one piercing is desired, this is the ideal location. It is not so far back as to be uncomfortable or uncontrollable, and not so far forward that it will be irritating or subject to snags.

Multiple tongue piercings are beyond the scope of this seminar, and should be performed only by experienced piercers. Placement must be very precise to avoid problems or discomfort for the piercee. And coincidentally, few piercees who get more than one tongue piercing end up keeping them for more than a year.

Once you have made the top mark, use the gentian violet saturated toothpick to make a vertical reference line along one side of the tongue to help align your marks. Ask the piercee to try to touch their tongue to their nose, and find the lingual frenulum. Mark just on the near side of it, along the center seam, and check this mark against your vertical line. 90% of the time, your marks will only require clarification.

Gentian violet is a very intense dye. Use it sparingly. Blot on a tissue and make only light impressions until your marks are satisfactory. When they are, allow the piercee to swallow several times while you get prepared.

TECHNICALITIES

Because this piercing is vertical, in an internal, personal site, and the piercee has little control over the powerful muscle, there is always the possibility of a severe needle stick. Add to this a couple of special precautions. Having a piercee faint or vomit with a needle in their

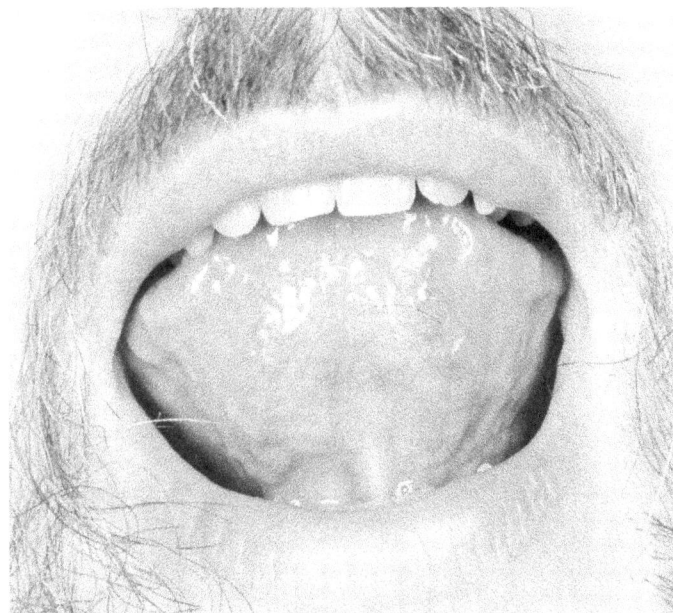

mouth is not a pleasant experience. Do not proceed until the piercee, assistant, and piercer ALL feel absolutely prepared.

You will need to decide whether or not to use an assistant to hold the forceps while you pierce. For less experienced piercers, this is usually the safest method. It is also used by many experienced piercers, for convenience and safety. Some piercers, however, would not perform a tongue piercing as safely with an assistant as without. Many piercers use an assitant after the piercing itself has been performed, to steady the forceps during jewelry transfer. Readers of this manual are encouraged to utilize an assistant until they have gained sufficient confidence and experience to attempt a solo run.

Assistants should ideally be chosen from among the staff, but a responsible, prepared friend of the piercee is an acceptable choice. Be alert! Friends have been known to faint while the piercee is unphased.

If calm and prepared, the piercee may serve as an assistant, although a coworker is probably a better choice. Whoever is chosen, the assistant needs to prepare by scrubbing their hands thoroughly with antibacterial soap, avoid touching anything afterwards, and wear a fresh pair of gloves for the procedure. The assistant, particularly if inexperienced, needs to receive complete instructions on their role.

Another point of contention is how to transfer jewelry. Most inexperienced piercers find it safest to use the standard method of piercing, then inserting the jewelry separately. As you gain confidence and skill, you may wish to experiment with this method: Using a very secure connecting wire, attach the barbell to the needle. Treating the barbell as an extension of the needle, you can acheive the piercing and insertion in one smooth motion. This saves many uncomfortable seconds for the piercee, but don't try it until you've gotten the basics down pat.

Chapter 10—
Female Genital Piercings

✦ Inner Labia

DIFFICULTY LEVEL: 4
This is an early intermediate level piercing. Provided that the piercer is sufficiently skilled in other piercings, and remains conscientious at all times, this is a good place to begin learning female genital piercings.

JEWELRY
The tissue of the inner labia is extraordinarily thin and elastic, and piercings in it will enlarge easily. A barbell or other open-ended piece of jewelry is likely to be lost within months. Therefore, stick with closed rings.

The very smallest ring a woman can safely wear in her inner labia is 16 ga, ⅜″. However, for the vast majority of women, this could be an uncomfortable and unattractive choice. As well as being elastic, this tissue can tear rather easily, and the labia of most women get moved about quite a bit in the course of an average day. Thicker jewelry minimizes the risk of tearing. Unless the labia are quite petite, chose a ring large enough to allow centered, secure placement. A fairly standard size is 14 ga, ½″. For the smaller ones 14 ga ⅜″ is preferable to 16 ga. If a woman plans to stretch or otherwise play with her piercings after they've healed, 12 ga would be better.

Many piercees imagine a much smaller, thinner ring. They may have even seen a friend wearing a tiny little earring. Discuss the risk of tearing, and NEVER pierce with smaller than a 16 gauge, ⅜″ diameter ring, and then only if the anatomy warrants it.

UNIQUE CONSIDERATIONS
In ancient Greece and Rome and some Arabic cultures, even today, labia piercings have been locked together to insure a woman's chastity. Nowadays these piercings usually serve a very different purpose. A shiny ring gleaming forth from ones personal parts can add a tremendous boost to sexual desire. The effect is, in the case of this piercing, largely visual and psychological. There aren't many pleasure receptors in this tissue. Women seeking a more physiologically stimulating piercing can try the clit hood, clitoris, or triangle piercing.

The inner labia is a very easy place to heal a piercing, and a very attractive place to hang jewelry.

PLACEMENT & MARKING
Arrange the inner labia to lay flat against the outer labia on both sides so that you can clearly see the symmetry (or asymmetry). If you do this right after cleaning the labia with povidone-iodine, they tend to stick where you place them. Since there are innumerable different types and shapes of inner labia, you will have to customize each piercing to its wearer.

Most women have one side of the inner labia that is much smaller than the other. This is completely normal, as the human body is not a symmetrical thing. If the piercee doesn't have a clear idea as to which labium to pierce, suggest the smaller one. Piercing tends to elongate the labia somewhat, and you may create more of a balance by having a ring there.

Most labia tend to follow a distinct shape, narrow top and bottom and flaring outward in the center. For ideal placement, set the piercing very slightly above the widest part of the flare. For medium or well-developed lips, mark placement at least ½″ in from the edge. If the lips are small, narrow, or thin place the mark(s) as far in from the edge as anatomy permits. This placement looks beautiful, and won't be affected as much by friction, either sexual or clothing induced.

Once marked, use calipers to check ring size. For medium or well-developed labia minimum ring diameter should be ½″. For the petite ⅜″ rings may be more appropriate. Just be sure nothing inhibits the free motion of the tissue. Don't pierce in such a way as to connect the inner to the outer, for example.

If both labia are to be pierced, it's usually best to mark them individually, that is, allow your placement to be guided by each labium's folds and flares, rather than attempting to

> ### Tray Setup for Labia Piercings:
> - Povidone-iodine swabs
> - Benzalkonium chloride swabs
> - Marking pen or India ink and toothpicks
> - Regular or mini forceps
> - Sterile piercing needle
> - Rubber band
> - Cork (thimble: optional)

align the two piercings opposite each other. This looks better, and the rings are less likely to hang up on one another. In some cases, as when infibulation is the goal, symmetry of the rings is more desirable.

This tissue is so thin that marking it on both sides is usually unnecessary. If care is taken not to distort the tissue when applying the forceps, they won't need that much adjustment. Make a careful, precise mark on the inside only. This will require you to pierce from the unmarked side of one lip, but by careful examination of the marked side, this should present no problem.

TECHNICALITIES

At some point, you may wish to discuss the sensations that will follow. Genital piercings make most women nervous. The piercing itself is only an instantaneous flash of heat, then nothing at all, or perhaps a pleasant, spreading warmth. In other words, no big deal. Let piercees know that the fear that goes before the piercing is worse than the actual piercing. Slow, deep breathing helps quite a bit.

The piercee needs to spread her legs as wide as possible, and hold them still. Remind her of that whenever necessary. If necessary, an assistant can hold the piercee's legs, or hands, if this would make her more comfortable.

This is a mucous membrane piercing, so, if a marking pen is used, it will need to be discarded after contact with the tissue.

✦ CLIT HOOD — HORIZONTAL

Functional yet not so daunting as clits or triangles, clit hoods are probably the most popular female genital piercing. The horizontal hood piercing is more versatile, in that it can be flipped out of the way when so desired. This piercing stimulates by providing additional, indirect pressure to the shaft of the clitoris. Any woman with a fairly developed hood is a good candidate for this piercing.

DIFFICULTY LEVEL: 5

This is an intermediate level piercing. Do not attempt it until you have acquired sufficient experience with easier piercings, such as the inner labia. Remember that proper placement and clamping are crucial to avoid damage to the shaft of the clitoris.

JEWELRY

The tissue of the clit hood is extraordinarily elastic. A barbell or other open-ended piece of jewelry could easily be lost within months. Therefore, stick with rings.

Assuming it is appropriate for the anatomy, the very tiniest ring one could wear in her hood, vertical or horizontal, is 16 ga, ⅜″. But for most women this could be an uncomfortable and unattractive piece of jewelry. As well as being elastic, this tissue can tear easily, and the genitalia of most women gets moved about quite a bit in the course of an average day. Jewelry needs to be both thick enough to minimize tearing, and large enough to allow centered, secure placement. A fairly standard size is 14 ga, ½″. If the hood is very small, 14 ga

⅜″ is preferable to 16 ga. If a woman plans to stretch or otherwise play with her piercings after they've healed, 12 ga would be a better choice.

PLACEMENT & MARKING

Arrange the folds of the hood so that you can clearly see the symmetry (or asymmetry). There are innumerable different types and shapes of clit hoods, so you will have to customize each piercing to its wearer.

Many womens' hoods favor, or lean toward, one side. This is completely normal, as the human body is not a symmetrical thing. Generally it looks better and feels more comfortable if you respect the wishes of the body, and follow this lean when marking. Make your piercing symmetrical from wherever the center seam may happen to lie.

For maximum comfort of horizontal clit hood piercings, be sure the marks aren't too deep or too shallow. Usually spacing the width of the piercing at between ⅜″ and 7⁄16″ for a ½″ ring is appropriate.

If the hood is exceptionally small, a ⅜″ ring may be more appropriate. Use calipers as you feel the area to find out how far into the tissue you can safely place the piercing. Go as deeply as you can without inhibiting the free motion of the tissue. Avoid piercing any blood vessels, and especially avoid piercing the stem of the clitoris.

TECHNICALITIES

It is often a good idea to make the woman aware what you will be doing through each step of the piercing process. Genital piercings make most women nervous. The actual piercing itself lasts only a second and may be perceived as an instantaneous flash of heat followed by nothing at all or perhaps a pleasant, spreading warmth. In other words, not such a big deal, after all. Let piercees know that the fear that goes before the piercing is worse than the actual piercing. Slow, deep breathing helps quite a bit.

The piercee needs to spread her legs as wide as possible, and hold them still. Remind her of this if necessary.

This is a mucous membrane piercing, so, if a marking pen is used, it will need to be discarded after contact with the tissue.

Tray Setup for Clit Hood Piercings:
- Povidone-iodine swabs
- Benzalkonium chloride swabs
- Marking pen/ink & toothpicks
- NRT (not flared) for vertical piercings
- Regular or mini forceps
- Sterile piercing needle
- Rubber band
- Cork/thimble

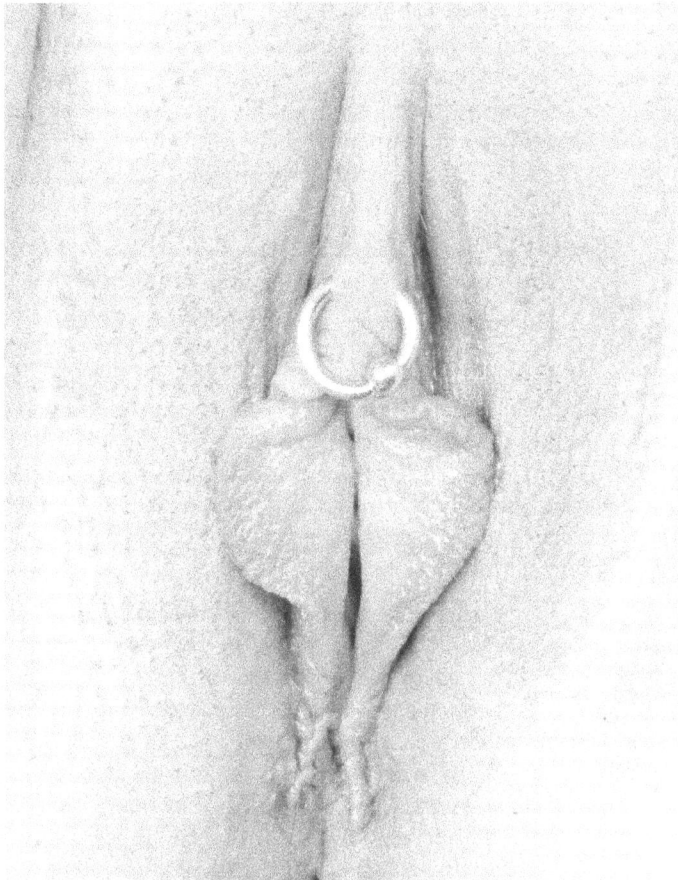

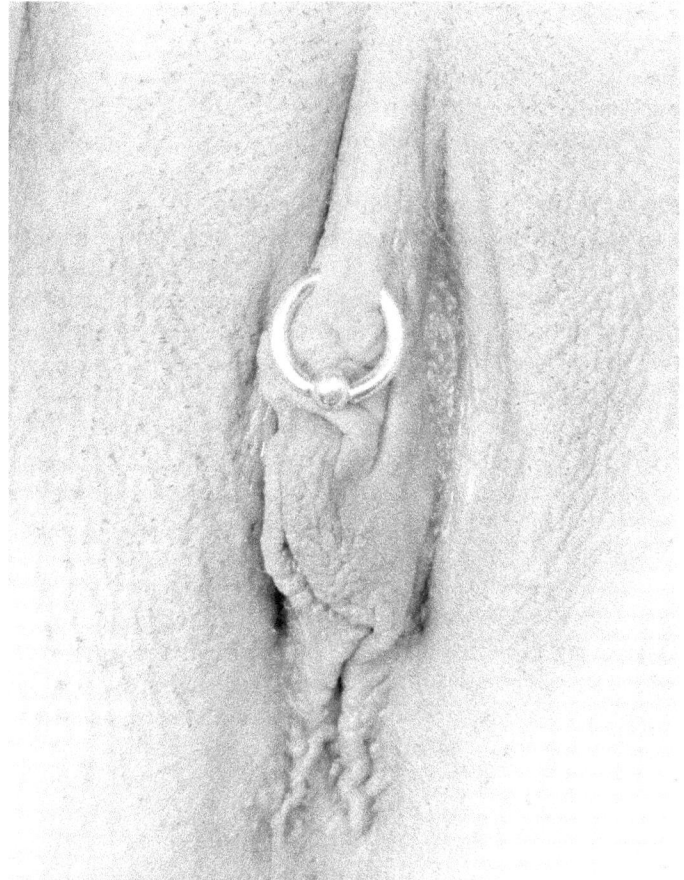

◉ Outer Labia

DIFFICULTY LEVEL: 5

This is an intermediate level piercing, and should not be confused with inner labia piercings in that respect. Placement is very specific, and crucial to the comfort and healing experience of the piercee. Piercers should have acquired sufficient experience with inner labia, clit hood, and scrotal piercings before attempting the outer labia.

JEWELRY

To minimize friction problems, the jewelry must be placed deeply enough to be protected by tissue, but not so deeply that it can't move freely if need be. For most women, the diameters which best accomplish this are ½″ or ⅝″. If unsure, bring both sizes into the room with you. ½″ is the absolute minimum diameter, and larger than ⅝″ tends to get excessive movement.

Regarding gauge, anything smaller than 14 ga is apt to tear through the tissue. Therefore choose 14 ga or 12 ga.

Most women choose a bead or captive ring, and rightly so: circular barbells can hang up on themselves, various body parts and clothing, and other people's jewelry. Barbells are not suggested as starter jewelry except for women who are experiencing friction problems. Remember, as always, to allow an extra ⅛″ for cleaning.

UNIQUE CONSIDERATIONS

Outer labia piercings can also be used to enforce chastity, although inner labia piercings are much more practical for this purpose. These piercings are now primarily for show. A shiny ring gleaming forth from ones personal parts can add a wonderful boost to sexual drive. The effect is, in the case of this piercing, largely psychological since there aren't many pleasure receptors in this tissue. Women who are seeking a more functional piercing, have large thighs, or whose legs are close together, might be wise to consider clit hood, clitoris, or triangle piercings for more sensation and fewer problems with friction.

PLACEMENT & MARKING

Try to arrange the outer labia in such a way as to make symmetry and centering easier. You may need to gently "plump" the area with your fingers. Also check out how and where the labia fold when the woman is standing.

Some women, particularly heavier women, have very prominent outer labia. Others, particularly smaller women, have very small, insignificant outer labia. In any case, remember to mark neither too deeply nor too shallowly, and always make sure the diameter of the jewelry is ⅛″ more than the depth of the piercing.

A common mistake with this piercing is to place the center marks too high up, near the clit hood. This places the jewelry directly in a place where friction and discomfort are significant possibilities. Placing the marks too low results in similar problems especially for women with heavy thighs or whose legs are close together. The center mark is ideally placed just slightly above the exact center of the labia.

It is sometimes difficult to find the leading edge, especially if the outer labia is hairy or not well defined. Sometimes this is easier to see when the woman is standing. Otherwise it may need to be located by feel. Outer labia tissue is soft and fatty. Avoid the pubic tendons. You want to stay within the outer labia tissue, so don't go as deep as the join between inner and outer labia, and stay away from where the outer labia joins regular skin. Where possible, marking the leading edge can be a great help in finding placement. This way calipers set for the proper depth can be used to measure equidistant on either side of the line.

The angle at which the piercing is set can significantly affect comfort and make a great deal of difference when clothing or inner thighs begin to rub against the jewelry. Follow the natural planes and curves of the body. Usually this results in an angle which turns very slightly down and inward, but every body is unique, and variations may certainly occur.

After you have made your three marks (center, entry and exit), gently stretch the tissue and measure again with the calipers. The marks, even when stretched, should be no more than ⅛″ less than the diameter of the jewelry. This writer has often encountered ½″ diameter rings crying out for release from ⅞″ deep piercings! Measure twice, pierce once.

TECHNICALITIES
Many women get nervous having their genitals pierced. Customers tend to be more at ease if they know what is happening, so explain what you are going to be doing each step of the process and what they can expect. The piercing itself is usually no more than an instantaneous flash of heat followed by nothing or perhaps a pleasant, spreading warmth. No big deal! Let piercees know that the fear that goes before the piercing is worse than the actual piercing. Slow, deep breathing (but not hyperventilation) helps quite a bit.

The piercee needs to spread her legs as wide as possible and hold them still. Remind her if necessary.

✦ FOURCHETTE

DIFFICULTY LEVEL: 6
This is an intermediate level piercing. You should acquire sufficient experience with clit hood and labia piercings before attempting to perform a fourchette. Placement can be tricky. Since the piercing is vertical, take special care to avoid a needle stick.

JEWELRY
The jewelry best suited for this piercing is a barbell, owing to its tight, vertical placement. A 14 ga or 12 ga, ⁷⁄₁₆″ to ½″ long barbell is very comfortable for daily wear, as well as for sexual play. Unfortunately, because this tissue is quite elastic, after a few months, the piercee could hear a tinkling noise in the shower, and look down just in time to see her pretty barbell wash down the drain. For this reason, a ring is much more commonly worn. The usual size is 14 ga or 12 ga ½″, but some smaller women could have a better time with a ⅜″ ring.

UNIQUE CONSIDERATIONS
This piercing is a beautiful addition to a woman's genitals. Healing time is minimal and jewelry can create a tantalizing pressure on the perineum, particularly during anal and oral sex. The downside to the fourchette is that for some women its location may inhibit vaginal penetration. The elasticity of the tissue comes into play particularly at this time, and a barbell could be pulled through the piercing. A ring is definitely a better choice for piercees for whom vaginal penetration is common.

MARKING AND PLACEMENT
Placement for the fourchette is largely determined by individual anatomy. With the piercee's legs comfortably spread, examine the tissue. The fourchette is a small pocket located at the very bottom of the vagina where the two inner labia join. Some women's fourchettes are very pronounced, but many need to be coaxed out. Pull on the tissue until you can clearly see the leading edge of the tissue. Mark this edge, then measure to the very limits on the inside and the outside. Be very clear that

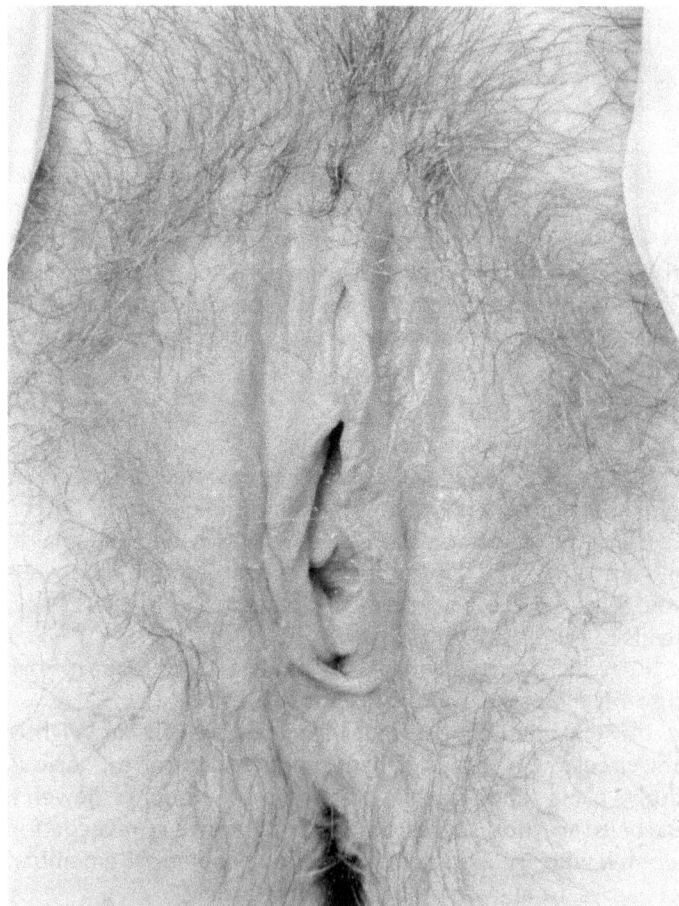

you aren't inhibiting any of the body's natural motions.

Mark only the easily pulled fourchette. Depth of placement is determined by how far the tissue stretches naturally. Simulate this a few times to be sure. For most women, the piercing will be marked exactly as deep as the inside diameter of the jewelry.

TECHNICALITIES

As some tissue is usually lost during healing, it's likely that the piercee may want to come back for a smaller piece of jewelry.

This is a vertical piercing, in a very tight space. Be very careful with cork centering and remain focused to avoid a needle stick.

✦ CLIT HOOD — VERTICAL

Functional yet not so daunting as clits or triangles, clit hoods are probably the most popular female genital piercing. The vertical hood piercing is much less common. While its placement provides generally more direct stimulation to the shaft of the clitoris, a small number of women have experienced overstimulation, which leads to a reversible sensation of numbness. This piercing is sometimes better suited for women with heavy thighs or whose legs are close together, situations which can cause problems with a horizontal hood piercing.

DIFFICULTY LEVEL: 6

This is an intermediate level piercing. Being a vertical, freehand piercing, it is slightly more difficult and more dangerous to perform than a horizontal clit hood. Do not attempt it until you have acquired sufficient experience with horizontal hood piercings. Remember that proper placement and smooth, secure piercing are crucial to avoid damage to the shaft of the clitoris.

JEWELRY

The tissue of the clit hood is extraordinarily elastic. A barbell or other open-ended piece of jewelry could be lost within months. Therefore, stick with rings.

Depending upon anatomy, the very tiniest ring one could theoretically wear in her hood, vertical or horizontal, is 16 ga, ⅜″ though this is usually not the most comfortable or attractive jewelry choice. As well as being elastic, this tissue can tear easily, and the genitalia of most women gets moved about quite a bit in the course of an average day. Jewelry needs to be both thick enough to withstand tearing and large enough to allow centered, secure placement. A fairly standard size is 14 ga, ½″. If the hood is very small, 14 ga ⅜″ is preferable to 16 ga. If a woman plans to stretch or otherwise play with her piercings after they've healed, 12 ga would be better, but be sure she has a well-developed hood that will carry it.

Many piercees imagine a much smaller, thinner ring. They may have even seen a friend wearing a tiny little earring. Discuss the risk of tearing, and NEVER pierce with smaller than a 16 gauge, ⅜″ diameter ring.

PLACEMENT & MARKING

Arrange the folds of the hood so that you can clearly see the symmetry (or asymmetry). There are innumerable different types and shapes of clit hoods, so you will have to customize each piercing to its wearer.

Many women's hoods favor, or lean toward, one side. This is quite common, as the human body is seldom a symmetrical thing. Generally it looks better and feels more comfortable if you respect the design of the body, and follow this lean when marking. Make your piercing symmetrical from wherever the center seam may happen to lie.

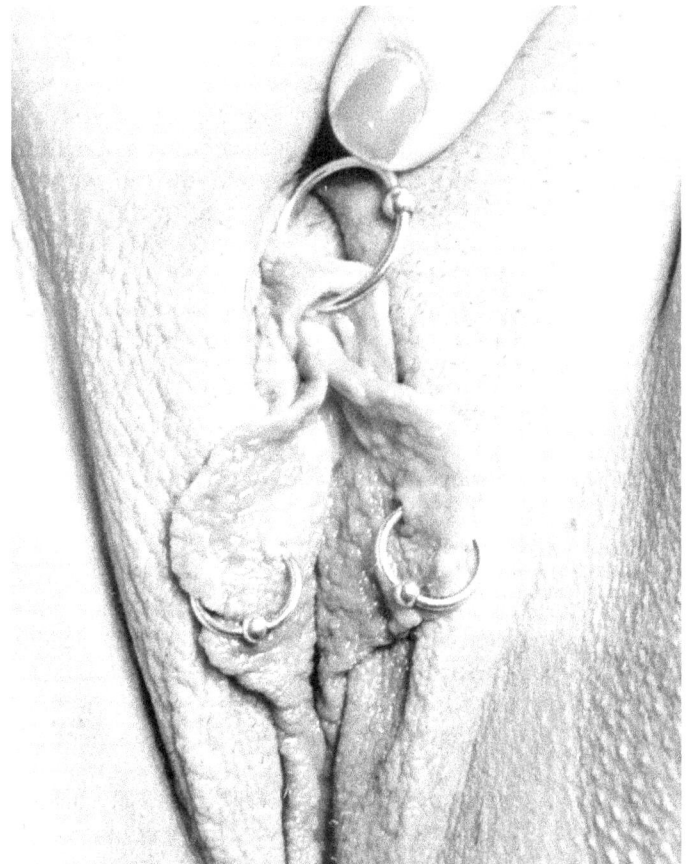

Vertical clit hood and inner labia piercings

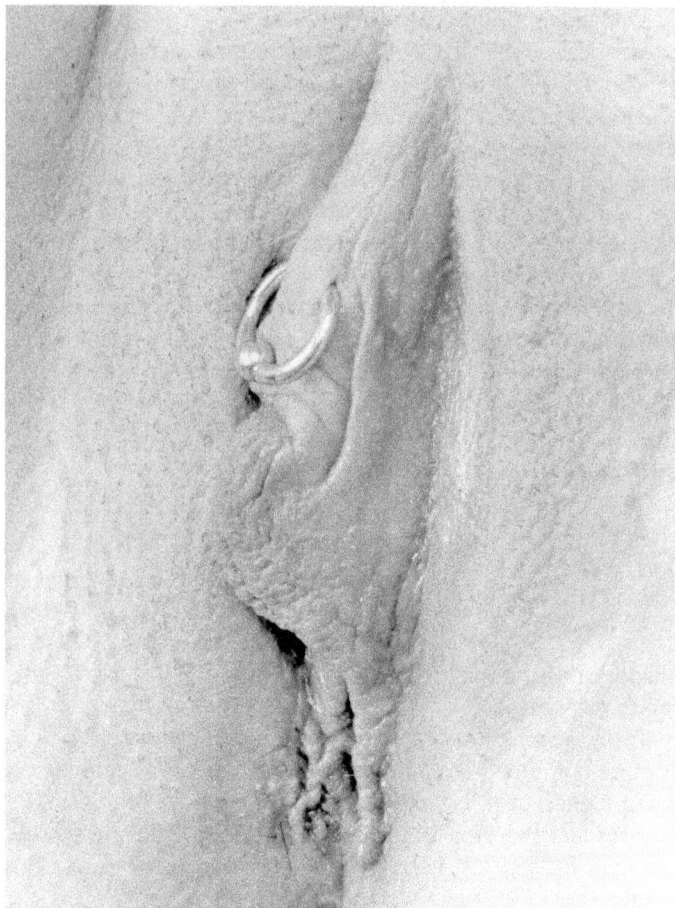

Horizontal clit hood piercing

If the hood is exceptionally small, a ⅜″ ring may be appropriate. Regardless, always check with calipers as you feel the area to find out how far into the tissue you can safely set the piercing, and make sure it doesn't exceed the diameter of the ring. Go as deeply as you can without inhibiting the free motion of the tissue. Avoid piercing blood vessels or the clitoris.

For a vertical piercing, you may need to insert the NRT under the hood as part of your marking procedure. Never pierce higher than the NRT will comfortably fit. The bead of the ring should fall directly against the clit.

TECHNICALITIES

At some point, you may wish to discuss the sensations that will follow. Genital piercings make most women nervous. The piercing itself is only an instantaneous flash of heat, then nothing at all, or perhaps a pleasant, spreading warmth. In other words, no big deal. Let piercees know that the fear that goes before the piercing is worse than the actual piercing. Slow, deep breathing helps quite a bit.

The piercee needs to spread her legs as wide as possible, and hold them still. Remind her of that whenever necessary.

This is a mucous membrane piercing, so, if a marking pen is used, it will need to be discarded after contact with the tissue.

✦ TRIANGLE

DIFFICULTY LEVEL: 10

In difficulty of precise marking, placement, piercing, and healing, the triangle is equal only to the clitoris and the dydoes. Piercers should have reached a very advanced level of experience, and should be observed closely by a senior or master piercer. A detailed knowledge of the female anatomy is essential. Even very experienced piercers have typically had difficulty with the triangle. Potential for lasting damage is very high. Do not attempt this piercing before you are absolutely ready!!!

This is a very difficult, deep piercing. Extreme concentration and a high level of skill are needed to place this piercing in the right location, while avoiding potentially serious accidents. There are piercers who should know better asserting that this is just a deep clit hood piercing. This is NOT the case. It passes through very different tissue, requires a much longer healing time, and produces very different sensations.

JEWELRY

Before you begin to select jewelry, examine the piercee to determine whether she is a suitable candidate for the triangle piercing. If her hood and inner labia are small, and stay close to the larger outer labia, she should consider a different piercing. If, however, her hood and inner labia are prominent, and appear almost separate from the rest of her genitalia, she stands a good chance of healing the piercing without incident. She should be made aware of the fact that approximately one fourth of women who initially seem like good candidates end up removing the jewelry because of friction-related problems.

This piercing initially requires a ring with a standard thickness of 12 ga, and a diameter from ½″ to ⅝″, depending on the build of the piercee. In some cases where friction becomes a problem, barbells may help, but if friction is presenting a problem, it's possible that the piercing won't be successful.

Tray Setup for Triangle Piercings:
- Povidone-iodine swabs
- Benzalkonium chloride swabs
- Marking pen or India ink and toothpicks
- Small german, matte paki, or mini forceps
- Sterile piercing needle
- Needle pusher
- Rubber band
- Cork (thimble: optional)
- Knowledge of anatomy

UNIQUE CONSIDERATIONS

Many women have genitalia that aren't appropriately formed for smooth healing of a triangle. If a piercee is considering this piercing, arrange for a consultation so that you can examine and discuss the situation.

This piercing is, for many women, at least as functional as a clit piercing. It provides enhanced pressure on the shaft of the clit, from underneath.

PLACEMENT & MARKING

Placement for this piercing is very particular, and marking can be quite difficult. Begin by examining the entire area very carefully. Feel for the shaft of the clitoris by tugging gently on the hood. Stretch the tissue to see where the hood, labia, and mons veneris meet.

The most common placement errors can result in either a *very* deep clit hood piercing or two *very* high inner labia piercings. These could be unattractive, uncomfortable, and even need to be removed. Both can be avoided by careful marking, and a careful and accurate application of the forceps. Always double, triple, and quadruple check your marks. Use calipers and stretch the tissue with your fingers. You should be able to feel the stem of the clit just above the marks you have made. Your marks must be level, and not be so deep that they prevent the hood from moving freely away from the mons/labia.

TECHNICALITIES

At some point, you may wish to discuss the sensations that will follow. Genital piercings make most women nervous. Triangle piercings can be very intense, but fortunately, when performed by a knowledgeable professional, are over in an instant. Try not to alarm a client or add to their fears, but be honest and let piercees know what to expect. Slow, deep breathing (but not hyperventilation) helps quite a bit. And don't be startled if the client should let out a scream when you do this one.

Clamping for the triangle is every bit as important as marking. Rubber band tension should be fairly tight, without crushing. Lift the clit hood and shaft of the clitoris out and away from the body, while sliding the forceps under and upwards. The result should require that the tissue is adjusted for depth, and the shaft of the clitoris is secured and protected by being well beyond the triangular head of the forceps. Check before piercing to be sure that the clit hasn't moved from that spot.

The piercee needs to spread her legs as wide as possible, and hold them still. If desired, an assistant can hold the piercee's legs, or hands, assuming this would make her more comfortable.

This is a mucous membrane piercing, so, if a marking pen is used, it will need to be discarded after contact with the tissue.

✦ CLItoRIs

DIFFICULTY LEVEL: 10

The clitoris is, perhaps, the most difficult, dangerous, technically advanced piercing of all. No one with less than three years of full-time expe-

rience and close supervision should even consider attempting to perform a clitoris piercing. The piercee is usually highly agitated, the area to be pierced is often less than ¼" wide, and the slightest misstep could result in serious, permanent damage to the clitoris, the source of a woman's sexual pleasure. We cannot emphasize enough: do NOT attempt this piercing without an extremely advanced level of skill and close supervision by a senior or master level piercer.

JEWELRY

The vast majority of women just don't have a large enough clitoris to pierce. Unless you can easily clamp it, you certainly can't pierce it.

Those women who are candidates for a clit piercing usually fare best with a 16 ga, ⅜" bead ring. A very, very tiny minority can be pierced with a 14 ga ⅜" captive, but that is a most unusual situation.

Minibars have been used, particularly for vertical clit piercings, but remember to wax the threading, and remember that threading the bead onto the post may be very tricky after such an intense piercing.

UNIQUE CONSIDERATIONS

This is probably the rarest, most difficult of all piercings. Very few women possess the appropriate anatomical proportions to properly place and heal the piercing, and very few piercers possess the very high level of skill, experience, and concentration to pull

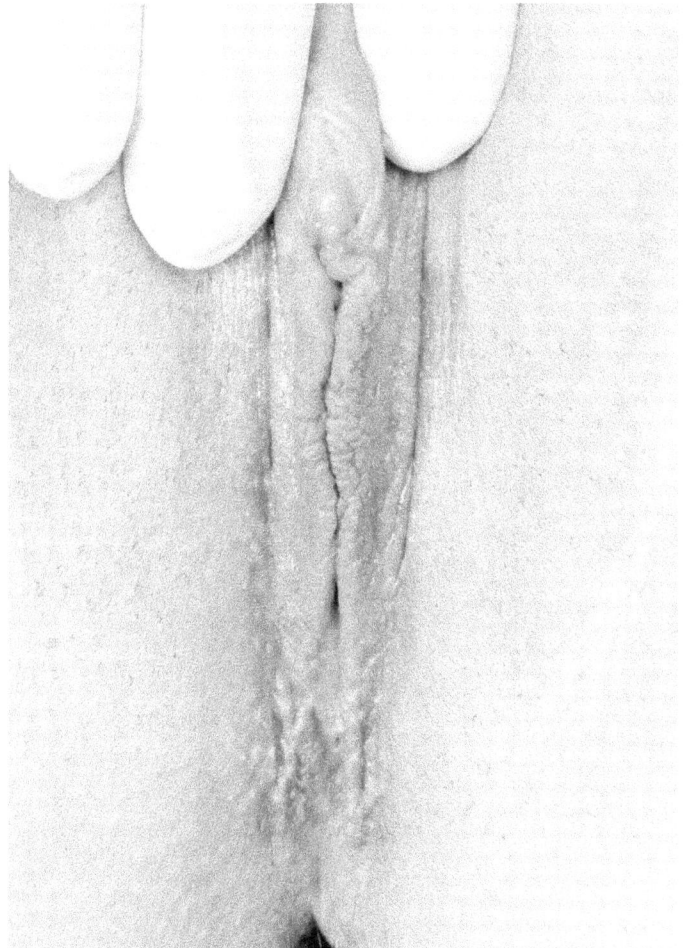

Tray Setup for Clitoris Piercings:

- Povidone-iodine swabs
- Benzalkonium chloride swabs
- Marking pen or India ink and toothpicks
- Small german, matte paki, or mini forceps
- Sterile piercing needle
- Rubber band
- Cork (thimble: optional)

it off satisfactorily. To be a suitable candidate the clit must be well-developed and readily exposed. Pass on small clits and those swathed in hood tissue.

Although the technique appears at first glance to be a manageable clamp-and-pierce, the area is so small, so sensitive, and so full of nerve endings—over 200 in a dot the size of a pencil eraser—that it should be obvious to sensible people that this is no ordinary piercing. For those fortunate enough to be built for it, it is a very functional piercing, providing extraordinarily heightened sensations. Done improperly, it could easily impair the pleasure center of the body forever. When considering your ability to perform this piercing, please ask yourself if you are willing to take that risk. How confident are you in your skill? Could you be any more prepared for such an undertaking? Would a few more months or years of experience make this piercing safer?

PLACEMENT & MARKING

The area in which you are working is very delicate, and very small. Gently pull back the hood until the clit pops forward. If necessary dry it with a clean tissue or cotton swab.

Look at the proportions. Is it asymmetrical? Where does the clitoris attach to the hood? To the top of the labia? Place two very precise, careful marks in the deepest, most centered spot possible. It is crucial to avoid piercing into the hood or inner labia.

When you have made your marks, let the hood fall, to get some idea of the interaction between ring and hood. If necessary, you may need to make careful, minor adjustments.

TECHNICALITIES

At some point, you may wish to discuss the sensations that will follow. Genital piercings make most women nervous. Clit piercings can be very intense, but fortunately, when performed by a knowledgeable professional, are over in an instant. Try not to alarm a client or add to their fears, but be honest and let piercees know what to expect. Slow, deep breathing (but not hyperventilation) helps quite a bit. And don't be startled if the client should let out a scream when you do this one.

The piercee needs to spread her legs as wide as possible, and hold them still. Remind her of that whenever necessary. If necessary, an assistant can hold the piercee's legs, or hands, if this would make her more comfortable.

This is a mucous membrane piercing, so, if a marking pen is used, it will need to be discarded after contact with the tissue.

Chapter 11—
Male Genital Piercings

✦ Frenum

DIFFICULTY LEVEL: 5
This is an intermediate level piercing. Be very conscious of placement and have sufficient experience with easier piercings before attempting a frenum.

JEWELRY
Barbells are the most comfortable jewelry choice for frenum piercings. The size is pretty standard: ⅝″ long, 12 or 10 gauge. While 14 ga is an acceptable choice, thicker studs are much more comfortable. Men who are uncircumcised and have a very tight foreskin may require a slightly shorter stud so the foreskin can be rolled down over the piercing, if desired. The lorum piercing, a frenum at the base of the penis, offers the alternative choices of the standard barbell or a ¾″ ring.

The reason for the stud length seems to evade some people because frenum piercings are so commonly misplaced. We don't want to continue this practice. Choose a ⅝″ barbell, and mark the piercing just slightly less (see placement section below).

Men who are endowed with a well-flared, mushroom-shaped penis head have the option of wearing a large ring or frenum loop that encircles the shaft, though these are best reserved for after the piercing has healed.

Although 12 or 10 ga, ½″ rings can be worn, they can get in the way of oral sex and intercourse.

UNIQUE CONSIDERATIONS
Passing through a nerve-rich point of the male anatomy, the frenum piercing is considered by many to be one of the two most sensuous penis piercings. This can be pleasurable for a woman also assuming the man can wear a beaded frenum loop or large ring around the penis. These can be very stimulating during intercourse.

Some individuals into bondage and discipline have used the frenum with other piercings as a means to enforce male chastity. By locking the frenum to a lower frenum (lorum), scrotum, or guiche piercing, erection or masturbation is rendered difficult and intercourse impossible.

PLACEMENT & MARKING
There are two main types of frenums—sometimes also called frenulums. The first, commonly found on uncircumcised men but also seen on some circumcised, is distinguished by a thin web of tissue which connects the penis head and shaft (see drawing on page 90). Piercers who don't know better frequently put frenum piercings through this web, a placement which is seldom satisfactory. The tissue isn't strong enough to endure the rigors of masturbation or intercourse and will usually tear or heal out in a short period of time. During the process of circumcision, men often lose this web (see photo on next page). This is characteristic of the second type of frenum.

After carefully examining the area the piercer retracts the foreskin, if there is one, and/or all loose flesh back towards the base of the penis thus creating an easy tautness similar to that which would be experienced during erection. S/he first draws a reference line following the frenum seam. If this seam is distinctly off center or wanders erratically to one side or the other, the piercer may have to compensate. The line should be centered in relationship to the center of the head and the urethra which can be seen and felt as a distinct, rounded ridge running the length of the penis just under the skin. Next, visualizing the penis as a cylinder (see drawing on next page), s/he proceeds to draw a short reference line on the underside of the penis directly opposite the upper edge of the corona. This crosses the first line and indicates the proper placement for the piercing in relationship to the tip of the penis. In most cases it will fall in a fleshy area ideally suited for anchoring a permanent piercing. Using these two lines as a guide, the piercer will now draw two dots, one about ⁵⁄₁₆″ to ⅜″ equidistant on either side of the center, lengthwise line and just beyond the ends of the cross-mark. Once satisfied that the

Tray Setup for Frenum Piercings:
- Povidone-iodine swabs
- Benzalkonium chloride swabs
- Marking pen or India ink and toothpicks
- Regular or mini forceps
- Sterile piercing needle
- Rubber band
- Cork (thimble: optional)
- Barbell connecting wire

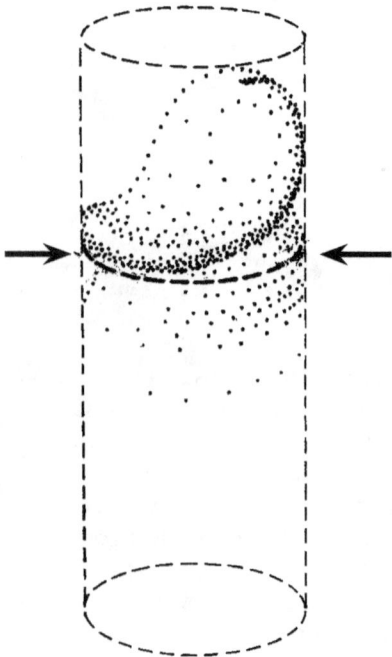

Left: **To find the correct frenum placement first pull the tissue on the shaft of the penis somewhat taut as it might be with an erection. Then, visualizing the penis as a cylinder, place your marks on the bottom of the penis opposite where the edge of the glans meets the shaft on the upper side.**

marks are even and properly aligned, the piercer allows the tissue to relax, checks to see if the marks still line up properly, then measures the distance between the dots. For a standard ⅝″ barbell they should be about ⁹⁄₁₆″ apart. If necessary the piercer can change, correct, or clarify the marks by removing old ones with alcohol and redrawing them.

As you gain experience with frenum piercings, you will, no doubt, be called upon to perform "ladders" of frenums evenly spaced along the shaft. These should always follow the center seam. This can be difficult, especially when the seam isn't

straight. It is almost always best, where possible, to follow the natural lines of the body. If the seam is crooked, use the center of the urethra as your guide. Do the marking with the tissue relaxed and space the piercings no less than ⁷⁄₁₆″ apart. ½″ is generally more attractive and comfortable.

TECHNICALITIES

This area of the penis is very vascular. Once the tissue has been clamped into the forceps, it can be helpful to shine light through it with a small flashlight. Any blood vessels in the path of the needle will be easy to see. If necessary, these can easily be repositioned inside the forceps.

It is always in everyone's best interest if you are reasonably candid with your clients regarding the pain they can anticipate. This doesn't necessitate going into gory detail. Expect the piercee to be nervous, and attempt to put him at ease by explaining each step of the process as you proceed. The frenum piercing should not be that intense: a quick flash of heat, then nothing at all, or perhaps a spreading warmth. Often the pinching of the forceps hurts worse than the piercing. In other words, this shouldn't be a big deal. Let piercees know it's okay to be nervous. Encourage them to breath deeply and slowly. This will help quite a bit.

The piercee needs to hold fairly still. Remind him of that whenever necessary.

✦ SCROTUM

DIFFICULTY LEVEL: 5

This is an intermediate level piercing. Be very conscious of placement and have sufficient experience with easier piercings before attempting a scrotum.

JEWELRY

The scrotum covers a fair amount of genital real estate, and virtually every square inch is pierceable, though some areas are more suitable than others.

The choice of jewelry is fairly broad. Depending largely upon personal preference, a ring or a barbell may be worn, according to aesthetics and function.

View of a typical circumcised penis.

> **Tray Setup for Scrotum Piercings:**
> • Povidone-iodine swabs
> • Benzalkonium chloride swabs
> • Marking pen or India ink and toothpicks
> • Regular or mini forceps
> • Sterile piercing needle
> • Needle pusher
> • Rubber band
> • Cork (thimble: optional)

If a ring is the desired item of jewelry, 12 or 10 gauge, ⅝″ is the preferred size though ¾″ is an option. 14 ga may be worn, but is less comfortable for most people. In many cases, the tissue rejects somewhat. Therefore, you really shouldn't pierce with less than a ⅝″ ring. When the piercing has healed, ½″ rings usually can be worn, if desired.

The barbell for scrotal piercings is pretty standard, usually ⅝″ long, 12 or 10 gauge. Though 14 ga may be worn, it's usually less comfortable. Longer barbells, up to ¾″, may be worn if a piercee has a particular design idea in mind, but these have a tendency to snag on clothing and bedding.

UNIQUE CONSIDERATIONS

Doug Malloy claimed that there was a traditional piercing high on the scrotum on either side of the base of the penis. Called a hafada, it was allegedly native to Kuwait. All other scrotum piercings Doug often referred to as "bag" piercings.

Stories often surface regarding deep piercings which pass through the scrotum being done by this or that tribe in some part of the world. The feasibility of such piercings makes their likelihood doubtful. To heal them successfully would require a surgical procedure beyond the capabilities of most experienced piercers, never mind a native without benefit of basic hygiene. Scrotum piercings must be kept superficial, through surface tissue only.

If desired, a frenum ladder can be continued down and around the scrotum to the guiche.

PLACEMENT & MARKING

It is generally a good idea to assess, and sometimes to mark, the scrotum with the piercee standing. This tissue has the rather frustrating tendency to shrink, stretch, and twist all by itself. The piercee has no control over it. Sometimes the changes can dramatically alter your dots. Your best approach will be to mark where you think the piercing should be, then wait and watch. Invariably the tissue will shift. Adjust your marks and wait some more. Eventually you will find a placement which, though possibly not perfect, is acceptable. If it remains reasonably level and doesn't move too drastically, go for it.

If you will be piercing a fold of tissue, as you might for hafadas, it is often a good idea to mark the center of that fold. You can then use your calipers to measure equidistant either side of the line. Distance between the two dots when the tissue is relaxed and unstretched should be as close to ⅝″. If you are trying to create symmetrical piercings, try using a level made of a folded facial tissue to help you visualize and balance the marks. Remember that this tissue stretches and shrinks constantly! If in doubt, wait a few minutes and recheck your marks.

Give some thought to how scrotum piercings will be impacted upon by clothing and/or walking. It is often a good idea to avoid the sides of the scrotum for this reason, since piercings there would get a lot more irritation than elsewhere.

If you will be continuing a frenum ladder, try to follow the center seam. This can be difficult, especially when the seam wanders. Wherever possible follow the natural lines of the body. Piercings in this area should be spaced no less than ⁷⁄₁₆″ apart, though ½″ is generally more attractive and comfortable.

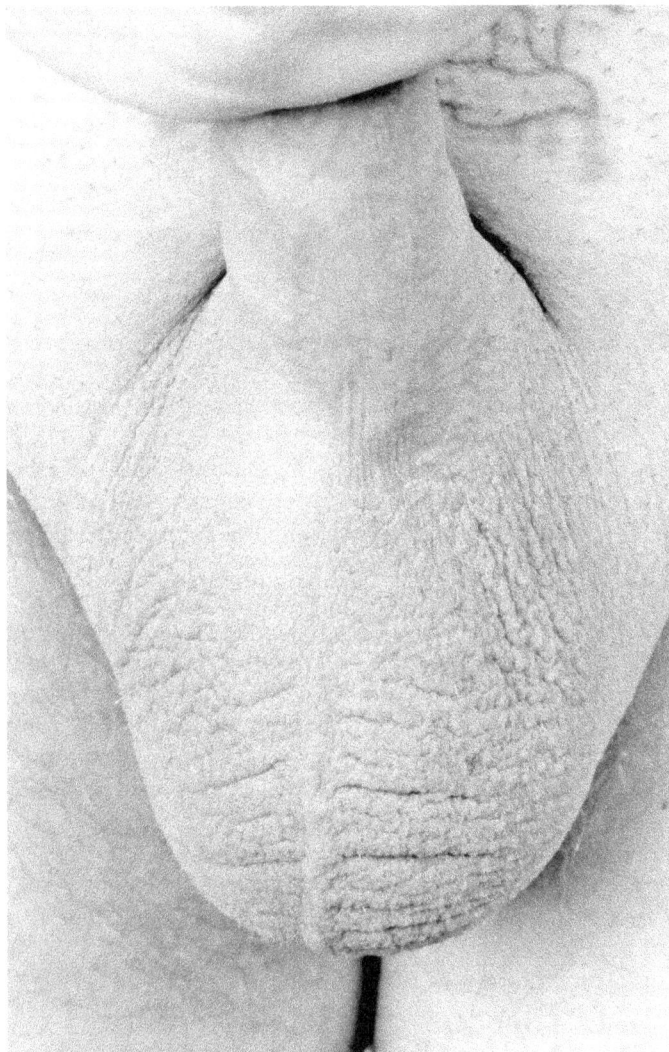

TECHNICALITIES

This area is very vascular. Once the tissue has been clamped into the forceps, it can be helpful to shine light through it with a small flashlight. Any blood vessels in the path of the needle will be easy to see and avoid. If necessary, these can easily be repositioned inside the forceps.

To help reduce your client's anxiety, it is always beneficial to explain each step of the piercings process as you are doing it. Yes, there may be a little bit of pain, but more likely an instantaneous flash of heat, then nothing at all, or perhaps a pleasant, spreading warmth. In other words, not such a big deal after all. Let piercees know that the fear that goes before the piercing is worse than the actual piercing. Deep breathing help quite a bit.

The piercee needs to hold fairly still. Remind him of that whenever necessary.

✦ ⌘ Prince Albert

DIFFICULTY LEVEL: 5

This is an intermediate level piercing. Piercees should have acquired sufficient skill with nostrils and other, easier freehand piercings before attempting a PA. Care must be taken to avoid any damage to the urethra.

JEWELRY

This piercing is done with either a ring or a circular barbell. If the piercee foresees frequent removal of the jewelry, a circular barbell would be the better option. Because the tissue is so thin, it would easily tear if thinner than 14 ga jewelry were inserted. Consider 12 ga your minimum. Most piercees find 10 ga to be the most comfortable size, and, in fact, can't wait to stretch to 8 ga or beyond!

To determine diameter, it is always wise to measure the piercee. A man with a small urethral opening situated high on the head will usually require a ¾″ ring. A man with a wide, low urethral opening usually is more comfortable with a ⅝″ ring. A few men require as small as ½″ or as large as ⅞″ ring, though these are fairly rare.

Foreskin can be a problem if it is kept in a retracted state by the ring. In this case, measure for the smallest possible ring, and make piercees aware of the possibility of problems.

If a piercee returns a few weeks later with a swollen, shiny, discharging piercing, it is possible that the ring is either too small or too large. Hot soaks and a jewelry change will often correct the problem.

UNIQUE CONSIDERATIONS

It is not known whether Prince Albert himself actually had this piercing (also called a dressing ring), but it was quite fashionable for men of the day to have one. Victorian pants were very tight, and it has been said the ring was used to strap the penis tight to the leg to minimize any unsightly bulge.

Nowadays, this piercing is done almost exclusively for erotic enhancement. While this is primarily for the possessor, some men's partners also find it stimulating, but for others, it may be uncomfortable, particularly during oral or anal sex. Fortunately this piercing is in a very vascular area and heals so quickly and completely that it may be removed for short periods as early as three months after piercing.

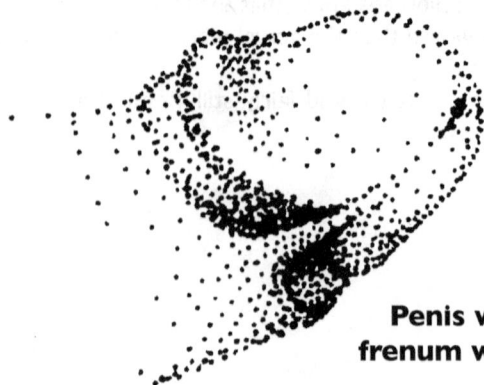

Penis with frenum web.

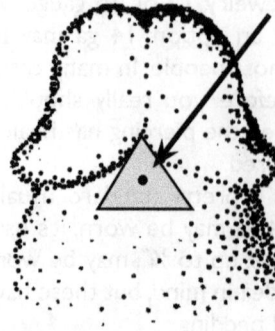

The PA triangle: place a *Prince Albert* piercing in the center of an imaginary triangle, the apex of which falls where the glans joins and the base of which falls on the frenum piercing line. If there is a frenum web, place it to one side as close to the center as possible.

For some men, the PA becomes a "PE" (pee everywhere). In some cases it necessitates that the piercee sit down for urination. Generally speaking this doesn't happen unless the piercing is stretched beyond about 8 ga.

Like the frenum piercing, the PA is sometimes used in combination with other genital piercings to enforce chastity.

PLACEMENT & MARKING

Examine the head and shaft of the penis carefully, from as many angles as possible. Turn it upside down and sideways. Note any irregularities, slopes, or asymmetries which may influence your placement. If both are placed correctly, any man can have both a frenum and Prince Albert piercing, but there should be at least ¼″ between them.

If there is a thin, frenum web, you will need to mark and pierce slightly to one side of it. If not, place the piercing in the center of an imaginary triangle, the apex of which falls where the corona joins and the base of which falls on the frenum piercing line. Never place the piercing in the head.

TECHNICALITIES

If you are using a topical anesthetic ointment or the NRT has been lubricated with Bacitracin, be sure to wipe these off your gloves before doing the piercing so you'll have a better grip and there will be less likelihood of a slip or needle stick.

**Tray Setup
for Prince Albert Piercings:**

- Povidone-iodine swabs
- Benzalkonium chloride swabs
- Marking pen or India ink and toothpicks
- NRT (not flared)
- Sterile piercing needle
- Rubber band
- Cork (thimble: optional)
- *Optional:*
- Cotton swab
- Topical anaesthetic ointment

Also be sure the needle point is well inside the NRT and clear of the urethra before withdrawing the NRT.

It is always in everyones' best interest if you are reasonably candid with your clients regarding the pain they can anticipate. This doesn't necessitate going into gory detail. Expect the piercee to be nervous, and attempt to put him at ease by explaining each step of the process as you proceed. In the hands of a skilled professional, the Prince Albert piercing is not that intense: an intense moment and it's over. Let piercees know it's okay to be nervous. Encourage them to breath deeply and slowly. This will help quite a bit.

The piercee needs to hold fairly still. Remind him of that whenever necessary.

✦ GUICHE

DIFFICULTY LEVEL: 6

This is an intermediate level piercing. The placement and marking are very important to the comfort and function of the guiche. The location may increase the potential for a needle stick. Piercers should acquire sufficient experience with frenum and scrotal piercings before attempting a guiche.

JEWELRY

In Tahiti where this piercing originated, men don't wear trousers. But in this part of the world we usually do. Consequently, in terms of comfort, there is no ideal piece of jewelry. A standard or captive bead ring is the best choice, though some men have reported success wearing a barbell for several weeks. However, the piercing should be checked frequently to make sure a ball isn't working its way into the piercing. A nylon monofilament retainer may also help in such circumstances.

Standard size is 12 or 10 gauge, ⅝″ diameter. In some cases, there may be a little tissue loss. Therefore, you really shouldn't pierce with less than a ⅝″ ring. A larger diameter tends to get more movement and irritation especially from walking and sitting. When the piercing has healed, ½″ rings can often be worn, if desired.

"Worms-eye" view showing ideal placement for the guiche piercing, the center of another triangle.

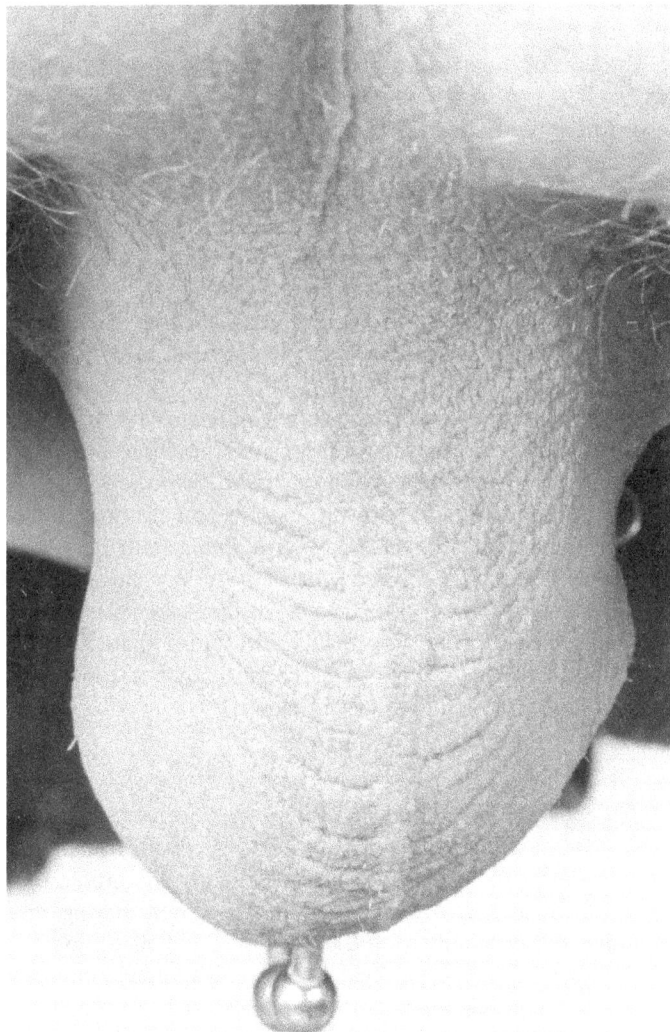

Tray Setup for Guiche Piercings:
• Povidone-iodine swabs
• Benzalkonium chloride swabs
• Marking pen or India ink and toothpicks
• Regular or mini forceps
• Sterile piercing needle
• Needle pusher
• Rubber band
• Cork (thimble: optional)

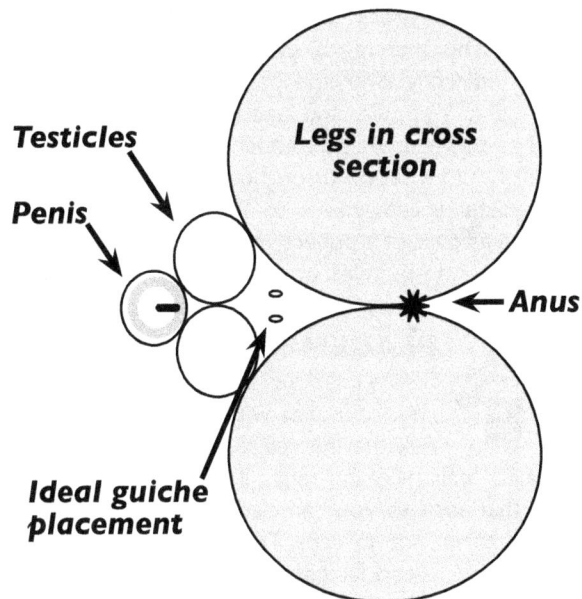

UNIQUE CONSIDERATIONS

This piercing is placed at the root chakra, and directly over the perineum muscle, making it a very popular and functional choice. Many men like to wear weights attached to the healed piercing, for a delightful sensation throughout the day.

The guiche is indigenous to Tahiti and was traditionally performed as part of a puberty rite.

Men who ride bicycles or motorcycles could find this an uncomfortable piercing especially during healing.

PLACEMENT & MARKING

Before marking, remove any excess hair and clean the area with a povidone-iodine swab. Ask the piercee if one particular spot in the guiche area feels nice and tingly. If they say yes, ask them to indicate that spot so you can clamp it using a clip such as a wire clothespin, not forceps. Then check the spot out for practicality. If it is too far back, the piercing will get constant irritation from walking, and its proximity to the anus could be a source of infection. If the piercee has no special spot or if the one they have indicated is too far back, place the piercing in the center of the "guiche triangle," the open space between the legs and the scrotum (see diagram). Once you are satisfied with the front-to-back location, mark it with a small reference line, and remove the clip.

The rest of the marking procedure and the piercing itself is easiest if the piercee assumes a "doggy style" position, on their knees with their body twisted at the waist and one shoulder braced against the table. While you could proceed with the piercee on his back, his scrotum would dangle in your way and if pulled too tightly upward, could stretch and distort the tissue you are attempting to work with. Consequently, the first position is preferable.

Once the piercee is in position, use another povidone-iodine swab and reclean the area. You are now ready for final marking.

Locate and draw a second reference line down the center seam (the perineum), which for most men is obvious. Although this seam may occasionally appear to be asymmetrical, it is almost always reliable. Wherever possible, you are best to follow the natural lines of the body. Now, equidistant on either side of this line, at the place where the first reference line would cross it, place a dot. Overall distance between these two dots should be no less than ½" or more than 9/16". If it would assist you in getting the marks perfectly horizontal, use a level made from a folded facial tissue.

TECHNICALITIES

Whether you choose to have the piercee on his back or adopt the "doggy-style" position for this piercing, be sure he holds still when you pierce him. If he jerks or lurches, you are particularly vulnerable to a needle stick as his legs try to come together. Having one shoulder and no hands on the table helps minimize the risk.

It is always in everyones' best interest if you are reasonably candid with your clients regarding the pain they can anticipate. This doesn't necessitate going into gory detail. Expect the piercee to be nervous, and attempt to put him at ease by explaining each step of the process as you proceed. The guiche piercing should not be that intense: a quick flash of heat, then nothing at all, or perhaps a spreading warmth. Often the pinching of the forceps hurts worse than the piercing. In other words, this shouldn't be a big deal. Let piercees know it's okay to be nervous. Encourage them to breath deeply and slowly. This will help quite a bit.

The piercee needs to hold fairly still. Remind him of that whenever necessary.

✦ FORESKIN

DIFFICULTY LEVEL: 7

This is an advanced intermediate level piercing. Although the clamp-and-pierce technique is fairly straightforward for an experienced piercer, it can be very tricky to locate just the right spots for marking. This situation is exacerbated by the fact that since most foreskin piercings are done in pairs, it is desirable for them to be symmetrical. Piercers should acquire sufficient experience with frenums, scrotal and related piercings before attempting this piercing.

JEWELRY

Because the tissue is so pliable, as it needs to be to compensate for the radical changes the penis goes through from erect to flaccid, jewelry must be able to accommodate these changes, at least during healing. Rings are usually best. For most men, 12 ga 5/8" rings are ideal. While 14 ga may be used, it tends to be sharper and less comfortable, and could inhibit healing. 10 ga tends, by virtue of weight, to be irritating. There is often some tissue loss which rings smaller than 5/8" can exacerbate. Rings larger than 5/8" move and cause irritation.

UNIQUE CONSIDERATIONS

The ancient Greeks and Romans used foreskin piercings to enforce chastity among slaves; a locking device through opposing piercings makes erection difficult and intercourse impossible. Most people don't use it for such purposes anymore. The rings create enhanced stimulation for both the wearer and his partner.

PLACEMENT & MARKING

It can be very difficult to mark and pierce a foreskin if the penis is erect. The piercer needs to be able to see how the foreskin folds and lies when the man is flaccid. In this relaxed state check to make certain there is no bunched up tissue, then, with the marker draw a reference line around the leading edge of the foreskin. Theoretically, piercings can be placed anywhere around this circle although they are usually horizontally centered on the left and right side. By looking carefully at the penis head-on it should be easy to determine the most attractive, central placement. Place a small reference mark on the leading edge at these locations. The first of your dots go on the outside about ½" from the leading edge. To mark the inside, gently retract the foreskin and place the

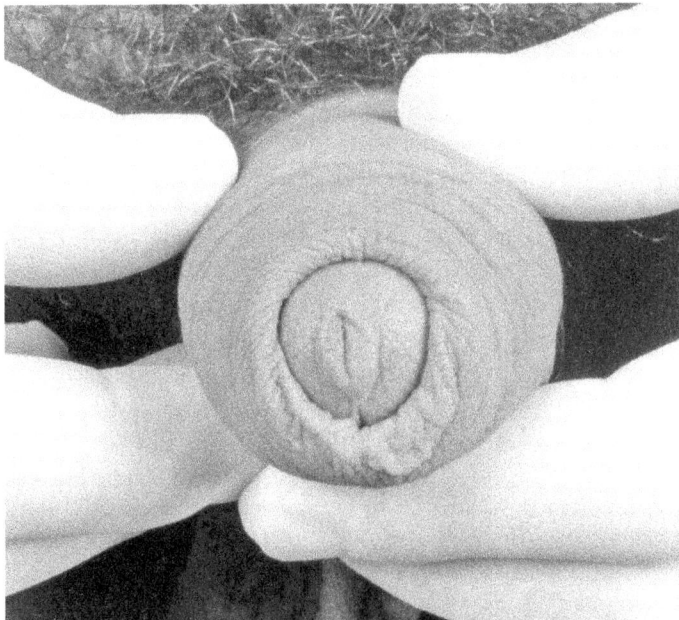

Two views of a typical foreskin. Marking should begin by drawing a reference line around the leading edge (above). Piercings are typically placed centered on opposite sides, usually left and right.

Tray Setup for Foreskin Piercings:
- Povidone-iodine swabs
- Benzalkonium chloride swabs
- Marking pen or India ink and toothpicks
- Regular or mini forceps
- Sterile piercing needle
- Rubber band
- Cork (thimble: optional)

second marks the same distance from the leading edge. Now let the tissue relax again. Pull the foreskin forward and carefully compare the marks. Will the piercing be level? Is the center mark still on the leading edge? If paired, do your placement match? The tissue is very pliable, and several adjustments are often necessary. Please don't rush through this important marking process.

TECHNICALITIES

This area of the penis is very vascular. Once the tissue has been clamped into the forceps, it can be helpful to shine light through it with a small flashlight. Any blood vessels in the path of the needle will be easy to see. If necessary, these can easily be repositioned inside the forceps.

It is always in everyone's best interest if you are reasonably candid with your clients regarding the pain they can anticipate. This doesn't necessitate going into gory detail. Expect the piercee to be nervous, and attempt to put him at ease by

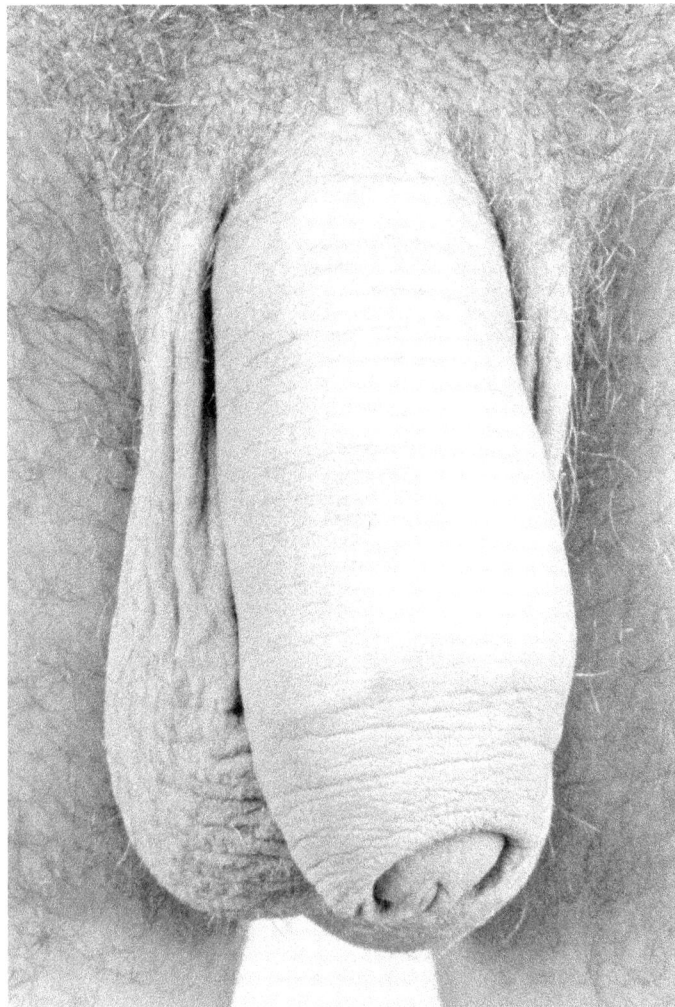

explaining each step of the process as you proceed. The foreskin piercing should not be that intense: a quick flash of heat, then nothing at all, or, at worst, a spreading warmth. Often the pinching of the forceps hurts worse than the piercing. In other words, this shouldn't be a big deal. Let piercees know it's okay to be nervous. Encourage them to breathe deeply and slowly but not to hyperventilate. This can help a great deal.

The piercee needs to hold fairly still. Remind him of that whenever necessary.

✦ AMPALLANG & APADRAVYA

Apadravya—

DIFFICULTY LEVEL: 8 to 9

This is by far one of the most advanced piercings, although slightly easier than an ampallang to mark and pierce. Placement is specific and crucial, the piercee is usually very nervous, and the necessary freehand technique greatly elevates your chances of a needle stick. Furthermore, this piercing passes through as much as an inch of tissue which can be as tough as shoe leather. Even for an experienced, skilled professional, an apadravya can take twice as long to perform as a more common piercing.

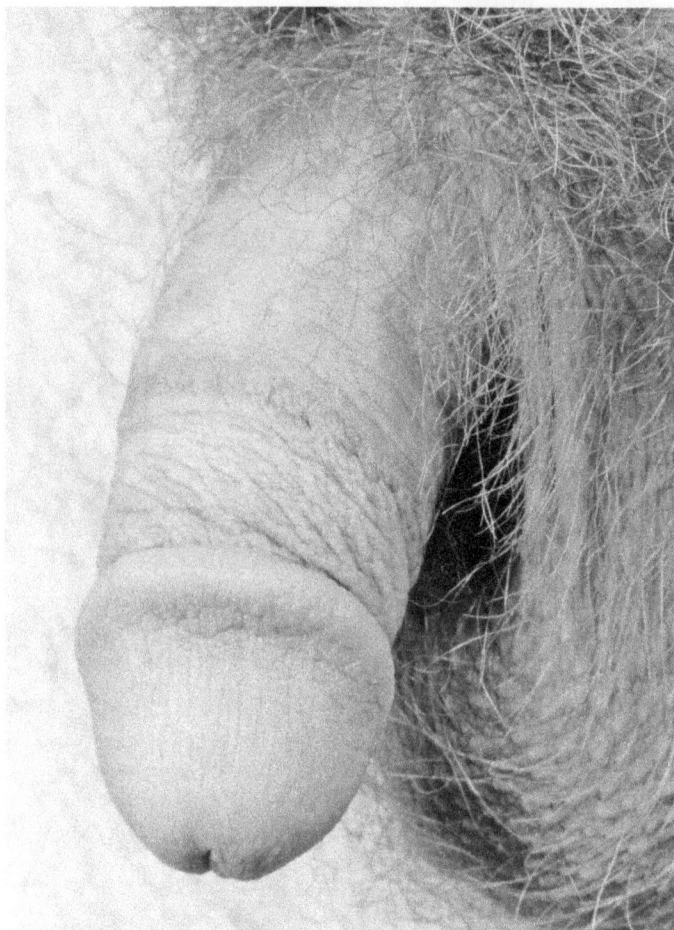

Ampallang—

DIFFICULTY LEVEL: 9

This is by far one of the most advanced piercings. Placement is specific and crucial, the piercee is usually very nervous, and the necessary freehand technique greatly increases your risk of a needle stick. Furthermore, this piercing can pass through more than an inch of tissue which is sometimes as tough as shoe leather; the time required to perform an ampallang, even for an experienced piercer, can be more than twice as long as for most other piercings.

JEWELRY

The jewelry worn in these piercings is a barbell, 14 ga, 12 ga, or, rarely, 10 ga. The length is determined by the anatomy.

To determine the proper length, clean the area with povidone-iodine and make two cursory marks in the approximate location of the piercing. Give the piercee a pair of dial calipers and instructions in their use. Instruct him on how not to contaminate the room, then leave him alone or send him to the bathroom to take his measurement. The piercee should attempt to achieve an erection (not always easy just before a piercing) and measure the distance between your two marks. When he is ready for you, put on a clean pair of gloves, and check the calipers to see what size stud he will need. If a full erection isn't possible, you and he will have to make an educated guess. It's better to overestimate than

underestimate. Hopefully, he will be in town for a few days so you can change jewelry if necessary.

Depending somewhat on placement, the barbell length can vary from $^{15}/_{16}''$ to almost 2″, with most piercees falling somewhere between $1^{1}/_{8}''$ and $1^{1}/_{2}''$. Apadravyas usually require just a bit less length than do ampallangs. Most piercees end up coming in for a slightly smaller barbell a few days after the piercing because these piercings seem to be more comfortable when they are just a little tight. A stud that is too long catches on clothing and bedding.

UNIQUE CONSIDERATIONS

These piercings have had long, well-documented histories. The ampallang has traditionally been worn by men in New Guinea and Borneo for the pleasure of their consorts, and the apadravya was described in the Kama Sutra as a gift to ones lover. All things being relative, it is safe to say that the functions of these piercings has remained more or less unchanged. Those who wear these piercings are able to report that they are also gifts to oneself, providing heightened sensation and adding beauty to pleasure.

These piercings are performed freehand, on some of the deepest, toughest, most sensitive tissue you will likely encounter. The placement also requires a skilled eye and extraordinary patience. The tough nature of the tissue often causes the piercing to take significantly longer than other piercings. Needle sticks are a real and serious risk, every time these piercings are done. Placement should always be in the penis head. Piercing through the shaft could cause serious, or even permanent, damage to the piercee. When considering your ability to perform this piercing, please ask yourself how confident you are in your skill. Could you be any more prepared for such an undertaking? Would a few more months or years of experience make this piercing safer?

MARKING & PLACEMENT

Examine the head of the penis carefully, from as many angles as possible. Look at it in a mirror. Turn it upside down and sideways. Note

---

Tray Setup for Ampallang & Apadravya Piercings:

- Povidone-iodine swabs
- Benzalkonium chloride swabs
- Marking pen or India ink and toothpicks
- Sterile piercing needle
- Needle pusher
- Barbell connecting wire
- Cork (to secure the point after piercing)
  Optional:
- Topical anaesthetic ointment
- Cotton swabs

---

any irregularities, slopes, or asymmetries which may influence your placement. Ask the piercee where he envisions the placement. Use your calipers, but don't depend too heavily on them. This area is very seldom mathematically symmetrical. Your eye, and that of your piercee, are the final authority. Make a couple of marks, discuss them with the piercee, adjust them as necessary. Patience is very important. It is not unheard of for a less experienced piercer to spend a half hour, or even longer, on marking alone. The time will likely decrease with experience.

Apadravya —

If the piercee has a Prince Albert, you may use it as the entry hole for this piercing. If there is no PA, mark the spot where a PA would normally go as your first dot. The top mark should be centered and placed in the bottom of the shallow valley about ¼" from the corona. This piercing must pass through the urethra which is a mucous membrane. A topical anesthetic may be used, if desired, to help minimize discomfort.

Ampallang —

Anthropological texts differ as to whether the ampallang passes through the urethra or above it. It really doesn't matter that much, but, if possible, going above the urethra is preferred. What is more important is to make certain the piercing is not too shallow, too near the top surface of the head. This common misplacement can result in discomfort and increased risk of rejection or tissue loss. Look at the penis head-on. Place marks just slightly above the center of the head. Now look at it from the top, and place marks about one half the distance between the tip of the penis and the edge of the corona. Some piercers prefer to go further back to the bottom of the shallow valley about two thirds of the way from the tip. While there is technically nothing wrong with this placement, the additional tissue will add significantly to healing time, and the placement would interfere with the piercee's ability to have dydoe piercings, should such be in his future.

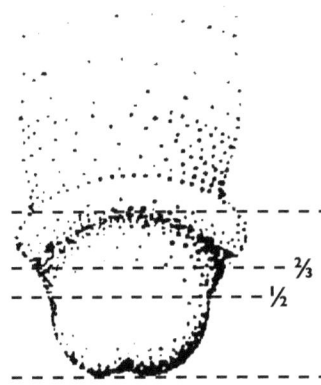

Ampallang placement is usually best about one half the distance between the tip of the penis and the edge of the glans although up to two thirds is viable unless the man also plans on having dydoe piercings.

TECHNICALITIES

It is always in everyone's best interest if you are reasonably candid with your clients regarding the pain they can anticipate. Certainly one can expect ampallangs and apadravyas to be fairly painful, but you needn't go into gory detail when you are discussing the matter with your client. This only makes them more anxious. The best thing you can do to minimize discomfort is to perfect your skill so the piercing can be done as quickly as possible.

Let piercees know it is okay to be nervous. Encourage them to breathe deeply and slowly but not to hyperventilate. This can help a lot. Also remind them to hold as still as possible. And don't be startled if they let out a yell when you are doing the piercing.

We guarantee you'll regret it if you neglect to include a needle pusher in your basic setup. This tissue can be unbelievably tough which adds to the risk of needle sticks.

For most piercees (and piercers!), it's a very good idea to have a little rest and a glass of water or juice between piercing and insertion. Be sure that the point of the needle is well-secured in a cork.

Choose a barbell connecting wire that is long enough and fits securely in both the stud and needle. The insertion can easily be botched if the needle and jewelry don't stay together.

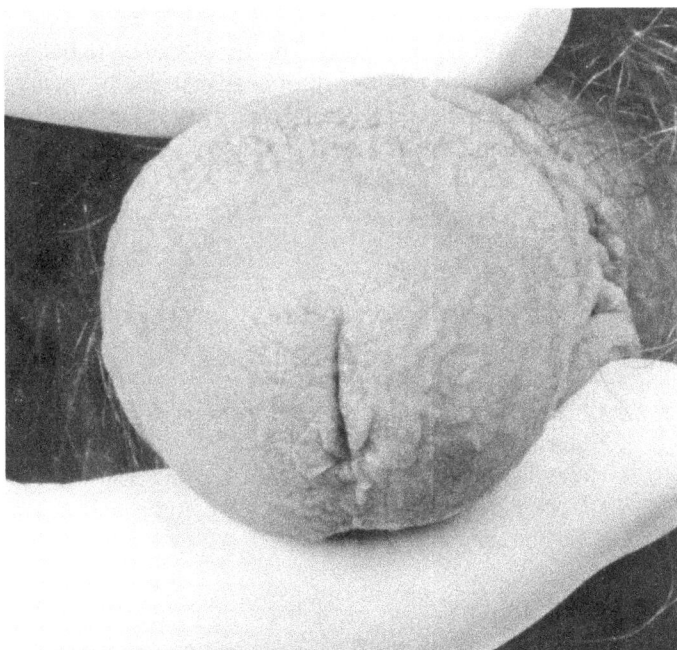

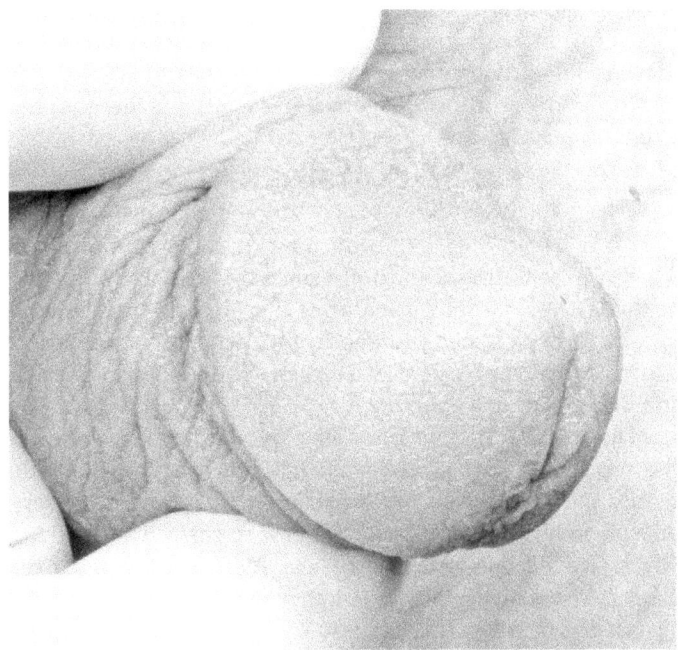

These piercings frequently swell and put out discharge for several weeks. The tissue may also become bruised. This is a normal part of healing such complex tissue. Urine may sting the piercing for the first few days, but reassure piercees that they needn't be concerned. Their urine is sterile to their bodies. Pouring warm water over the piercing during urination will help reduce stinging.

Many men find erections uncomfortable, or even painful, for a few days after the piercing. Keeping a bowl of cool water near the bed may provide relief in the event of a night time erection.

The piercing may ache or be highly sensitive for several days. Care should be taken to protect the piercing from anything which might disturb it for several weeks, including sexual contact, tight clothing, or excessive friction.

These piercings may bleed for four or five days. A panty liner or cotton pad can protect the area and catch any fluids.

✦ DYDOES

DIFFICULTY LEVEL: 10

These are among the most difficult of piercings. Dydoes should only be attempted by advanced level piercers with sufficient experience performing ampallangs and apadravyas. As dydoes are usually performed in pairs, placement is very specific. The piercee is usually very nervous, and the much smaller amount of tissue, requiring a tough push, increases the risk of a needle stick.

JEWELRY

Before you select jewelry, examine the piercee to determine whether he is a good candidate for dydoe piercings. If the corona is not very pronounced and well developed, it would be wise to go no further or consider something alternative.

The best jewelry choice is either a minibar or barbell stud. Rings would be very uncomfortable. Average initial stud length is usually ⅜″ to ⁷⁄₁₆″ though longer sizes are occasionally called for. Allow approximately ⅛″ for swelling. It's better to overestimate than underestimate. Don't be surprised if there is some tissue loss as the piercing heals. Most piercees end up coming in for a slightly smaller stud a few months after the piercing.

UNIQUE CONSIDERATIONS

Although Doug Malloy claimed that dydoes were performed by Jewish men to regain some of the sensation lost to circumcision, it is likely that he was the real inventor of this piercing, usually done in pairs through the edge of the corona. When they are healed, it is true that they enhance sensation. They can also provide stimulation for one's partner.

Many people imagine one single dydoe piercing, alone on the top of the corona. Unfortunately, this area has too little tissue, and receives so much friction, that is would be very difficult to heal such a piercing. It's best to stay along the sides, which are difficult enough to heal. Men who wear boxer shorts, or none, may notice irritation on the side which rubs against the pant leg. This can lead to rejection or tissue loss.

These are freehand piercings, and in some ways, more difficult to perform than ampallangs or apadravyas. The placement requires a skilled eye and extraordinary patience. Needle sticks are a real and serious risk every time these piercings are done. When considering your ability to perform this piercing, please ask yourself if you are willing to take these risks. How confident are you in your ability? Would a few months make a difference in your ability to perform this piercing safely?

PLACEMENT & MARKING

Dydoes are usually done in pairs. After first cleaning the area with povidone-iodine, examine the penis head-on. Place a reference dot on the edge of the corona at the three and nine o'clock positions. Now turn the penis to the side and place two dots above and below the reference dot on a line perpendicular to the edge of the corona. The first dot should be right at the edge of the corona where it joins the shaft. The second dot is placed in the shallow valley on the head. Once you are satisfied the marks are correct, repeat the process on the opposite side. Check your marks with calipers to make sure the two piercings will match and that the jewelry is the proper length.

TECHNICALITIES

It is always in everyone's best interest if you are reasonably candid with your clients regarding the pain they can anticipate. Certainly one can expect dydoes to be fairly painful, but you needn't go into gory detail when you are discussing the matter with your client. This only makes them more anxious. The best thing you can do to minimize discomfort is to perfect your skill so the piercing can be done as quickly as possible.

Let piercees know it is okay to be nervous. Encourage them to breathe deeply and slowly but not to hyperventilate. This can help a lot. Also remind them to hold as still as possible. And don't be startled if they let out a yell when you are doing the piercing.

We guarantee you'll regret it if you neglect to include a needle pusher in your basic setup. This tissue can be unbelievably tough which adds to the risk of needle sticks.

For most piercees (and piercers!), it's a very good idea to have a little rest and a glass of water or juice between piercing

---

Tray Setup for Dydoe Piercings:
- Povidone-iodine swabs
- Benzalkonium chloride swabs
- Marking pen or India ink and toothpicks
- Sterile piercing needle
- Needle pusher
- Cork (thimble: optional)
- Barbell connecting wire

Dydoes should be placed perpendicular to the rim of the glans.

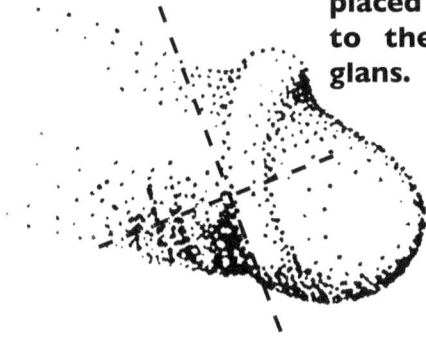

and insertion. Be sure that the point of the needle is well-secured in a cork.

Choose a barbell connecting wire that is long enough and fits securely in both the stud and needle. The insertion can easily be botched if the needle and jewelry don't stay together.

These piercings frequently swell and discharge for several weeks. The tissue may also become bruised. This is a normal part of healing such complex tissue. Urine may sting the piercing for the first few days, but reassure piercees that they needn't be concerned. Their urine is sterile to their bodies. Pouring warm water over the piercing during urination will help reduce stinging.

Many men find erections uncomfortable, or even painful, for a few days after the piercing. Keeping a bowl of cool water near the bed may provide relief in the event of a night time erection.

The piercing may ache or be highly sensitive for several days. Care should be taken to protect the piercing from anything which might disturb it for several weeks, including sexual contact, tight clothing, or excessive friction.

These piercings may bleed for four or five days. A panty liner or cotton pad can protect the area and catch any fluids.

CHAPTER 12 — THE UNUSUAL, THE WEIRD, & THE WACKY

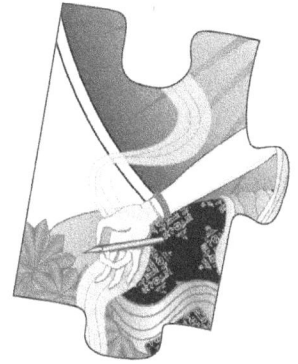

MULTIPLE PIERCINGS: 7-10

As piercings have become more mainstream, and piercees gradually use up their available piercing space, multiples have become popular.

Knowing how to appropriately and safely perform one of any given piercing does not automatically translate into knowing how to perform a second or third in that same area. It is strongly suggested that you become very skilled at performing a nipple piercing, for example, before you move onto pairs of nipples; then learn all about pairs before attempting any double nipple piercings.

Performing multiple piercings requires that you fully understand not only *how* and *where*, but *why* placements are made. This will help you make difficult decisions in the vague area of aesthetics (e.g. two eyebrow piercings: both off-center, or one centered and the other too high … or too low), and plan ahead for circumstances like tissue rejection and shape changes. Another example: many people's nipples are permanently enlarged by piercing. When marking for a second, it's important to plan for there to be additional enlargement and place the new jewelry accordingly. Full understanding of all the factors is developed slowly, as you gain experience in the specifics of each new piercing.

NEW TAKES ON TRADITIONAL PIERCINGS: 7-10

Occasionally a piercee will request a navel, nipple, or other piercing that's a bit deeper or more shallow than you'd normally do, or off at an unusual angle. Perhaps they'd like to connect two piercings with one piece of jewelry. Perhaps they intend for the piercing to perform some particular task, e.g. a "foreskin" piercing on a circumcised man for the purpose of stretching the tissue to regain something akin to a foreskin. Unique ideas and variations are valid and your piercees deserve your best, most creative efforts to individualize their piercings. Most variations, such as a diagonally placed nipples, don't radically diverge from their ancestors. Of course, you can't dance Swan Lake before you've learned how to do a demi-plie, you can't play Paganini without practicing hours of scales, and you shouldn't attempt any divergence from traditional piercings until you have nearly perfected the basic technique.

There are some variations, such as many of the examples just given, which require a great deal of expertise and intensive preplanning. These would have to be considered under the next category.

UNUSUAL & SURFACE-TO-SURFACE PIERCINGS: 10

There are many piercings being performed today that defy any of the previous categories. We acknowledge that the temptation to create something new or experiment with the boundaries of the human body is very strong, and valid when exercised *RESPONSIBLY*. However, there is a fine line between "cutting edge" and "over the edge." Many piercers today have no clue where that line exists and have clearly crossed it.

Earlier in the manual, we compared piercing to other skills and art forms. Like artists, woodworkers, or metalsmiths, we are constrained in our creative efforts by the limitations of the medium. The medium of the piercer is the human body. This medium hasn't undergone any really drastic changes in thousands of years, and is unlikely to do so in our lifetime. It is essential that you learn and respect the limitations presented by anatomy. You ignore them at great risk!

Let's examine a hypothetical situation. You are approached by a piercee who would like to have an unusual piercing, let's say a handweb, an "earl" (nose-bridge) or a "madison" (near the clavicle). These piercings are fairly well-known; they even have names. Why not just jump in and do one? People have been doing them for a long time.

Consider your own abilities foremost. If you have not reached a senior or master level in your abilities, it is unlikely that you will possess the technical skills, confidence, or troubleshooting information necessary to perform such an unusual piercing. You probably won't even know how to determine whether the piercee is a good candidate for the piercing without several years of experience with the more mundane piercings.

Do you have any personal experience with this piercing? Do you know the factors involved in candidacy for this piercing? Do you understand the healing process? Do you have a clear awareness of the underlying anatomy and how it might influence the danger, the success or failure of this piercing? What sort of things will you need to be aware of, to avoid accidents or serious injury to the piercee during the piercing? What sort of equipment and jewelry will you use?

If there is any chance that critical nerves or large veins pass through the area, research it carefully. Discuss the placement, depth, and choice of jewelry with other piercers, doctors, and the piercee. If there seems no way to do it with the odds significantly in the piercee's favor, DON'T DO IT. It's really that simple. There is no guarantee, but by explaining your refusal you will hopefully win respect from your piercees.

If you decide to perform such a piercing, it's a very good idea to get a second opinion on such matters as placement, jewelry, and aftercare. Call a coworker, another piercer, or the Gauntlet hotline. Has this type of piercing been done in this manner before? How did it turn out?

Once you have determined that the piercing can be safely done and has a fair chance of success, consider the piercee. How well do you know her/him? Is s/he a tourist breezing through town, someone you probably won't be able to do any follow-up visits with? Maybe it's someone you know to be irresponsible with their aftercare. How wise would it be to pierce someone living on the street without access to a shower and clean clothes? It is suggested that you reserve unusual piercings for regular piercees with whom you share a mutual level of trust and respect. These piercees have extensive experience with the aftercare process, and won't hesitate to contact you for any follow-up care. All piercings, but especially unusual ones, are truly a team effort on the part of you and the piercee.

After you have determined your comfort level with the piercee, it's time to make him/her *fully* aware of the commitment s/he will be making. Clearly inform them of any risks. If you've never done this piercing before, the piercee deserves to know. Might this piercing reject? Could it scar? What about infections? How long will they be caring for it, and how involved is the aftercare process? Do they or you have access to a piercing-aware medical practitioner in the event of any problems? Many piercees haven't really thought these all-too-important details out for themselves and may well determine that they'd be better off with something less complicated. But if you have earned the trust of a regular piercee who has fully considered the risks and still wants the piercing, it may be appropriate to go ahead and do it.

Let's review the steps in deciding whether or not to perform an unusual piercing:
• Do you have enough experience to perform the piercing safely?
• How much do you already know about the piercing?
• How much information can you gather to fill in the gaps in your knowledge?
• Is the piercing potentially dangerous?
• What is the safest possible way to perform the piercing?
• Do you feel comfortable with the piercee?
• Does the piercee fully understand the commitments and risks involved?

We have been discussing those unusual piercings for which there is some precedent. When you are considering a piercing that is not well-known, or may have never been done before, the risks multiply exponentially. After asking yourself all of the above questions, you should then ask the following:
• Is there any chance whatsoever, even a worst-case scenario, that this piercing could paralyze, mutilate, or kill the piercee?
• Are you legally and financially covered in the event of an accident? Are you willing to face the risk of a lawsuit?
• What kind of repercussions will your actions have in the long term? How will they affect the piercing community at large?

You may feel absolutely confident in your ability to perform this particular piercing. But what about those folks who see the one you did, and ask the ear gun-toting fool down the street to do it for them? In some sense, you are responsible for the damage done to that piercee. And if s/he ends up seriously maimed, all piercers will suffer, because legislators do not distinguish between your shop and that of the ear-gun hacker. Enough minor accidents, or one really serious accident, and we could all be shut down.

Before you accept the challenge of that untried piercing, consider carefully what kinds of contributions you wish to make to the history of piercing.

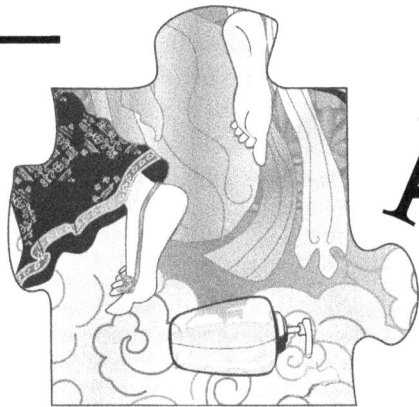

CHAPTER 13 —

AFTERCARE

At some point in this whole process, either before or after the piercing, you will need to discuss aftercare with the piercee. It is not enough to simply hand someone a printed sheet. Not only can written information be misleading, incomplete and unclear, but handing a newly pierced person a sheet of paper and shoving them out the door with a smile is certain to result in a widespread perception that you are rude, inaccessible, or uncaring.

Printed information can be, of course, extremely helpful. The piercee has a reference to bring home. Use any printed or videotaped aftercare material to reinforce the important information you discuss with the clients.

It is important to note that a piercer is neither a medical professional, nor is s/he an "aftercare police officer." It is only your responsibility to fully convey all the information you know, and be available to answer future questions to the best of your knowledge. It is entirely the piercee's responsibility to choose aftercare products, behaviors, and techniques that will give them the desired results.

Along the same lines, it is equally important to note that the bulk of information around aftercare has been acquired primarily through trial and error, and is constantly evolving. Individual piercings require individual treatments, and what works for one will not work for all. However, the suggestions below are generally the safest bet for healing.

Piercers are not doctors. Likewise, doctors are not piercers. Many piercees

bring their minor infection or irritation to a doctor, only to be told that the jewelry must be removed. This is often due to ignorance of or prejudice against piercings, and not to any medical reality. All piercers should try to find a truly piercing-friendly doctor in their area, to whom they can refer questions and clients. Of course, even a doctor ignorant of piercing can and should be referred to if a piercer and piercee cannot satisfactorily solve an aftercare problem.

SUMMARY —
1. Printed or videotaped aftercare information is helpful, but should only be used supplement verbal information.
2. The piercer is responsible for conveying what they know or have experienced regarding aftercare.
3. The piercee is responsible for caring for their piercing, using information given to them by the piercer or health care worker, and based on their own awareness of their body.
4. Piercers are not doctors. You could run afoul of the medical profession if you "recommend" anything. Consequently, only make "suggestions." All aftercare information is anecdotal and based on observations by piercers and piercees over many years.
5. While doctors and other health care workers are a valuable source of aftercare assistance, many are not well-versed in the care of piercings and may give inaccurate or prejudiced recommendations. Seek out a piercing-friendly physician.

• DISCUSSION TIME

There are pros and cons to discussing aftercare either before or after the piercing. Before the piercing, clients will be nervous and excited. Afterwards, they will be high on endorphins and excited. Having the piercee read or view aftercare information before the piercing can entertain while you are preparing the room. Having the piercee absorb aftercare information after the piercing will give important time to rest before re-entering the outside world. Whenever you transmit the information, tell the piercee several times that they are welcome to call you at any time to get any bits that are almost certain to slip past them right now. Encourage them to come by or call in for a checkup at some point in their healing process.

• THE HEALING PROCESS

Skin is not a one-piece garment. The human body is comprised of over 100 trillion cells, many trillions of which are dispersed over several layers of skin tissue. Cells are highly specialized units of matter, made of protoplasm, also called plasma. A very thin, soluble membrane surrounds the cell, protecting and defining it. The cell will grow and prosper as long as it has ample supplies of food, oxygen, and water, is maintained at a favorable temperature, and is able to dispose of its waste products. When one or all of these basic needs are not met, the cell dies, the membrane dissolves, and the plasma begins to decay. The body's immune system then removes it. Some types of human cells are not equipped to reproduce themselves; however, skin cells, those with which we are concerned, reproduce themselves throughout a person's life. The type of cell pattern found on the surface of the skin is simple squamous epithelial tissue. It is anchored on the inside to connective tissue (called aureolar tissue), which nourishes it by means of many blood vessels.

Cartilage is another type of tissue that we pierce. The ear cartilage is known as elastic cartilage, because of its comparative resilience. There are fewer blood vessels in cartilage, which accounts for the slower healing times of piercings in this area.

Some piercings pass through mucous membranes, tissue very similar to epithelial tissue except that it produces lubrication. Piercings through mucous membranes generally heal the fastest, due to their excellent blood supply.

When you perform a piercing, you are essentially cutting a hole through hundreds of layers of tissue. To heal the holes, the body sends white blood cells (leukocytes) via the bloodstream to fight any organisms that may have slipped in, and begins to sew up the damage with scar tissue (fibrin strands). As new material is grown, the old, dead matter must be discarded. This shows up as a whitish-yellowish material which crusts up on the jewelry and around the edges of the piercing (scab). This matter is primarily blood plasma, and is NOT pus. Its function is to protect the wound while healing. Crusted matter indicates a normal, healing piercing; the piercing is healed when no more crusted matter is generated. The more vascular the area, the faster healing occurs, sometimes so quickly that the piercing is itchy. The healing is also hastened if the tissue has an adequate supply of oxygen. In areas such as the ear cartilage, where very few capillaries exist, it can take up to a year for the layers of scar tissue to be built up adequately.

Of course, a larger surface area (a deeper piercing or larger hole) will also generally require more healing time. But this does not mean that the thinnest piece of jewelry will always result in a fast-healing piercing. Take into account the fact that although the surface of the jewelry is smooth and round, the thinner it is the more of a cutting edge it becomes. The wire used in a cheese cutter is also smooth and round. Since the surface is not broad enough to support the tension and pressure of the cheese around it, it cuts easily through the cheese. If the piercee anticipates more than purely decorative function for his/her new jewelry, the minimum gauge is often insufficient.

Many piercees assume that healing a piercing means healing an infection. Infection is the presence of hostile foreign matter in the body. Help ease your piercees concerns by emphasizing that they will not be bringing any organisms home with them that they didn't bring in themselves. However, it is important that they understand that they can pick up bacteria at any time. They are most vulnerable during the initial period that the body is developing its first few layers of scar tissue.

HEALING — Migratory Phase
Granulation Tissue

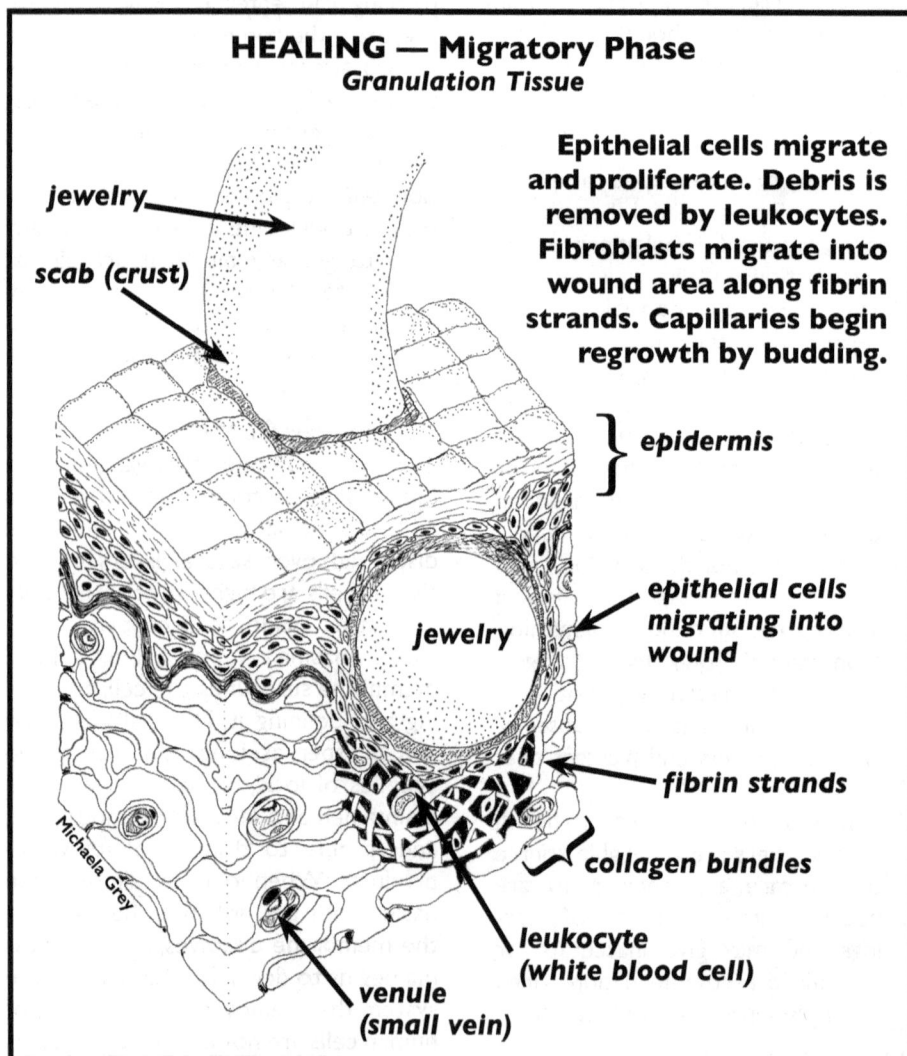

Epithelial cells migrate and proliferate. Debris is removed by leukocytes. Fibroblasts migrate into wound area along fibrin strands. Capillaries begin regrowth by budding.

jewelry

scab (crust)

epidermis

jewelry

epithelial cells migrating into wound

fibrin strands

collagen bundles

leukocyte (white blood cell)

venule (small vein)

Michaela Grey

SUMMARY —
1. Simple squamous epithelial tissue is found on the outer surfaces of most areas that are pierced.
2. Skin is made of thousands of layers of skin cells, which in turn are made of protoplasm, or plasma.
3. Healing a piercing means regenerating skin cells to replace the ones destroyed by the piercing.
4. Blood vessels bring nutrients, oxygen, and fluids to the healing tissue, and carry away waste products. The more blood vessels in the area, the faster this can occur.
5. Cartilage tissue has relatively few blood vessels, so it generally requires a longer healing time.
6. Mucous membranes have an abundant supply of blood vessels, so they heal rapidly.

7. Jewelry that is too thick or too thin inhibits the healing process.
8. Infections are not common. A skilled piercer will not transmit any infection-causing material into a piercing.

• BASIC PIERCING CARE

The piercee must treat the new piercing with almost as much sterility awareness as you did when you pierced it. Nine times out of 10, an infection is caused by handling a piercing with dirty hands, premature oral contact, or just one dip in a hot tub or lake. Piercees should avoid these practices as long as possible, but at least for the first several weeks after the piercing. As we have seen, thousands of organisms exist on the body. No one but the piercee should handle the piercing, even lightly and then only with clean hands. These must always be washed before contact. Obviously, heavy pressure or play is undesirable when the piercing is new.

At all times care must be taken to avoid getting any matter into the piercing. Saliva and other bodily fluids are a particularly rich source of foreign agents. Even the piercee's own saliva should not come into contact with a new piercing. Many people assume that the injunction against bodily fluids is due to a risk of STD's, and so neglect to avoid the fluids of their significant other. No matter long you have been with someone or how often you have exchanged bodily fluids, the bacteria in your bloodstream is very different from the bacteria in theirs, and you can get a nasty infection if their fluids enter your piercing.

Bodies of water, both natural and of human origin, are teeming with organisms. In hot tubs or other chlorinated bodies, these organisms are mostly dead, but their little corpses can still clog up a new piercing. Resistant organisms can often thrive in the warm environment. Piercees should wait at least a month before taking the plunge. Make sure they take their antibacterial cleaner with them to perform a thorough scrubbing immediately after their immersion.

On the other hand a hot bath at home can work wonders for drawing out fluids, encouraging blood flow, loosening crusted matter, and soothing aches. The tub must be scrubbed extra carefully prior to the soak, and occupied only by the piercee. Oils, fragrances, or scented salts will only irritate the new piercing, but sea salt is a wonderful healing aid. Add ½ cup to the tub to increase the benefits of a soak.

For some piercings, such as nipple, navel, and penis piercings, soaks can also be done without having to sit in a tub. Mix ¼ teaspoon sea salt with 1 cup of clean hot water, and press the cup over the concerned body part, or dangle the body part in it. Soaks can aid in treatment of infections, irritations, and other problems, and can be a wonderful adjunct to a normal healing process. Used alone, however, without antibacterial soaps, they simply aren't effective enough.

Dirty clothes or bedding can also be a source of problems, as can cosmetics or oils. Also avoid getting the area sunburned. Of course, the healing always moves along faster in a healthy body, so suggest that clients get plenty of rest, eat well, and take care of themselves.

Vitamins and minerals, particularly zinc and vitamin C, will boost the regeneration effort. Alcohol, nicotine, and caffeine can cause swelling in oral piercings. Have piercees avoid these. If soreness or swelling occurs, suggest ibuprofin for its anti-inflammatory properties. Avoid aspirin.

Piercees need to take good care of themselves in other ways. Staying up all night, eating poorly, drinking alcohol, ingesting drugs, or getting stressed out are real burdens on the immune system. The body can hardly bother to heal a little piercing when it must commit so many of its resources to such matters.

SUMMARY —
1. New piercings should only be handled with freshly washed hands.
2. Even light pressure, friction, and play should be avoided for several months.
3. Bodily fluids teem with bacteria. Keep them out of new piercings.
4. Piercees should avoid bodies of water such as lakes, oceans, pools, hot tubs, and rivers for at least a month after their piercings.

5. A very clean bathtub filled with clean water and a little sea salt, is an excellent place to soak a new piercing.
6. Vitamins and minerals, particularly vitamin C and zinc will help the body regenerate tissue and fight off infection.
7. For the fastest, easiest healing, piercees should eat well, get plenty of rest, avoid alcohol, caffeine, nicotine and other drugs, and stay as stress-free as possible.

• SPECIFIC PIERCING CARE

For Piercings above the Neck

Piercings above the neck generally receive plenty of assistance from the bloodstream, and heal pretty quickly (approximate healing times are found in the chart on page 106). Piercees must remember not to touch or pick at their piercings while they are healing. Many people have found success using an ear care product containing benzalkonium chloride or benzalthonium chloride. Twice daily cleaning is appropriate; more tends to damage the delicate scar tissue and prolong healing. Makeup, shampoo, or soap can clog and irritate the piercing.

For Oral Piercings

Oral piercings require special attention. In addition to twice daily cleaning with a product containing carbamide peroxide (Peroxyl, Gly-oxide, etc), the piercee must rinse the area with an antibacterial mouthwash such as Listerine or Biotene any time food, liquids, or other material enters the mouth. Since antibacterial mouthwash is quite strong, it may kill delicate cells if not diluted with water, up to 75%.

Hot, spicy, or crunchy foods can cause irritation and swelling. Avoid alcohol, aspirin, caffeine, and tobacco. Sucking on ice and/or drinking cold liquids for the first 48 hours will keep swelling to a minimum as will ibuprofin.

For Piercings of the Torso

Torso area piercings, i.e. nipples and navels, require a stronger cleaning agent. For years, people used Hibiclens (chlorhexidine gluconate) or povidone-iodine to clean these piercings. However, many people had problems with Hibiclens and its relatives (Briancare, Hibitaine, etc.), to the extent that these products are currently being reclassified by the FDA. In the future, they may be available only by prescription. If a piercee desires to use any product containing chlorhexidine gluconate, make them aware that there could be a possible reaction to it. It is important that they read the label and follow the instructions carefully. Hibiclens, et al, can cause blindness and deafness if they get in the eyes or ears. It should therefore NEVER be used above the neck for ANY purpose. The frequent occurrence of reactions to chlorhexidine gluconate in genital piercings, suggests that it not be used below the navel.

As for povidone-iodine, it continues to be the product used for prep scrub. But for some individuals, prolonged contact with povidone-iodine has led to allergic reactions. Persons severely allergic to shellfish are, due to the iodine present, possibly already allergic to povidone-iodine. Povidone-iodine is no longer used in some hospitals as an aftercare product due to its ability to *lyse* new tissue. In layman's terms, it enters the baby cell and expands the walls until the tissue collapses. Povidone-iodine also stains skin and clothing. If a customer desires to cleanse with povidone-iodine, make them aware of these facts.

Povidone-iodine is the active ingredient in a number of products including Betadine. The solution is the form we use to prepare skin before piercing. Use the surgical scrub form for aftercare. Betadine also comes in ointment form and a douche.

Another iodine-based cleaning agent is Clearly Natural. This appears to be a milder product than Povidone-iodine and thus less likely to cause problems at least in people who are not allergic to iodine.

Most people now clean their nipples and navels with a mild liquid antibacterial soap, just like the ones piercers use to wash their hands. Many companies market one: Dial, Softsoap, Lever 2000 to name just a few. The active ingredient in these products is triclosan. Although those named above contain fragrance to which some piercees may be sensitive, Almay

and Johnson & Johnson offer unscented products with the same active ingredient. Once again, twice daily is the appropriate cleaning schedule.

The piercee may also wish to avoid clothing which is tight or causes friction, at least during the healing period. However, they may want to wear a sports bra, tank top, or snug clean T-shirt to bed for a few weeks, to keep the piercings clean and prevent snagging on bedclothes.

For Genital Piercings

Healing times and experiences vary quite a bit in the genital area. Some piercings, such as the inner labia, are located in very thin, vascular tissue and heal almost immediately, while others, such as the ampallang, are rather deep, requiring more time and effort to heal.

The tissue found in the genital area is delicate and sensitive. Cleansers used there should be strong enough to be effective but mild enought not to cause irritation. The low/no fragrance antibacterial soaps containing triclosan or povidone-iodine are appropriate for most people. Products containing chlorhexidine gluconate are best avoided in the genital area.

Friction caused by walking, clothing, sexual activity, or bicycle/motorcycle seats can really irritate these piercings, causing pain, discharge, even keloiding or rejection. Avoid or adjust activities or clothing that cause discomfort or irritation as long as necessary.

SUMMARY —

1. Avoid friction and anything which might contaminate the piercing including dirty hands or clothing, cosmetics, oils, or bodily fluids.
2. Benzalkonium chloride or benzelthonium chloride are the best antiseptics for use above the neck.
3. Carbamide peroxide, the active ingredient in Gly-Oxide, Peroxyl, and other oral antibacterial cleansers, is the cleaning agent suggested for use in oral piercings. Additionally, the mouth should be rinsed frequently with an antibacterial mouthwash such as Listerine or Biotene, diluted, if necessary, to avoid irritation.

---

4. Antibacterial soaps containing triclosan (Dial, Softsoap, and Lever 2000) or povidone-iodine (Betadine or Clearly Natural) are suggested for cleansing piercings of the torso and genitals.

• DUBIOUS CLEANING AGENTS

Many people think they know more than you do and will initially reject your suggestions for various cleaning agents. They will insist on using rubbing alcohol, hydrogen peroxide, oral antibiotics, or Windex instead. It is not our responsibility to police behavior. All we can do is provide accurate information in a friendly, non-aggressive manner, and invite them to contact us if and when any problems occur. Some people have, in fact, healed their piercings using nothing but water, or soap and water, but this is rare. At the very least, the vast majority of persons using the following, less-than-ideal agents to clean piercings experience a lengthy and troublesome healing period. At worst, many piercings have had to be removed, and infections or severe reactions to the cleaning agent have badly scarred the surrounding tissue. This said, the responsibility for aftercare lies completely with the piercee.

Alcohol

Many naive piercees assume that rubbing alcohol is an appropriate cleaning agent, especially for ear piercings. In fact, many assume that ear care solutions containing benzalkonium chloride are just overpriced, scented alcohol (it actually sells for about $3.00), and will refuse your offer to sell it to them. Alcohol, even the 70% alcohol used by piercers to perform very minor disinfection procedures, is an inefficient antibacterial agent where broken, healing tissue is concerned. Many types of pathogens are unphased by this weak liquid. It is, however, quite strong enough to dry, sting, and kill extremely delicate growing tissue. A healing undertaken with alcohol as the primary cleanser will be prolonged and often troublesome.

Hydrogen Peroxide

Another popular alternative to that "expensive" antiseptic you're trying to push on your customers, hydrogen peroxide possesses the same harsh, drying properties as alcohol. While its bubbling action may, in fact, be cleansing undesireable organisms out of the piercing, it is also bubbling away new skin cells which are attempting to heal the wound. Peroxide does have some limited use when confronting problem situations, which will be discussed in the troubleshooting portion of this manual, but for routine aftercare it is a poor choice.

Vaseline

Believe it or not, people sometimes assert that they plan to use Vaseline (petroleum jelly) as a "cleanser." Petroleum jelly has no redeeming value in this function. It is not antibacterial in any way. Furthermore, it promotes the growth of organisms in its warm, oxygen-blocking jelly. There is a carbolated Vaseline which is somewhat antibacterial, however, like its plain cousin it seals out oxygen which helps wounds heal.

Unless a piercing is very well healed, never use Vaseline to lubricate the jewelry. There are many, much cleaner alternatives, a gel-suspended water solution being one.

Witch Hazel, Sea Breeze, Etc.

Some ignorant people, often saying they want to use something "natural" will choose some derivative of alcohol such as witch hazel or facial astringent. All the facts that pertain to alcohol pertain here, with the added complication of fragrances, numbing agents, etc. Not wise!

Bath Soap

While some people certainly have used bar soaps to clean their piercings, it is not the best choice for most. Soaps are generally formulated with lye which makes them very alkaline. The tissue inside a healthy human should be neutral to slightly acid. In layman's terms, soap will burn and irritate growing skin. The fragrance and other additives present in even "99⁴⁴/₁₀₀% pure" type soaps will only aggravate the situation. To top it all off, most soaps are not antibacterial in the way that a new piercing needs them to be.

Some piercing studios suggest liquid Dr. Bronner's baby soap. Perhaps this is milder, but is still alkaline, and its antibacterial properties are unknown. It's usually best to stick with triclosan or povidone-iodine based liquid antibacterial soaps.

• ANTIBIOTICS

Given the shabby state of health education in this country, it should not surprise you to know that, for many piercees, the terms "healing period" and "infection" are synonymous. They believe that any opening in the skin automatically becomes infected, and that their purpose in cleansing is to "kill" something. While some organisms may, in fact, find their way into the piercing (hence the antibacterial soaps), infections usually occur only among the unthinking or slovenly. There is little that requires killing in the average piercing. What may be killed instead of the pathogens are one's own delicate building cells.

We have become so conditioned that, at the first suspicion that something might be wrong with our piercing, we reach for an antibiotic. Without the supervision of a knowledgable health care professional, this is foolhardy. First of all, antibiotics are effective only against bacteria, not viruses, fungi, or other pathogens. Second, there are many different antibiotics, each effective against certain specific organisms but not others. Consequently, unless the appropriate drug is used, the treatment will be ineffective.

Ointments & Creams

To some extent antibiotic ointments and creams can be used on a fresh piercing to help prevent an infection, but once an infection has occurred, antibiotic ointments, especially the over-the-counter variety, are of limited benefit. The harm has already been done, and the invading organisms have taken up residence out of reach of the ointment.

In piercings, bacteria like to "hide" along the surface of the jewelry, making them difficult to flush out. Furthermore, they can quickly develop a tolerance to antibiotics. If antibiotics haven't done their job within a week, they should usually be abandoned.

If used in large quantities, or for longer than a week, antibiotic ointments can block the oxygen supply to the piercing, while creating an ideal breeding ground for newly resistant bacteria in its jelly base.

Over-the-counter topical antibiotics are usually adequate, but in the case of advanced or viral infections, a prescription drug may be necessary. Viral infections occur most frequently in navel piercings, and manifest as slimy, reddish pink bumps on the inside of the navel. They may be connected to the breakdown and corrosion of porous stones such as malachite, lapis lazuli, or tiger's eye, so don't put these beads near new piercings, especially navel, oral, and genital piercings.

To use antibiotics properly, apply a very, very small amount to the ring and pass it through the piercing several times. Ointment should not be applied more than twice a day, and for no longer than a week at a time.

Oral Antibiotics

Like topical antibiotics, oral ones should only be taken under a doctor's supervision. While a piercee who happens to be on a cycle of oral antibiotics at the time of piercing will get a temporary boost in protection, it is manual antibacterial scrubbing that will keep the piercing free of organisms.

Topical or oral antibiotics may help to clear up an infection, if one is present. However, there are alternatives. For most minor infections, hot compresses and thorough cleansing are more than adequate. Soak a clean washcloth in 1 cup clean hot water mixed with ¼ tsp sea salt. Apply the cloth to the piercing, using firm yet gentle pressure, and turn the ring through the piercing every few minutes. Do this two times daily for 10 or 15 minutes to draw out fluids, soften deposits, and encourage blood flow.

• HEALING TIMES

The time it takes for a piercing to heal is determined by the type of skin cells present in the area, the area's vascularity, and of course, the type of aftercare it receives. The healing process of any piercing, even one of a pair done at the same time under the same circumstances on the same person, will be unique.

During the initial healing time, the jewelry should not be changed or removed unless it is causing or contributing to a chronic problem.

INITIAL HEALING TIMES
(Approximate)

Ampallang	4-6 mos.
Apadravya	4-6 mos.
Cartilage	2-3 mos.,
	sometimes up to 1 yr.
Clit Hood	4-6 wks.
Clitoris	4-6 wks.
Conch	2-3 mos.
Dydoe	2-3 mos.
Earl	6-8 wks.
Earlobe	6-8 wks.
Eyebrow	6-8 wks.
Fourchette	6-8 wks.
Frenum	2-3 mos.
Guiche	2-3 mos.
Hand web	3 mos.-1 yr.
Labia, Inner	4-6 wks.
Labia, Outer	2-3 mos.
Labret/Cheek	6-8wks.,
	sometimes up to 3 mos.
Lip	6-8 wks.
Navel	6-9 mos.,
	sometimes up to 1 yr.
Nipple, Female	4-6 mos.
Nipple, Male	2-3 mos.
Nostril	2-3 mos.,
	sometimes up to 6 mos.
Prince Albert	4-6 wks.
Scrotum	2-3 mos.
Septum	4-6 wks.
Surface Piercings	Varies
	(not recommended)
Tragus	2-3 mos.
Triangle	2-3 mos.

• REMOVING THE JEWELRY

Sometimes a piercee will decide they no longer want a piercing and will request that you remove the jewelry for them. This may be done safely at any time in the healing process. If the piercing is extremely well-healed, a small indentation may remain, and the piercing, although shrunken, may stay open. If the piercee was experiencing infection, irritation, or keloiding, some scar tissue may remain or develop. To reduce the risk of scarring, have the piercee use a warm compress several times daily for a week or so after the removal, as though the jewelry were still in the piercing. If the piercing was new, and matter is still crusting on the outside, have the piercee continue to clean the piercing as though the jewelry were still present, until the piercing is completely healed. The sooner the jewelry is removed, the less likelihood of scarring of any kind. Remember that there are times when removing the jewelry would prevent escape of matter from the piercing, resulting in a possible abscess.

Many people are not able to wear their jewelry full-time, or need to remove it for surgery, jail, or X-rays. Some people think that once the hole is made, it is automatically permanent, and that they can remove and replace the jewelry at will after the first day or week of healing. Unfortunately, as we know, it takes skin cells much longer than a few days to completely regenerate themselves. Removing jewelry, even for a few seconds, minutes, or hours, usually results in disaster.

If piercees anticipate the need for removal at any time in the healing process, advise them not to get pierced until such time as no removal will be necessary.

The body is designed to heal itself. Remove jewelry too soon and the opening of the piercing will rapidly begin to knit up with scar tissue. The frustrated piercee will find it almost impossible to reinsert the jewelry. Sometimes a piercer can use an insertion taper to gently open and stretch the hole enough to accept the jewelry, but success is not guaranteed and this procedure is seldom pain free. Of course, the sooner a piercee returns to you, the better chance of success.

As for when jewelry may be safely removed, and how long it may stay out without problems, that is a very individual situation, varying according to the healing ability of the body, the type of tissue, the location and size of the piercing, and just plain luck. Some people are amazingly able to remove jewelry from their relatively new piercings for days or even months without losing them. Others have a piercing for years, remove the jewelry for one hour, and find reinsertion impossible. Most people fall somewhere in the middle.

For a list of average times when temporary removal is feasible for most people, see the accompanying chart. Notice that these times fall well beyond the initial healing times. This is because most piercings require much longer than that initial time to develop the full amount of scar tissue necessary to allow removal. By no means is this list a guarantee that a piercee will be able to safely remove the jewelry from their piercing at the given time; it is merely a guide to approximate times when many piercees have successfully gone without jewelry.

If a piercee wants to remove their jewelry at any time after the initial healing process, advise them to ease into it slowly. Have them keep the jewelry with them, in a clean plastic baggie, and reinsert it or an insertion taper of the same gauge every few hours using a small amount of antibiotic ointment as lubricant. If the jewelry begins to feel tight at any time, the piercing is shrinking, and the piercee will need to reinsert the jewelry if they wish to keep the piercing. Very few piercings can ever go more than a few days without jewelry, even after many years.

SUMMARY —
1. Permanent removal of jewelry can occur at any time, unless the risk of an abscess is present.
2. If jewelry is removed when tissue is still open and healing, continue aftercare methods until the tissue is healed.
3. If a piercee is unable to wear jewelry in a piercing for the full duration of the healing period, it is unlikely that the piercing will be successful.
4. Complete healing times, the times at which jewelry may be removed without losing the piercing, are much longer than initial healing times, and vary according to many different factors.

• TROUBLESHOOTING

As thoroughly as you may convey aftercare information, many are bound to disregard your advice and get themselves into trouble. Some people won't have success with your usual aftercare suggestions, and will need a customized regimen. And of course, some piercings seem determined to cause trouble, no matter how careful everyone is to avoid it. A good piercer will become a good troubleshooter, learning which questions to ask and what plan of action to follow. The best troubleshooters have almost a sixth sense which helps them zero in on the cause of a problem and its solution.

Infection

An infection is the presence of harmful organisms in the tissue. These organisms can be any one of countless bacteria, viruses, or other pathogens. Rather than healing the piercing, the body must concentrate on fighting the invaders. Infections are typified by swelling, redness, tenderness, and a detectable heat given off by the area. The wound may discharge a great deal of pus or there may be little or none (this will be discussed soon). The most common causes of an infected piercing are:
1. Handling with dirty hands
2. Contact with a contaminated object or surface (hair, the telephone)
3. Contact with bodily fluids, especially saliva
4. Contact with polluted water (rivers, lakes, oceans, swimming pools, hot tubs)

If you suspect an infection, ask if the piercee has had any contact of this kind. Unfortunately, you can't always take a negative response at face value as some people will be too embarrassed to tell you the truth or simply won't remember.

SUMMARY —
1. An infection is caused by harmful organisms getting into a piercing.
2. Infections are usually caused by handling with dirty hands, contact with contaminated surface, bodily fluids or polluted water.
3. Antibiotics can be ineffective against established infections.
4. Oral antibiotics and prescription topical antibiotics should be used only under the supervision of a doctor.
5. Unless otherwise directed by a medical doctor, use topical antibiotics sparingly, twice a day, for not more than one week, to avoid complications.

6. Hot compresses, using 1 cup hot water and ¼ tsp sea salt, twice daily for ten or fifteen minutes, are effective in clearing up most infections without antibiotics.

Abscesses

An abscess is a pocket of fluid which has become trapped under the skin. Fluid is added to the pocket steadily, but there is no escape vent through which fluid can drain. Since blood plasma decays rapidly, the fluid is infectious. This condition is very painful. There is no discharge, or very little discharge, from the swollen area which keeps expanding. Redness and heat are present. Abscesses are very unpleasant.

An abscess often occurs when a previously pierced area, often a nipple, is repierced. Matter that would normally have no option but to exit the body is redirected into the old piercing and begins to accumulate. If a piercing is the second one in that area, be sure that warm soaks and thorough cleanings are part of the aftercare regimen.

Abscesses also develop in piercings that have had the jewelry removed during an infection. The outer part of the piercing seals up quickly, trapping the infection inside. If at all possible don't remove the jewelry from an infected piercing. Instead, downsize the gauge of the jewelry to promote draining.

If an abscess is detected, try hot compresses, preferably with an herbal infusion and sea salt to increase drainage. This often breaks the seal quickly and, in some cases, dramatically. Continue the compresses for at least one full week after the drainage appears to be complete. Residual fluid can start the whole cycle all over again.

If compresses are ineffective after 24 to 48 hours, a doctor should be consulted. The doctor may need to lance the abscess, inject hydrocortisone into the area, and/or prescribe oral antibiotics. None of these is pleasant or inexpensive for the unfortunate piercee. Avoid situations that increase the chance of an abscess, and make piercees conscious of the potentials.

PERMANENT HEALING TIMES
(Approximate)

For most people, healing is complete:

After about 4-6 mos:
   Earlobes
   Eyebrows
   Septums
   Lips
   Labrets
   Clit hoods
   Clits
   Inner labia
   Prince Alberts
   Fourchettes

After about 1-1½ yrs:
   Outer labia
   Guiches
   Frenums
   Scrotums
   Triangles
   Dydoes

After about 2-3 yrs:
   Male nipples
   Female nipples
   Ampallangs
   Apadravyas
   Surface-to-surface piercings
   Navels
   Nostrils
   Ear cartilage

SUMMARY —
1. An abscess is a pocket of infectious fluid trapped under the skin.
2. Abscesses can occur when a repiercing is done, particularly on a nipple.
3. Abscesses can occur when jewelry is removed from an infected piercing.
4. Hot compresses, particularly herbal compresses can be very effective in draining an abscess.
5. If compresses are ineffective within 48 hours, refer the piercee to a doctor. The abscess will need more complex treatment.

Chemical Sensitivity

When a piercing gives trouble, most people immediately conclude the it is infected. Actually what may be going on is a reaction to either the cleaning agent or the metal of which the jewelry is made. The former is much more common. Like an infection, the piercing will put out lots of fluid, the piercing may enlarge, and rejection begin. Cleanser reactions can be quite extreme, or very subtle (a little tender, or a little itchy, or an extended healing time). Usually the fluid is clear, the tissue all around the piercing looks red and shiny. There may be a rash. If the piercee thinks they have an "infection," they increase cleaning to four or five times a day with the very cleanser that is irritating them.

For most people, the reaction begins when they overclean the piercing. Cleaning more than twice a day with antibacterial products, combining several different antibacterial products, or soaking it with sea salt/hot water for hours, is bound to kill off far more skin cells than it saves. Once the body has determined the cause of its woes, it often develops a sensitivity to that cleanser, and will react even if it is used appropriately. This is frustrating, and can be avoided by stressing to piercees that overcleaning is just as bad as not cleaning it at all. Twice a day is plenty of exposure to antibacterial agents, particularly when no bacteria is being introduced into the area.

Fragrance, numbing agents, or other additives may prove irritating, so try to avoid them.

Some cleansers such as chlorhexidine gluconate and povidone-iodine are quite strong, and many people react to even small amounts of them. These products should be used very cautiously, and heavily diluted, even by those people who have not yet experienced any sensitivity. Since allergic reactions can occur after cumulative exposure, someone who had no problems using Hibiclens last year could have a dramatic reaction to it this year.

Navels and genitals, particularly frenums and PAs, are exceptionally sensitive to strong cleansers. It is not suggested that any questionable cleanser be used in these areas, even by piercees who have had past success using them.

Some people may react to triclosan, the active ingredient in many antibacterial soaps, or benzalkonium chloride, the active ingredient in above-the-neck cleansers. Clearly Natural, a povidone-iodine-based soap, may alleviate this problem. Phisoderm or Phisohex may also be an effective solution.

A very small number of people react to almost every cleanser you can suggest. Although it is not preferable to an antibacterial cleanser, these highly sensitive people can try the following recipe three times daily:

⅓ saline solution
⅓ distilled water
⅓ hydrogen peroxide

In addition to this cleanser, a gentle antibacterial cleanser should be used at least twice a week.

> SUMMARY —
> 1. Irritation caused by cleansers is a common problem.
> 2. Overcleaning, combining cleansers, or using cleansers containing fragrance, numbing agents, or other additives, may cause irritation.
> 3. Some cleansers, such as chlorhexidine gluconate and povidone-iodine, are very strong, and more likely to cause irritation.
> 4. Sensitivity to cleansers is often cumulative. A reaction can occur after years of uneventful use.
> 5. The special cleanser recipe shown above is only to be used in cases where all other cleansers are too strong, and should be accompanied by occasional use of an antibacterial soap.

Metal Reactions

When you are presented with a problem piercing, your first steps should be to rule out infection and /or sensitivity to the cleaning agent as probable cause. What is left is a possible sensitivity to the material of which the jewelry is made. While this can be expected with silver, non-surgical stainless steel, gold-filled, gold-plated, or base metal jewelry, it can occur with even surgical stainless steel or 18 karat gold. The offender is often nickel or copper or other base metal. Don't rule out a metal reaction just because appropriate jewelry is worn. Sometimes something not in the actual piercing, but touching it, will cause reactions.

The vast majority of metal reactions follow two distinct patterns. Most commonly, the area is not particularly tender, but the openings of the piercing are greatly enlarged, with a pinkish-yellowish color. The body is drawing its tissue away from the offending jewelry. Rejection is the end result. This type of rejection is most common with frenums and navels, and can be aggravated by overcleaning. The other, much less common type of metal reaction is more subtle. The piercing appears to be healing normally, but suddenly begins to move the jewelry towards the surface. This type of metal reaction occurs most commonly in persons with immunosuppressed conditions such as diabetes, hypoglycemia, or AIDS.

If neither of these patterns is present, a metal reaction is unlikely. Still, don't rule it out. Lesser reactions can manifest in the form of heat, itchiness, or discharge soon after inserting the metal, though these symptoms usually indicate some other problem.

The obvious solution to a metal reaction is to exchange the jewelry for something less likely to react or, in a real pinch, a piece of monofilament nylon. A more gentle cleansing regime should also be used to give the tissue a better chance to regenerate, and warm soaks will ease discomfort and discourage scarring.

> SUMMARY —
> 1. Metal sensitivity can occur with any metal but especially nickel, copper, or other base metal.
> 2. A few very sensitive people may react to surgical stainless steel, solid 18k gold, niobium, or titanium, but it is less likely.
> 3. One type of reaction causes the piercing to greatly enlarge and take on a pinkish-yellowish color.
> 4. Another type of metal reaction causes the jewelry to be rapidly pushed out of the body, while appearing to heal normally in all other respects.
> 5. Metal contact can cause heat, itching, discharge or discomfort.
> 6. In cases of metal sensitivity, try jewelry of a different metal, usually niobium or titanium, or try monofilament nylon.

Jewelry Design

Barring a metal reaction, plenty of things could be going on with the jewelry itself. Check for any scratches, nicks, or irregularities on the surface of the jewelry. These can be very small, yet cause big problems. Also check for sharp edges. How is the size of the jewelry relative to the piercing? If the tissue on either side is looking pinched, swollen, or deformed, a larger diameter or longer post may be needed. A piercing which is weeping fluid and feels extremely tender when the jewelry is touched could need a smaller diameter or length. If the diameter is too large it tends to cause friction and get snagged easily, this is a possible cause of the problem. Also consider if a ring is being worn in a piercing that might be better suited to a barbell, or vice versa.

If the gauge is too thin, it too can manifest all the symptoms of a metal reaction. A thicker gauge (not too much at one time) will usually slip into the piercing quite easily indicating that the jewelry has cut a hole larger than itself through the tissue. At the other extreme, a too-thick piece of jewelry can be heavy enough to tear delicate tissue and prevent the escape of fluids. Immediately downsize the jewelry, and don't be surprised if there is a lot of fluid; you have probably just prevented (hopefully) an abscess.

Consider all these variables, and make adjustments as necessary. The piercing should get extra attention in the form of daily hot compresses until the irritation subsides. If the irritation does not begin to subside within about three days, something else is happening in the piercing.

SUMMARY —
1. Scratches, nicks, or deformities on the surface of the jewelry may cause irritation.
2. Jewelry that is too small or too large in diameter or length may cause irritation.
3. Jewelry of an inappropriate gauge may cause irritation.
4. Wearing an inappropriate style of jewelry may also cause irritation.

Irritation

If swelling, redness, tenderness, and discharge are present, but infection is unlikely (the piercee has not exposed the piercing to pathogens), the piercing may be in a state of irritation. Irritation is separate from infection, although the factors causing irritation frequently invite subsequent infection if left untreated. Irritation is caused by a bewildering number of factors. Let's look at some of the most common:

Friction

A common source of irritation is friction or frequent handling. The jewelry is moving around too much, or isn't being allowed to move at all. This pulls crusted matter back into the piercing, tearing the delicate edges. Often the surrounding tissue is red or very dark reddish-brown, indicating that many cells are dying. This happens quite commonly with navel piercings whose owners are overeager to wear that big belt, or in guiche piercings that get sat on constantly, or outer labia that are ground against the inner thigh, or ear piercings that get slept on.

If a jewelry change will help matters, for example inserting a barbell into the outer labia to minimize snags, by all means try it. Have the piercee wear something soft, clean, and absorbent next to the piercing. Women's pantyliners can be a lifesaver for troublesome guiche and scrotal piercings. A comfortable tank top, T shirt, or sports bra will prevent friction while one sleeps and during the day. Look for creative solutions. Avoid belts, tight pants, uncomfortable or unbreathable clothing. No amount of softness next to the piercing will help if the friction or pressure is too great.

Frequent warm soaks help reduce crusting, as will drying the area with clean tissues throughout the day.

SUMMARY —
1. Friction and pressure cause many incidents of irritation.
2. It is sometimes beneficial to change the style, size, or gauge of the jewelry when friction is presenting a problem.

3. Keep something soft and absorbent next to the piercing afflicted by friction.
4. When possible, avoid or alter behaviors that cause friction or pressure on new piercings.
5. Frequent warm soaks reduce the crusted matter and attendant damage associated with friction irritation.

Keloiding

A piercee shows you their ear cartilage, complaining of tightness and discomfort. It looks fine upon first glance, and you are puzzled. But as you inspect the backside, there appears to be a giant bump growing out of the piercing. What is it, and why is it so ugly? Most importantly, how do you get rid of it?

A keloid is technically an overgrowth of scar tissue. The body becomes a little overenthusiastic and piles layer upon layer of tissue in one inconvenient location. The more melanin (pigment) present in someones skin, the more likelihood there is that a keloid will occur. Often before the growth hardens into scar tissue, it is full of fluid. This fluid is not infectious, as it was produced by the body; however, if allowed to remain in the keloid, it creates a distinct possibility for opportunistic infections to occur. Abscesses may start out as keloids, although they can develop independently as well.

Sometimes the keloid makes sense; sometimes it doesn't. If jewelry is moving too much, a keloid is the body's "bandaid." This will also happen if friction is causing crusted matter to tear the inside of the piercing. If jewelry is too small, a keloid sometimes appears on one or both sides of the piercing, which makes less sense, as this expands the size of the piercing, making the jewelry even smaller by comparison.

If a keloid is present, you can usually make it leave quietly. Sometimes you can't. There are many methods which have proven successful, but that's no guarantee that any of them will work in any given situation.

The best plan is to avoid creating a condition that might encourage keloiding to occur. Alway pick the right jewelry, err on the side of caution every time, and place and angle piercings, especially outer labia, ear cartilage, and oral piercings, away from trouble.

Assuming that, in spite of all precautions, a keloid occurs, look first at the jewelry. Inappropriate or damaged jewelry is often the cause of the keloid. Changing it will probably eradicate the keloid. If the jewelry is not the cause, or if the keloid remains in spite of a change, try the following procedures, one at a time, in the order given. These methods range from most gentle to harshest. Often a more gentle process will be effective. Give each method a few weeks try before moving on, and don't confuse the body by mixing cleansers.

1. Use hot water and sea salt compresses two or three times daily, applying firm yet gentle pressure.
2. An herbal compress, using one or all of the following:
   - Sea salt
   - Comfrey
   - Chamomile
   - Echinacea
   - Goldenseal

   Make a hot, very strong infusion and apply in compress form to the area for a half hour twice daily. Clean the piercing with antibacterial soap afterwards. This method is very effective, and can also draw out abscesses.
3. Hydrogen peroxide, in gel or liquid form (gel is less messy), applied twice daily for not more than 10 minutes, to bubble off accumulated matter.

4. Tea tree oil, or grapefruit seed extract, applied sparingly twice daily, to dry up any fluids. In some people, these products can encourage tissue growth, so be careful.
5. Hydrocortisone cream, 1% to 5%, applied sparingly twice daily, or according to doctor's orders. Cortisone can cause discoloration of the area, and some people will react to it. People with immune disorders should consult a physician before using it.
6. Aspirin. If a piercee has no allergy to aspirin, a tablet can be moistened and applied directly to the keloid, literally burning it off. Don't do this more than twice a day, 15 minutes at a time. This method is pretty severe, and is most effective with oral keloids.
7. Removal of the jewelry. Sometimes this is necessary, when all else has failed. The keloid will usually reduce rapidly upon removal of jewelry, but just to be sure, continue hot compresses or other keloid-fighting method until the growth is completely gone.
8. Surgical removal. The keloid may stubbornly remain after the jewelry has been removed. In these cases, surgical removal by a doctor would be the expensive solution. Unfortunately, the surgical procedure itself may create another opportunity for keloiding, so even this method is no sure guarantee.

SUMMARY —

1. A keloid is a growth containing fluid or scar tissue, depending upon how well-established it is.
2. The more pigment in a piercee's skin, the more likely keloiding.
3. Keloiding is often a reaction to inappropriate jewelry or friction.
4. Changing the jewelry and soaking the piercing usually solves the problem of keloiding.
5. Persistent keloids are treated in a number of different ways, listed above.

Other possibilities

Rest assured you will encounter situations resembling none of those discussed above. Knowing the health status of the piercee helps in some cases. For example, if a piercee discloses that they are diabetic, you will know that their skin may be a little tougher to pierce, they may take longer to heal because of poor circulation, and may be more prone to infection or rejection. Pregnant or nursing women may have unusual developments, as may persons who are immunosuppressed.

Remember! You are not a physician. Some problems will elude you. Connect with a good, piercing-friendly doctor in your area, to whom you can refer piercees when problems mystify you.

✦ A Touch of Heresy

Throughout this manual we have presented a great deal of health and safety information. Most of it adheres closely the concepts and philosophies endorsed by the majority of health care professionals in the United States and the countries of Western Europe. And who would question the vital importance of hygiene and sterility in protecting the health and well-being of not only our clientele but the world at large? We, as responsible piercers, would not consider conducting our businesses in anything other than the most hygienic way possible. Rather, what we wish to present in this brief section is an alternative perspective to the orthodox view of the disease process and alternative methods of prevention and treatment.

The prevailing viewpoint of Western medicine, based primarily on the work of Robert Koch (1843-1910) and Louis Pasteur (1822-1895), is that each and every disease or infection results from an invasion by a specific microorganism. Thus, if a certain bacteria causes a certain disease, then logically, if we can kill that bacteria, we can end the disease. Thus we need only discover an agent that will destroy the invading pathogen. To that end researchers have devoted endless hours and pharmaceutical companies have spent billions of dollars. To them we owe the discovery of antibiotics and the other chemical drugs which have changed the face of medicine as we know it and, in the process, turned their discoverers into wealthy and powerful cartels.

No one can deny that these drugs have saved many lives, but unfortunately, behind their bright promise there is a dark and sinister side. Antibiotics and other chemical drugs exact a heavy toll upon all who take them. Their impact upon the body is harsh. And all too frequently they produce serious side-effects, occasionally even death. If taken regularly they can devastate a person's health. Ones internal ecological balance can be thrown off. As these drugs alter the pH (acid/alkaline) balance of the blood and tissues and as they destroy beneficial bacteria along with the bad, the individual is left open to invasion by fungi and other pathogens.

We face an alarming future as bacteria have become increasingly resistant to antibiotics, requiring stronger, more toxic drugs to bring them under control. What is even more alarming is that doctors continue to prescribe them, often for the most trivial of conditions. We are not likely to see that change any time in the foreseeable future, at least in US. The American Medical Association (AMA) and the Federal Drug Administration (FDA), which dictate how medicine is practiced and what drugs will be approved in this country, are controlled by and bow to the dictates of the rich and powerful pharmaceutical cartel.

With enormous profits from expensive drugs and therapies at stake, it should come as no surprise that the phamaceutical companies and their confederates have fought hard and bitterly to block the availability of safe, effective, reasonably priced alternatives. Most people probably don't even realize that such alternatives exist.

While most people have heard of Koch and Pasteur, few know the names of Antoine Béchamp (a contemporary of Pasteur) or Guenther Enderlein (1872-1968). The work of these and other pioneers in microbiology has gone largely unnoticed and ignored by the medical establishment. It was swept aside by the politics of power and money, and even attacked by Hitler and his henchmen in an effort to discredit scientists who differed with the Nazi doctrines of "racial purity."

Despite opposition, Professor Enderlein, in particular, researched, discovered, and developed a wide variety of highly effective medications based on biological products. Unlike antibiotics, which are also derived from biological

"People live statistically longer, but they are not necessarily healthier. Today we have sewage systems, water faucets, and better sanitary conditions that have helped eliminate mass epidemics, such as typhus, cholera and tuberculosis. But more people are becoming sick from heart disease, cancer, and intestinal illnesses than ever before. The idea that antibiotics and modern medicine deserve most of the credit for improving both the length and quality of people's lives is a fraud."

M. O. Bruker, M. D.
Our Nourishment, Our Destiny

substances, these non-toxic medicines do not directly kill disease causing pathogens, but, instead, work with the body and dismantle virulent organisms into benign forms. Unlike both antibiotics and vaccines (and chemical drugs as well) there are no side effects.

The Enderlein medications, which have been available in Europe for many years, are in the process of being approved by the FDA for sale in the US. Hopefully they will be available in the near future.

Responsible piercers continually seek ways to make the piercing experience safer for their clients and the healing process smoother and more problem free. The Enderlein products provide excellent alternatives to toxic antibiotics which are the stock in trade of the medical profession for dealing with infections. At present only European piercers can benefit from their ready accessibility. But once available in the US, American piercers and piercees alike can take advantage of these remarkable medicines. They will be worth seeking out.

The Enderlein products are manufactured by SANUM-Kehlbeck GmbH & Co. KG, D-2812 Hoya, Germany.

From any given biological resource, Sanum produces medicines in several different forms and strengths: capsules, drops, ointments, and injectable solutions. Most of these should be used under the supervision of a physician familiar with them. When they are available in the US, you will need a doctor's prescription to purchase them.

Two Enderlein formulas are of particular interest and usefulness to us as piercers:

Notakehl —

Derived from *Penicillium notatum*, but without the allergens found in penicillin, Notakehl is effective in preventing and fighting infections, especially strep and staph.

In doing a piercing it is standard procedure to lubricate the needle point with a little Bacitracin ointment. Notakehl ointment is an excellent substitute, especially for European piercers who may find Bacitracin ointment harder to locate. And any time an infection threatens, piercees would find it beneficial to reach for the Notakehl ointment instead of an antibiotic ointment. Should a serious infection develop the piercer should consult a health care professional familiar with the Sanum products and their use. Notakehl capsules or injections should be able to bring the problem under control.

Notakehl can be used in the aftercare regimen as follows: Wash the piercing(s) as described earlier in this chapter using an antibacterial soap. Dry on a clean towel and apply a little Notakehl ointment. Continue this procedure for two to four weeks. Reinitiate the regimen if signs of an infection should appear.

Mucokehl —

Derived from *Mucor Racemosus*, Mucokehl is useful for stimulating and improving healing (especially in slow-healing piercings) and for preventing the formation of scar tissue. It is also effective for reducing pain by stimulating circulation to the area. Whenever possible, wait three days after using Notakehl before using Mucokehl as they tend to reduce each others effectiveness.

The best protocol for these two products is to use the Notakehl for two to four weeks as described above, use neither for at least three days, then use Mucokehl in the same way until the piercing is healed. Return to Notakehl if an infection arises.

If you have never heard of or had any experience with biological medications, and if you are fortunate enough to have access to them, you might find them well worth exploring.

"These remarkable formulas [the Enderlein formulas] of biological and homeopathic preparations are used in Europe and are the product of the work of one of the truly great unrecognized medical geniuses of this century. It is a therapy based on the 'theory' of the pleomorphism of bacteria. This position is held by thousands of our best scientists, and thousands of papers have been written about it. They have been systematically ignored because they shake the foundations of the current allopathic approach of modern medicine and would render the stranglehold of the pharmaceutical industry impotent."
Robert E. Willner M.D., Ph.D
Deadly Deception

CHAPTER 14—
EMERGENCIES

• FIRST AID

Screening out drunk, drugged and unprepared piercees will almost eradicate the need to know first aid. But occasionally emergencies will arise. Keep on hand a well-stocked first aid kit with a good supply of bandages, gauze pads, cold packs, and other supplies. We feel very strongly that no one should be doing piercing who has not completed a Red Cross First Aid and CPR course. The course takes no more than two days, often only one, and will eliminate most of the frantic guesswork out of a sudden emergency. It is downright dangerous for a piercer to be ignorant of basic first aid.

• BLEEDING

When done skillfully most piercings are accomplished with scarcely more than a drop of blood, but some piercings are prone to immediate, profuse bleeding. These include the earlobe, cartilage, nostril, eyebrow, septum, Prince Albert, and inner labia. These areas are generally vascular, and the tissue pliable enough to allow blood to escape. While bleeding is more common with these particular piercings, it can just as easily occur elsewhere. This potential increases if the piercee has ingested alcohol, aspirin, caffeine, or other blood-thinning agents. Using a needle thicker than the jewelry, as is sometimes done with a cartilage or septum piercing, will practically guarantee some blood.

Always set a packet of benzalkonium chloride wipes on your setup tray. If bleeding is anticipated, have some cotton swabs and/or tissues close at hand. Whenever possible, carry a tissue with you when performing the jewelry transfer on an earlobe, eyebrow, nostril, or Prince Albert. Make sure to have a good supply of tissues in the room at all times, and try to avoid touching your "sterile" field with bloody gloves in a frantic grab for tissues. Be prepared; be conscious.

The proper way to stop normal bleeding is to apply two minutes of gentle but firm pressure with a clean tissue slightly above the area. When bleeding has slowed or stopped, gently clean the area with benzalkonium chloride. Handling the area roughly or overcleaning it may start the bleeding all over again, so be gentle.

For persistent bleeding, hydrogen peroxide may be useful. The liquid is fine, but the gel form is less messy.

Some people don't have time to wait for bleeding to stop, or may have a piercing that keeps on bleeding. Wearing a fresh pair of gloves, loosely apply a sterile gauze pad with surgical tape. Avoid taping directly over the piercing or jewelry. For Prince Albert piercings the penis can be wrapped with several tissues, covered with a small plastic bag or a spare latex glove, and secured with a rubber band.

SUMMARY—
1. There is an increased likelihood of bleeding with certain piercings, and when the piercee has ingested alcohol, caffeine, aspirin or blood-thinning drugs.
2. Prepare for the possibility of bleeding by setting out benzalkonium chloride wipes, tissues, cotton swabs, and whatever else you may need.
3. Stop most bleeding with two minutes of firm pressure using a clean tissue.

• FAINTING

If you screen out people who have been drinking or haven't eaten recently, it is unlikely that many of your clients will faint. When this does happen it can be very scary for all involved. The piercee will suddenly gaze far off into the distance or become incoherent, their eyes roll back in their head, and, if they are standing, they can drop like a rock.

It is crucial that you be alert for the signs of fainting. Some people give no warning. Others faint long before the piercing, a few right in the middle of a piercing, and most several minutes afterwards. Sometimes the piercee is fine, while a friend or significant other passes out! Remain calm. If they are still conscious insist that they sit or lie down, even if it has to be on the floor. Help them if necessary. If there is a needle in their body, try to cork it before proceeding. Continue talking to the fainter, even if they appear to be unconscious. Call their name and attempt to gain communication with them. Ask if they feel hot. Shut off some of the lights in the room. When they revive tell them where they are and what has happened. They may be disoriented. Don't let them get up yet. Calmly request a coworker to remain in the room while you prepare a cold pack (or wet some paper towels) and get a glass of fruit juice or lemonade.

Back in the room, place the cold pack on the fainter's forehead and have them drink some of the juice since fainting is often caused by a rapid drop in blood sugar levels.

Stay with the person as long as necessary, and only resume piercing, insertion, or other work when the person feels completely recovered. If necessary, have them return at a later date to finish up. Encourage them to eat something after they leave your shop.

SUMMARY —
1. Alcohol, drugs, fatigue, hunger, or nervousness are the common causes of fainting.
2. Always be alert for warning signs of fainting. Remain calm and act quickly.
3. Lie the fainter or prefainter down, shut off all extra lights, and do not leave them alone in the room.
4. Provide the fainter with a cold pack for their forehead, and give them some juice or candy to help regulate their blood sugar level.
5. Do not proceed until the situation is corrected.

• BEDSIDE MANNER

A subtle art, partly instinctive and partly developed, bedside manner can make or break one's success as a piercer. Bedside manner encompasses such diverse skills as putting a nervous piercee at ease, applying first aid techniques calmly to someone who has fainted, and chatting about aftercare on the phone. Some people develop a calm and reassuring bedside manner almost immediately, some need to

work at it a bit, developing the manner gradually. Unfortunately, some just don't have the innate ability to develop. Ideally members of this latter group should reconsider their choice of career, but sadly, many of them can't admit that something is lacking. However technically skilled one may be, it is irresponsible, unkind, and unprofessional to treat a client roughly, gruffly, rudely, coldly, or shyly.

• UNFAVORABLE CONDITIONS

The vast majority of people experience problems during a piercing only when they are poorly prepared for the experience. These people may be drunk, have taken some form of drug, have had nothing to eat for several hours. They may be ill, have not had a decent night's sleep, or simply be too nervous. Most of these conditions should be fairly easy to spot when you first meet them. Include screening questions on your release form. Talk with the client privately. Ask them to realistically gauge their ability and readiness to be pierced in their current condition. Approach them not with judgement but with professional concern and compassion. Many people will happily reschedule for later in the day or week, if the reasons are laid out for them.

Some people feel that they are capable of being pierced in their condition. It is then up to you to decide from the standpoint of your own safety and theirs, if you feel comfortable performing the piercing. Do they seem able to remain calm throughout the process? Will they be able to communicate vital information to you during the piercing? Are they likely to make any sudden moves, faint, or vomit? Are you comfortable enough in your current state to handle what is likely to be a more difficult piercing than usual? Are you able and willing to spend some extra time with this piercee?

If you decide that you do not feel comfortable with the piercing, for whatever reasons, ask them calmly and politely to return under different circumstances. Perhaps the person just needs to go have a little food. Perhaps they need to come back with friends so they feel more secure. Perhaps they

need to come back at a time when they haven't been drinking. Whatever the case, remain firm in your decision without appearing judgmental. Explain fully your reasons for not doing the piercing at that time and welcome them back under different circumstances. There is an excellent chance that their opinion of you and your establishment will greatly increase, even if they appear upset. Even if they aren't appreciative of your concern for safety, never pierce under circumstances that cause you doubt or discomfort.

Some health conditions, notably pregnancy, diabetes, recent or current illness, and immune deficiency problems, can be a contraindication for piercing. Be sure before piercing someone with any of these conditions that they have seen a doctor and gained their approval first. If they decline to consult with a physician and assert that they feel well enough to be pierced, use your discretion. Generally people with any of these conditions will experience a somewhat longer and more involved healing period, and the body may have to decide between healing the piercing and attending to the condition. Persons with low T-cell counts should be advised to maintain very stringent aftercare due to their increased vulnerability to opportunistic infections.

SUMMARY —
1. Screen all piercees for signs of alcohol, drugs, fatigue or other conditions that could negatively influence the piercing.
2. Ask questionable clients privately to gauge their own ability to be pierced.
3. Decide the risk factor and your own level of comfort in proceeding with the piercing.
4. Maintain professionalism and tact, even if asking a piercee to return at a later date.
5. Use this professionalism when deciding if piercing elevates someone's health risk.

114

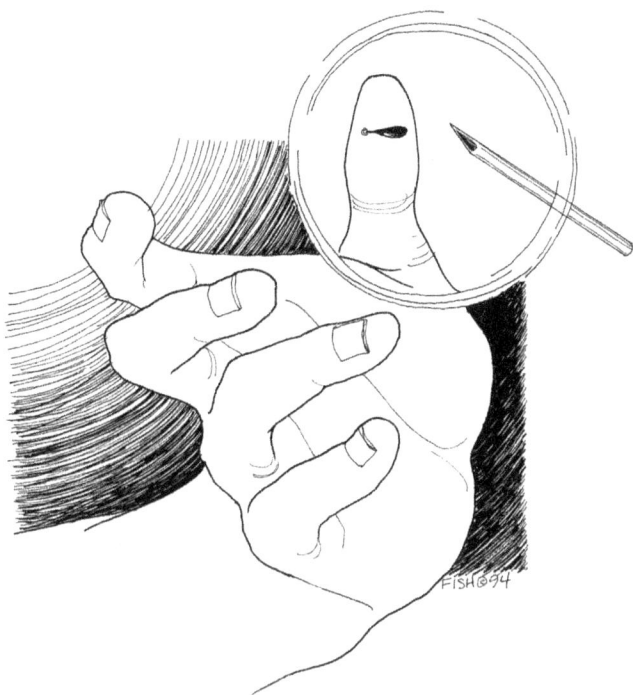

DEALING WITH NEEDLE STICKS

One of the risks we face as piercers is the daily possibility of an accidental needle stick with a contaminated piercing needle. By practicing the same kind of awareness we employ around sterility, we can do much to minimize the risk and avoid the terror, confusion, and uncertainty that follows a needle stick. The piercer who is alert, focused, and careful has little to worry about.

But accidents do happen. If you are accidentally stuck by a contaminated piercing needle, remain calm. Secure the needle point in a cork, and immediately tend to the stick. If necessary, call in a coworker to complete the piercing. Remember! the needle is now also contaminated with your own blood, so under no circumstances should the point be withdrawn back through the piercing nor should the needle be reused. It must be discarded immediately after the jewelry insertion.

Following a needle stick, take these steps:

1. Immediately remove your gloves and attempt to get the wound to bleed. Squeeze out as much blood as possible.
2. As you are milking the stuck area, immerse it in full strength bleach for 30 seconds to one full minute. This is strictly an emergency procedure.
3. Continue to encourage bleeding, and rinse the area with warm running water and antibacterial soap for several minutes.
4. Dry the area with a clean towel then apply a small amount of antibiotic ointment and a bandage.
5. When you are calm, return to the piercee. If necessary, complete the piercing and/or jewelry insertion.
6. Inform the piercee in a calm manner of your accident. Respectfully inquire into their health status. Hopefully they will be open to discussing their hepatitis and HIV status with you. Remember; it is possible that they may have something they don't know about, or they may not want to share that information with you. In some cases people are so ashamed of being HIV positive they may even lie about it. You cannot legally require anyone to divulge this confidential information to you.
7. If you have not received the hepatitis vaccine series, and may have been exposed to hepatitis, there is a 10 day series of shots that may prevent you from becoming ill. It is highly advisable to consult your physician about these shots if there is any chance you have been exposed. Some people can carry the virus without themselves being sick.
8. Antibodies indicating the possible presence of the HIV virus are not detectable for at least six months. If you think you may have been exposed to HIV, mark your calendar six months from the date of your stick, and consider being tested for it at that time.

   Try not to worry. The statistics are in your favor. Although many health care workers have been stuck with contaminated needles, few—some of the world's leading scientists say none—have contracted AIDS via this means. And while it is still controversial there is mounting evidence suggesting HIV, alone or in tandem with another organism, may not, in fact, be the cause of AIDS.
9. Finally, carefully consider how and why the needle stick occurred. How could it have been avoided? Make a clear plan to prevent and avoid another needle stick in the future.

CHAPTER 15 —

✦ AFTERWORD

• APPRENTICESHIP — THE NEXT STEP

Congratulations! You've completed the seminar! You have learned new things, reinforced what you already may have known, and hopefully made some great connections. You have every reason to feel proud. But what are you going to do with all this knowledge? Many of you are already piercing, and just wanted to clarify your path. Many of you took the seminars so that you'd be better able to pierce your friends or lovers. But probably most of you are perceiving these seminars as an introduction to piercing professionally. What's your next step, if that is your goal?

A mail-order correspondence course won't make you a tattoo artist any more than a two year course of study will produce a professional woodworker, plumber, or electrician. Two years in cosmetology school will not make you a Vidal Sasoon. Even eight years of highly specialized schooling fails to qualify one as a fully accredited physician. Nor will these seminars alone make you a skilled, professional piercer. What's missing? For every one of these trades, the most important element, without which the education is meaningless, is a period of apprenticeship or internship.

What is an apprenticeship? A prolonged period of study directly under a more experienced piercer. This usually lasts for a minimum of one year, full time. The senior piercer instructs, guides, and observes the apprentice, rounding out the educational aspects

and providing an exemplary model of professionalism. Truly, the ideal way to pursue your goal is in the closely supervised environment of an apprenticeship.

Unfortunately, this ideal assumes the existence of a reasonable number of experienced, skilled piercers, who were themselves well-trained. The craft of modern piercing is very new, and the information around it has been jealously guarded. The result, as we have already discussed, is a surplus of ignorant, attitude-laden charlatans. This manual contains more information than is possessed by many of those folks combined. Consequently, you can expect locating a suitable apprenticeship to be something of a challenge.

But don't be dissuaded! Call piercers in your area. Interview them carefully, just as they should be interviewing you. Ask them about their commitments to health and safety, the length of time they have been piercing, how they learned the craft. You should have gained enough from these seminars to be able to spot a genuine professional. With luck you will find a reputable, knowledgeable piercer in your area who just happens to be seeking an apprentice.

Realistically, as we have already stated, it's quite possible that you will already know more about certain aspects of piercing than your so-called "master." If this is the case, it may still be worthwhile to pursue an alliance with an open, available piercer whose ego is not so inflated that they will feel threatened by you or be closed to the valuable new information you could provide.

If there is absolutely no one in your area who merits your time, good luck. The learning process of a non-apprenticed trainee can be very rough, and time-consuming. Remember to seek out as much information as you possibly can. Subscribe to the APP health and safety newsletter. Strike up a relationship with the local health board and get to know some of your local physicians. Read the materials in the bibliography, and any other related publications. Call the Gauntlet hotline. Consult with other piercers or trainees, whenever possible. But most importantly, don't allow insecurity to lead to misrepresentation of your abilities or experience. This is irresponsible, dangerous, unethical, and plain tasteless. Information, aptitude, caution, and patience will be your unfailing guides. Keep your goal in sight, then, piece by piece, assemble the knowledge and experience that will one day make you a responsible AND a professional piercer.

• YOUR OWN BUSINESS

We encourage every student to "pay their dues" and serve an apprenticeship, and we know that sooner or later, prepared or not, many of you will want to start your own businesses. If we have succeeded at nothing else, we hope to have instilled in you a sense of ethics and responsibility that will stand you in good stead whenever that time comes.

Piercing can be done at home, for friends, or it can be done in a professional setting, in a piercing studio. Given that there is little enough time in a few days to impart even the technical information necessary to begin piercing, there is simply no time to cover how to start a business. In addition every state and country has its own laws and regulations which you should adhere to if you expect to be treated like a professional and not a shady, fly-by-night operation.

In the simplest of terms we include a few of the things you need to consider in starting a business. If you will be hiring employees, be prepared to deal with the regulations which that entails. While individual permit requirements, etcetera, will vary from place to place—some are handled on the city or county level, others on the state or federal—here are the basics required to operate a business in the state of California. Other states and countries may have very different requirements.

Get an Accounting Professional

When you first make the decision to go into business, connect with a good accounting professional. You will never regret it. This person can save you immeasurable trouble and aggravation. Not only can they steer you through much of the permit or registration process, telling you what government agencies you need to contact, but they can set up your books, help you open a bank account, inform you what records must be kept, how to keep them, and how to stay out of trouble with taxation authorities.

Permits & Registrations

The DBA—

When you come up with a name for your business, you are required to let the world at large know that you are "doing business as (DBA)"... This is done by publishing a notice several times in a local newspaper. Call around and find a paper which provides this service, then go to their office, fill out the necessary forms, and pay the fee.

The Resale Permit—

In California this is handled by the State Board of Equalization which has offices in all major cities. The resale permit allows you to make wholesale, tax-exempt purchases, and collect sales tax upon resale of this merchandise. Expect to make a tax deposit based on your estimated income for the coming year.

Business Permit—

The business permit is a form of registration and is usually a requirement of the city in which you will be doing business. Oddly, not every city requires one.

Health License/Permit —

If they are required, health licenses or permits may be handled at the state, county, or city level. You will have to do some calling around to find out. The regulating body may be the Board of Health, but in some states, the Board of Barbering and Cosmetology has lobbied for control of this industry. It is your legal responsibility to comply with the requirements of the regulating body, whether reasonable or not. It is your ethical and moral responsibility to exceed any minimal regulations, and to practice at the highest possible standards, regardless of the level of regulation in your area.

If you happen to live in a regulated area, your establishment may be subject to inspection before you open and/or periodically thereafter. You will be judged on the quality of your safety and hygiene methods, the overall cleanliness of your store, and on your compliance with OSHA requirements. For example, you may be fined if you have a non-wheelchair accessible bathroom, or if you have failed to clearly mark the biohazard areas in your shop.

Location

It has been said that the secret of a successful business is "location, location, location." Seek out a business site in an area frequented, more or less, by the type of clientele you wish to attract. If your reputation grows, more people will make a special trip to get to you. Choosing a location in a less desirable neighborhood may give customers the wrong impression, or discourage visits to your establishment.

The Space

Wherever you decide to set up shop, the building should be clean, and laid out in a manner conducive for piercings. This includes having sufficient electrical outlets and wiring that can handle the demands of an autoclave and other equipment, at least one bathroom with at least one sink, and separate rooms for the front counter and actual piercing room. A partitioned or recessed part of the plan may serve as the sterilization area, as long as it is well out of the way of normal traffic. If tattooing, massage, hair styling, or other services will be provided, you will need a separate area for each service.

Unless the space has just been freshly painted, a new coat of paint is a good idea before you move in. If this is not an option, then scrub every surface with disinfectant.

If carpeted, you will want to lay down some sort of non-porous flooring material in the actual piercing area. This can be as simple as the vinyl rug protectors found under office desks and chairs, or as complete as a whole new hardwood or tile floor.

Furnishings

In the front room, choose a counter surface such as glass, so that you can easily and thoroughly disinfect things throughout the day.

There are numerous ways of storing jewelry, including utility/ hardware boxes, chests, drawers, etc. Just be sure that all sizes and styles of jewelry have their own separate place, to avoid dangerous mixups. Your containers should also be nonporous, to allow for occasional sterilization.

Whatever furniture your autoclave and other sterilization equipment rests on should be nonporous and very solid and sturdy. Autoclaves are quite heavy and fragile. Ideally, the sterilization table also has drawers or shelving for storage.

For a list of piercing room furnishings refer to chapter 2.

Equipment

Chapter 2 will also provide a good list of equipment and supplies you will need. Also check out the resource guide at the end of the book.

When setting up your shop, you will need to invest in forceps, several pairs of each style, as well as nostril tubes & NRT's. While the latter two are readily available from Gauntlet, forceps can be unfortunately difficult to track down. If you locate a potential supplier, it's best to order just one to inspect the quality. Even poorly made forceps can be expensive, and may not be returnable.

Perhaps your greatest expense will

be an autoclave. These are available in medical and dental supply catalogs, several of which are listed in the resource list. While it is possible to locate a used autoclave for substantially less money, a new autoclave functions much more reliably. Autoclaves are very delicate pieces of equipment, requiring frequent and regular maintenance. Can you afford to suspend business until a broken autoclave is fixed?

Disposables, such as table paper, hard-surface wipes, Chex-all autoclave baggies, Betadine swabs, and the like, are available from a number of medical and dental supply houses. Experiment to find your favorite products, then order a large enough quantity to save money and avoid running out of any products. Autoclavable corks may be hard to come by; check your yellow pages for cork vendors in your area.

Office supply stores yield rubber bands and Sharpie fine point markers for piercings, as well as miscellaneous needs such as register paper, receipt paper, and the like. You may also find items such as circle templates there. Art supply stores are also excellent sources for supplies.

Dial calipers can be purchased from woodworking or machinist's supply stores. You should have several. Gauge wheels are found jeweler's supply stores.

Snap-on Tools make excellent pliers, though they aren't cheap. You may also find pliers at auto supply and hardware stores. Some types, such as large ring expanders, are available through Gauntlet.

Presterilized, disposable piercing needles and a large range of jewelry are available from Gauntlet. Should you choose to use needles or jewelry from another source, make a thorough inspection to be sure they are not of an inferior quality. The old saying, "You get what you pay for," is usually true.

Disposable medical sharps containers are available from medical and dental supply houses and some pharmacies. They are inexpensive, sometimes even free. When full, they are sealed, autoclaved, and taken to a participating hospital or pharmacy for exchange and disposal. This is either done for free, or for a nominal charge.

As you become more skilled, and your safety and comfort needs evolve, you will acquire additional equipment. Just remember to keep safety & hygiene foremost in your considerations when making any purchases. Think about how the equipment will be used, and envision a worst-case scenario. Will it stand up to your standards? Will it meet your needs? Would some similar item be safer? For example, pump dispensers are much safer than pour dispensers, since you are less likely to spill the contents or contaminate the bottle.

Paperwork

If you wish to be perceived as a professional, provide your clients with informational brochures and such topics as piercing aftercare and jewelry selection. A well-crafted brochure will be carried home and shared with potential customers. Remember that Gauntlet brochures and all other forms of Gauntlet paperwork are copyrighted, and may not be reproduced without permission. And, by using the information you are learning in this seminar, in addition to information gained from other reliable sources (health officials, health professionals, etc.), you should have no problem formulating your own personalized brochures.

Other paperwork is essential. In our litigious society you would be wise to get a release form filled out for every piercing you do. This form should have the piercee's name, age, and address, and a signature releasing you from legal responsibility. In addition, it should note the date, as well as the specific piercing or piercings being performed. If the person is under 25 ask for picture I.D. and note important numbers, etc. on the release. If the client is under age, insist that a parent or legal guardian be present to identify themselves, and sign the release. Even with parental consent, NEVER pierce anything below a minor's neck except their navel. Otherwise you could find yourself accused of sexual abuse.

A signed release form will not guarantee you won't get sued, but it does offer at least some protection. Save every release form you generate, and try to keep them in some sort of order; you never know when or why you will need to look something up.

You should also have clients fill out a different release form for insertions or stretchings. There should be a paper record for every occasion your gloved hands make contact with a person's body. For samples of standard release forms see the following page.

• LAST WRITES

We hope that you have found this course to be valuable and instructive. Gauntlet has always striven to maintain the highest quality and standards in the piercing field. Your feedback regarding these seminars and this manual would be greatly appreciated. Write:

Jim Ward
c/o Gauntlet Enterprises
584 Castro St., #357
San Francisco, CA 94114
mrjimw93@gmail.com

RELEASE

To induce _____ to pierce my _____, and in consideration of its doing so, I hereby release _____ and its employees and agents, from all manner of liabilities, claims, actions and demands, in law or in equity, which I or my heirs have or might have now or here-after by reason of complying with my request to be pierced.

I understand I will be pierced using appropriate instruments and techniques. To ensure proper healing of my piercing, I agree to follow the aftercare procedures outlined in Gauntlet's "Keep it Clean" pamphlet, until healing is complete. I understand that this type of piercing usually takes _____, or longer to heal. I have signed this release on _____, 20_____.

Name (print) _____

Address _____

City, State, & Zip _____

Age_____ Signature _____

RELEASE

To induce _____ to insert jewelry into my previously pierced _____ _____, and in consideration of its doing so, I hereby release _____ and its employees and agents, from all manner of liabilities, claims, actions and demands, in law or in equity, which I or my heirs have or might have now or hereafter by reason of complying with my request to be pierced. This (these) piercing(s) are _____ old.

I have signed this release on _____, 20_____.

Name (print) _____

Address _____

City, State, & Zip _____

Age_____ Signature _____

Jewelry style, size and gauge _____

120

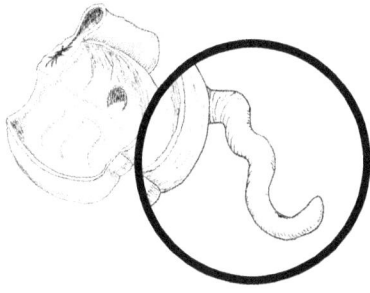

✦ APPENDIX— ANATOMICAL INFORMATION & ILLUSTRATIONS

Drawings by Phoebe Gloeckner

The information in this appendix is intended to serve as a broad overview of those anatomical factors which are likely to concern piercers. In no way can this small manual adequately cover this complex and important topic. We strongly urge all piercers to read all related material in the resource list, particularly the *Atlas of Human Anatomy* by Dr. Frank Netter.

• SKIN

Skin is the semi-porous outer protective coating of the body. It incorporates several complicated systems by which it can heat or cool the body, send messages about sensations to the brain: tighten, relax, etc.

Outer skin cells form epithelial tissue, most of which is called *simple squamous epithelial* cells. Cells are held together by a material called *intercellular cement.* Mucous membranes are also made of epithelial cells.

Erector pilii are the tiny erectile apparati which cause your individual hairs to stand on end. *Myoepithelial cells* are what contract the nipple. These are found throughout the surface of the skin. Nipples are primarily pigmented smooth muscle fibers, set in fibrous tissue.

Smooth muscle is the type which lines arteries, colons and other tissue that has to contract to squeeze air/blood/food through the passage. It is not, however, erectile tissue proper, which is found in parts of the genitalia only. *Erectile tissue* has large cavities so it can fill with blood and erect.

• CONNECTIVE TISSUE

Connective tissue is found throughout the body in various forms. It serves to bind together and support the other tissues and organs. It is made up of fibrils in a matrix of intercellular material.

Fascia

Fascia is a type of connective tissue. Superficial fascia is found just under the skin. It is made of several layers of loose or dense irregular fibrous tissue. Deep fascia envelopes skeletal muscle, supports viscera, connects superficial fascia to deeper muscle structures, and fills spaces between other tissues.

Cartilage

Cartilage is a connective tissue made of a matrix of cells suspended in gel. There is little blood supply to cartilaginous areas. There are three types of cartilage:

Hyaline—
Very fine collagenous tissue. It is found at the end and sides of the nose, and the supporting rings of the respiratory passage. Nostril and septum piercings pass through hyaline cartilage.

Elastic—
This is the type found in the ear and in part of the larynx.

Fibrocartilage—
This type is very rigid. It functions as a sort of bumper, and is found at the ends of bones and in intervertebral discs.

Bone

Bone is the most rigid connective tissue. It is made of very tightly knit fibril strands, and owes its hardness mainly to the presence of mineral salts such as calcium and potassium. Inside bones, the marrow produces new blood cells and forms part of the lymphatic system.

Blood

Blood is a connective tissue made of cells suspended in intercellular liquid. Its function is to transport nutrients and oxygen to the cells, and waste away from the cells. The amount of blood each person holds varies with respect to fat, weight, metabolism, and age, but the average 140 pound man holds about five quarts of blood, the cells of which are constantly dying and being regenerated in the marrow.

• NERVES

The central nervous system carries both sensory and motor function responses to and from the brain. The nerve canal carrying the nerves exits from between segments of the spinal vertebra. From the ocean source of the brain, to the rivers of the nerve roots exiting, the tributaries and rivulets of response and communication flow in patterns throughout the body. Major nerves generally run deep in the body and are more protected from surface intrusion. But the many nerves arising from these can run quite superficially. There are a few areas of the body, such as in the front/sides of the neck and lateral clavicular areas, where the muscle and fascia tissues are all that protect the deeper nerves from intrusion. Some understanding of the nerve pathways is responsibly correct for our work.

Nerves serve two purposes. The *anterior* (frontal), or *efferent* nerves connect to the gray matter and dispense motor instructions to the various parts of the body.

Severance or damage at or near the root of an efferent nerve results in loss of control of the motor functions in the area corresponding to the nerve. The *posterior* (rear), or *afferent* nerves connect to the base of the brain, what some call the reptile brain, and send it sensory information from the body. Severance or virus attack (neuralgia) at or near the root of an afferent nerve results in a loss of sensation in the area corresponding to the nerve.

The way in which nerves transmit their information is still not completely understood. It is thought that they release a chemical substance which causes an electro-chemical reaction in the brain.

There are 12 pairs of *cranial nerves*, nerves which serve the head and neck area. Cranial nerves serve the same side of the head from which they generate. Each pair serves a *dermatome*, an area of tendons, muscles, and skin. The primary cranial nerve with which piercers should be familiar is the *trigeminal nerve*. This large nerve has three main branches, and serves an area that covers most of the head. Within the trigeminal, the *maxillary branch* area serves the eyebrow and upper lip piercing locations, while the *mandibular branch* area serves the lower lip and tongue piercing locations. The other branch area of the trigeminal, the *auricular branch*, is probably too deep to be an issue for piercers.

Nerves, protected in the spinal column by the *dura mater* ("tough mother," a tough, flexible membrane with its own distinct body rhythm) exit from every spinal segment. There are 31 pairs of spinal nerves, each pair serving a dermatome. Spinal nerves serve the opposite side of the body from which they generate.

When the nervous system is responding to fear of stress it is said to be in a *sympathetic* state. Symptoms of this state are sweating, contraction, secretion, and salivation. Sound familiar? The goal of the piercer is to coax or encourage a *parasympathetic*, or *receptive* state in the piercee. This can be accomplished through soothing, steady talk, gentle, appropriate touch, and no surprises. The parasympathetic state enables the body to experience the piercing as a wholistic event rather than an emergency. Taking the one-day Craniosacral ShareCare course, or a similar form of touch instruction can be indispensible for piercers who are developing their bedside manner. For more information on nerves and pain management, see the bibliography.

There is a form of Tibetan massage involving over an hour spent massaging only the navel. This is because, as in foot reflexology, the entire nervous system is accessible from the navel. Consider this when you are dealing with that nervous piercee.

Veins and Arteries

Blood travels through the *circulatory system*, which is comprised of arteries, veins, and their smaller tributaries. The bloodstream can be likened to a vast network of rivers, streams, and rivulets.

There are two major pathways through which blood travels. The *pulmonary circuit*, containing only the pulmonary artery, has only one function. It carries blood from the heart where it is purified, to the lungs where it is oxygenated, back to the heart where it is distributed through the rest of the body via the *systemic* circuit which is comprised of arteries and veins. Arteries bring fresh red blood to the cells. Arteries branch into *arterioles*. Veins carry waste products and blue, oxygenless blood back to the heart. The entire circuit takes about one minute. The path of most veins roughly follows that of their companion arteries. Branching out from the veins are smaller veins which branch into *venules* which finally become *capillaries*. All are interconnected to provide a backup plan in the event of obstruction.

Most of the larger arteries and veins pass deeply under the surface, protected by muscle tissue. However, some are exposed, and could present a potential disaster for an incautious piercer.

On the neck, the *external jugular* passes OVER the muscles. This is the part that bulges when you tense your neck. The *anterior facial vein* arises from the external jugular, and passes under the chin. This makes any piercing performed under the chin, or high on the sides or front of the neck, highly suspect. Traditional placement for a superficial collarbone piercing, known as the "madison," is not in the path of these veins. The anterior facial vein also passes between the eyes, on either side of the nose bridge, site of a piercing called an "earl." If carefully placed, and not too deep, an earl would not be in the path of this vein.

The Lymphatic System

The *lymphatic system*, also known as the immune system, serves to defend the body. The thymus, bone marrow, spleen, lymph nodes, tonsils, and lymph tissues, as well as leukocytes and lymphocytes, comprise the system. Lymph activity includes resistance to invading organisms and removal of damaged, abnormal, or dead cells.

During normal body activity, excess fluid, including blood and lymphocytes, leaves the circulatory system and collects in surrounding tissue. The lymph system includes a series of lymphatic capillaries which gather the excess and transport it to larger lymph vessels and finally drain into two large veins in the neck. Along the way, the fluid is filtered through lymph nodes.

At times of increased activity, for example, when the body is in a sympathetic or autonomous state (fight or flight), or has been traumatized, drainage is heavy and the lymph system is overwhelmed. The tissue surrounding the traumatized area remains swollen and tender for several days following such an experience. This is another reason why it is extremely important to develop a calming, steady bedside manner. The piercee's aftercare experience will be directly related to how receptive the piercer was able to make them feel during the piercing.

EYEBROW

brow bone

orbicularis oculi
muscle

fat

inside lid:
tarsal glands

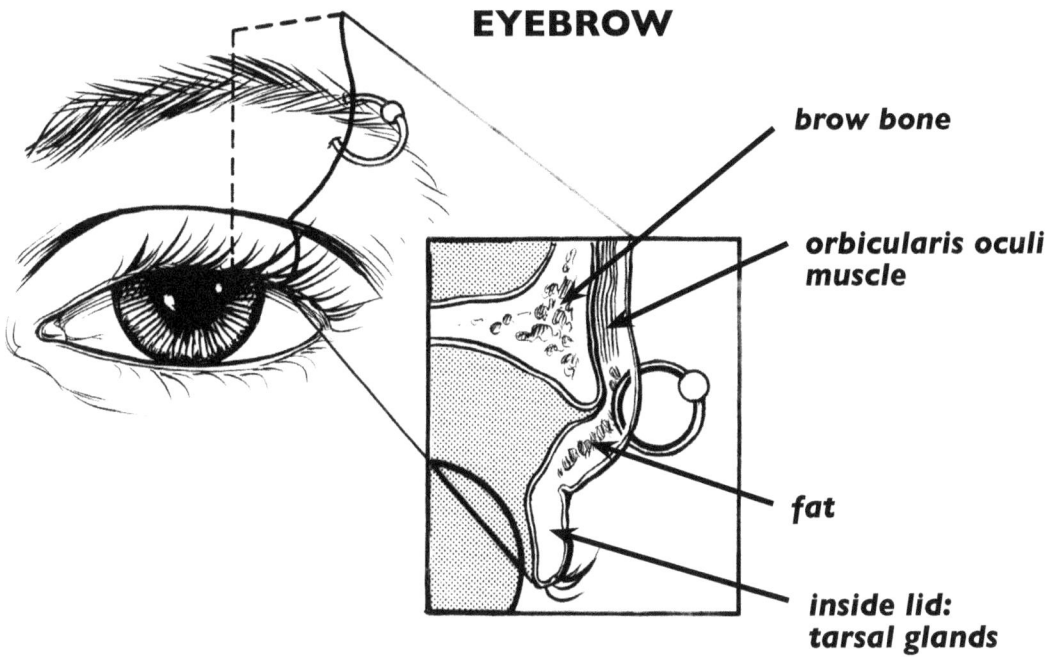

◆ The Eye
&
External
Ear

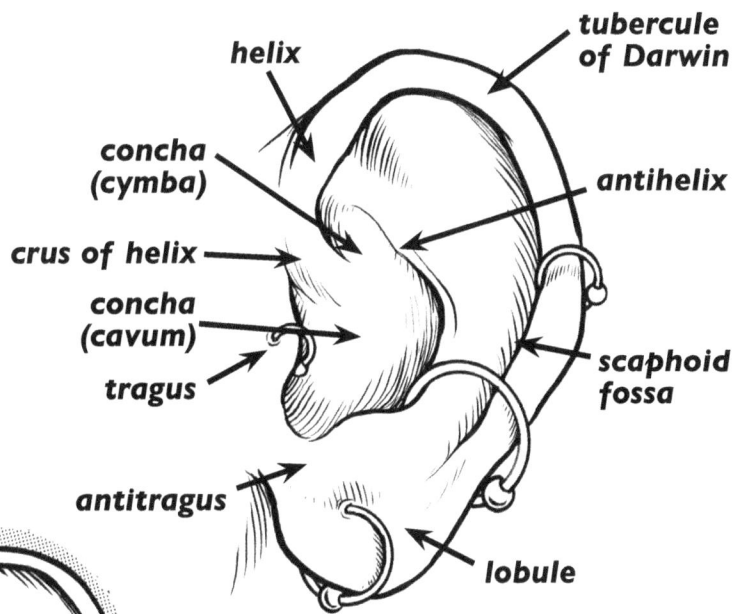

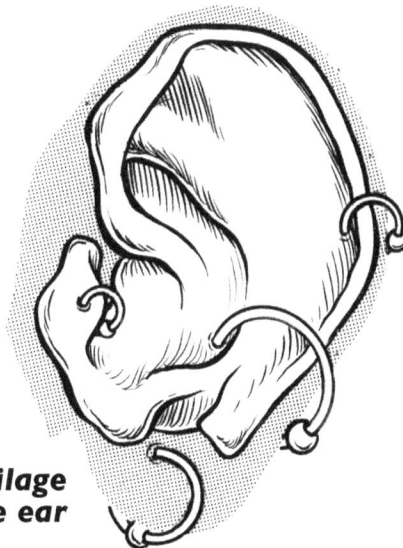

helix

tubercule
of Darwin

concha
(cymba)

antihelix

crus of helix

concha
(cavum)

scaphoid
fossa

tragus

antitragus

lobule

EXTERNAL EAR
OR AURICLE

elastic cartilage
structure in the ear

✦ THE NOSE & MOUTH

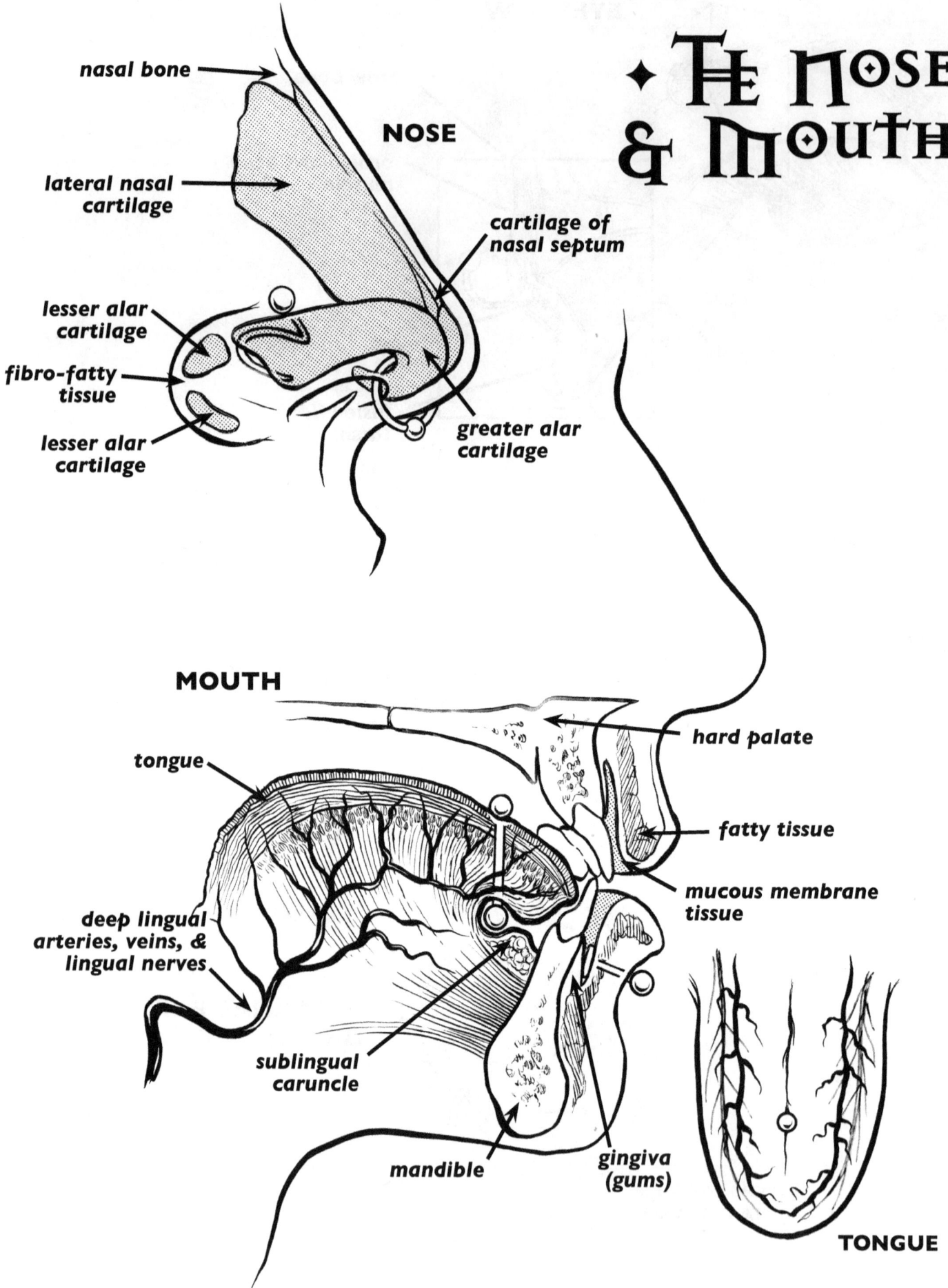

NOSE

nasal bone

lateral nasal cartilage

cartilage of nasal septum

lesser alar cartilage

fibro-fatty tissue

lesser alar cartilage

greater alar cartilage

MOUTH

tongue

deep lingual arteries, veins, & lingual nerves

sublingual caruncle

mandible

gingiva (gums)

hard palate

fatty tissue

mucous membrane tissue

TONGUE

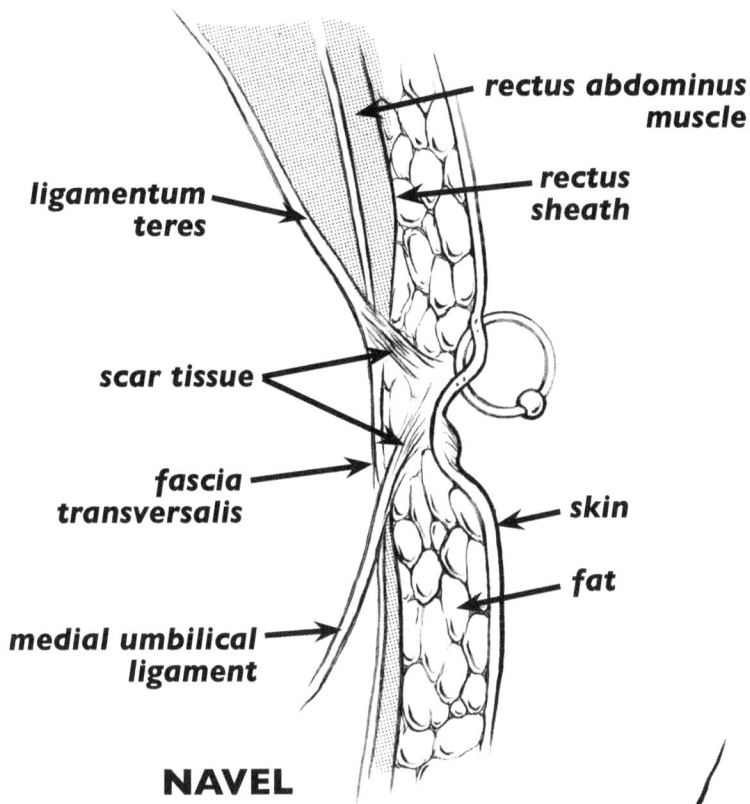

THE NAVEL & NIPPLE

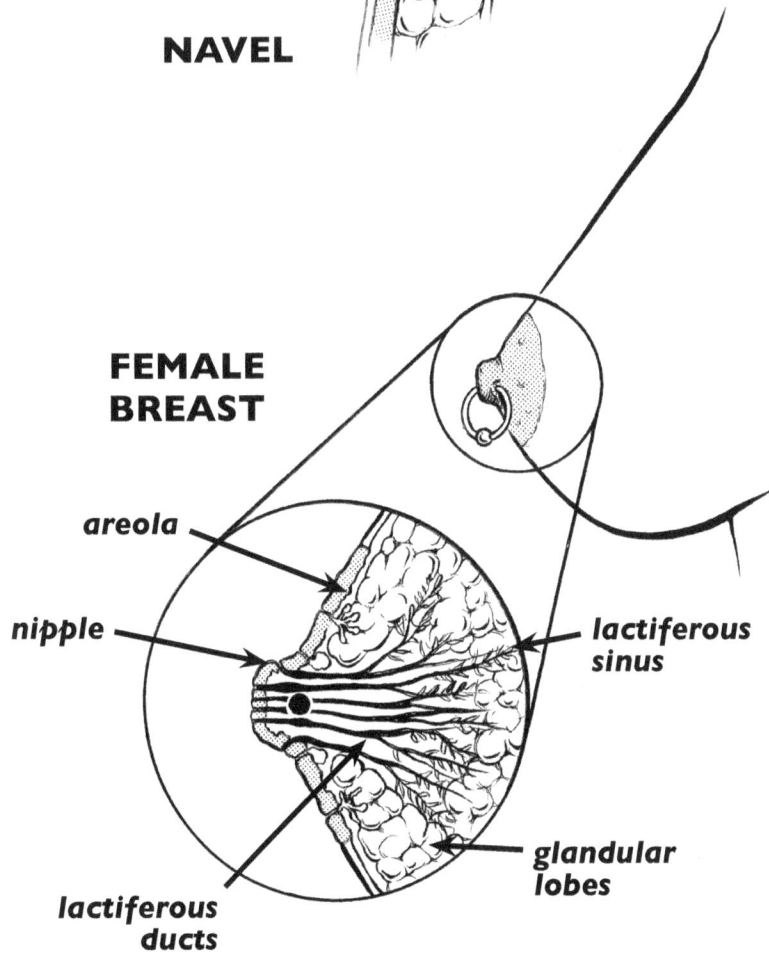

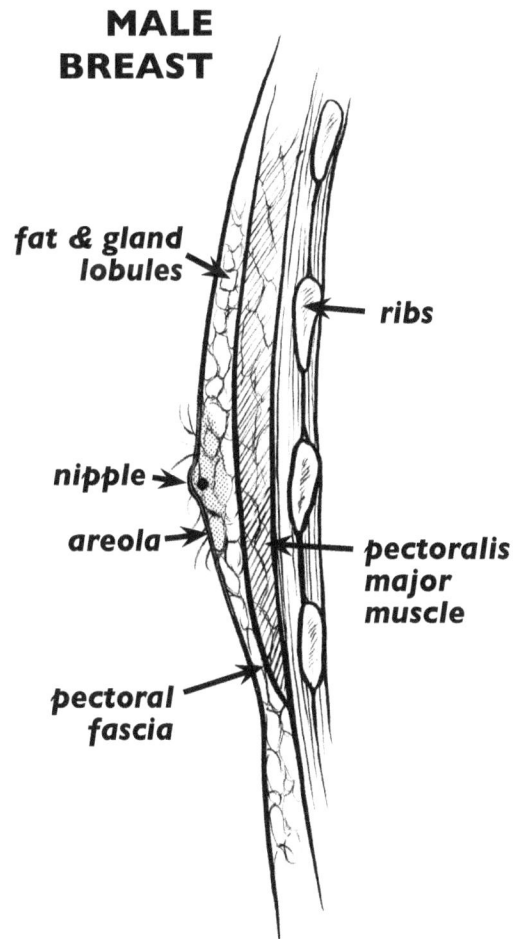

NAVEL

- rectus abdominus muscle
- rectus sheath
- ligamentum teres
- scar tissue
- fascia transversalis
- skin
- fat
- medial umbilical ligament

FEMALE BREAST

- areola
- nipple
- lactiferous ducts
- lactiferous sinus
- glandular lobes

MALE BREAST

- fat & gland lobules
- ribs
- nipple
- areola
- pectoralis major muscle
- pectoral fascia

CONSULT AN EXPERIENCED PROFESSIONAL PIERCER FOR THE LATEST INFORMATION

A.5

✦ THE MALE GENITALS

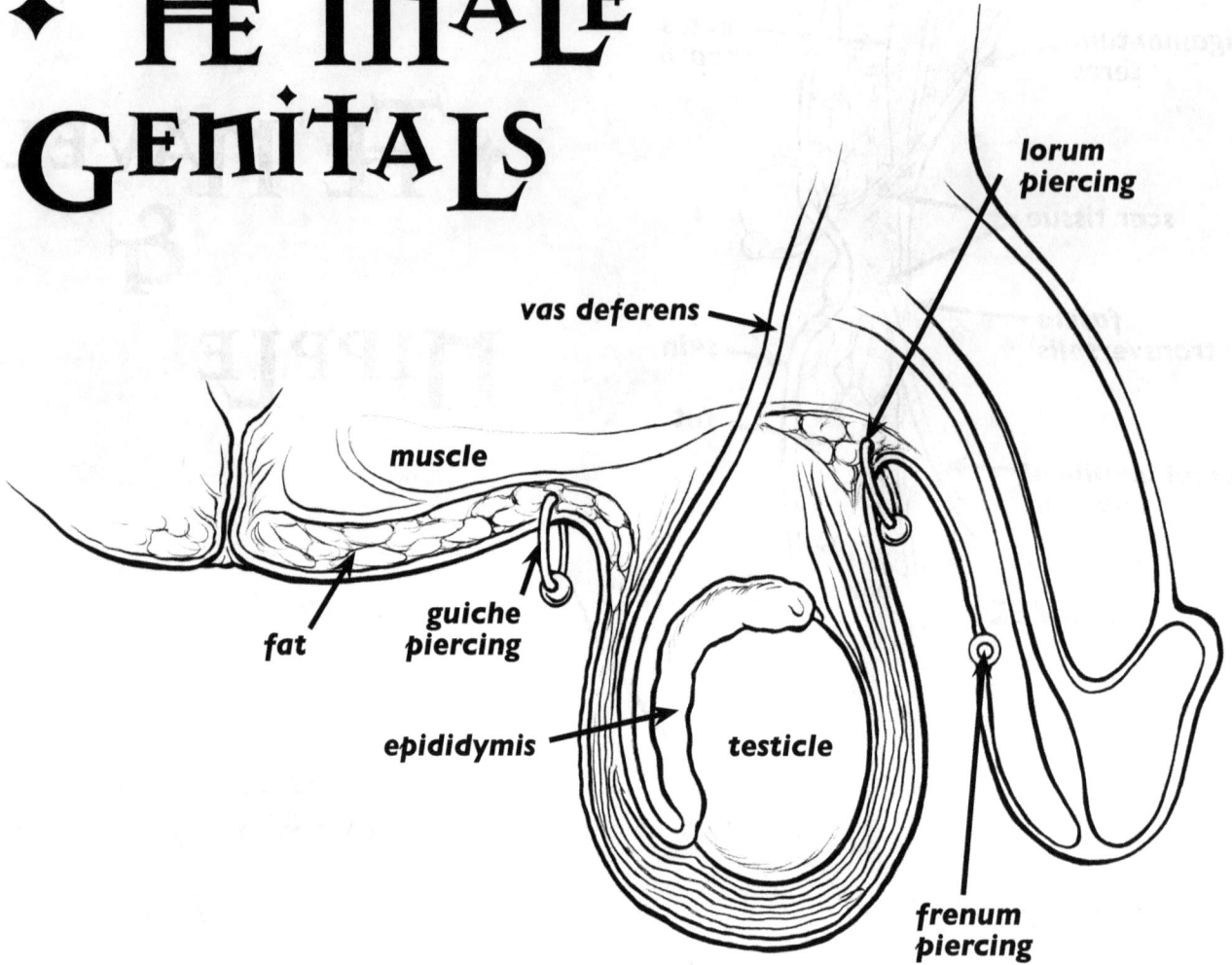

lorum piercing

vas deferens

muscle

guiche piercing

fat

epididymis

testicle

frenum piercing

DORSAL (TOP) VIEW

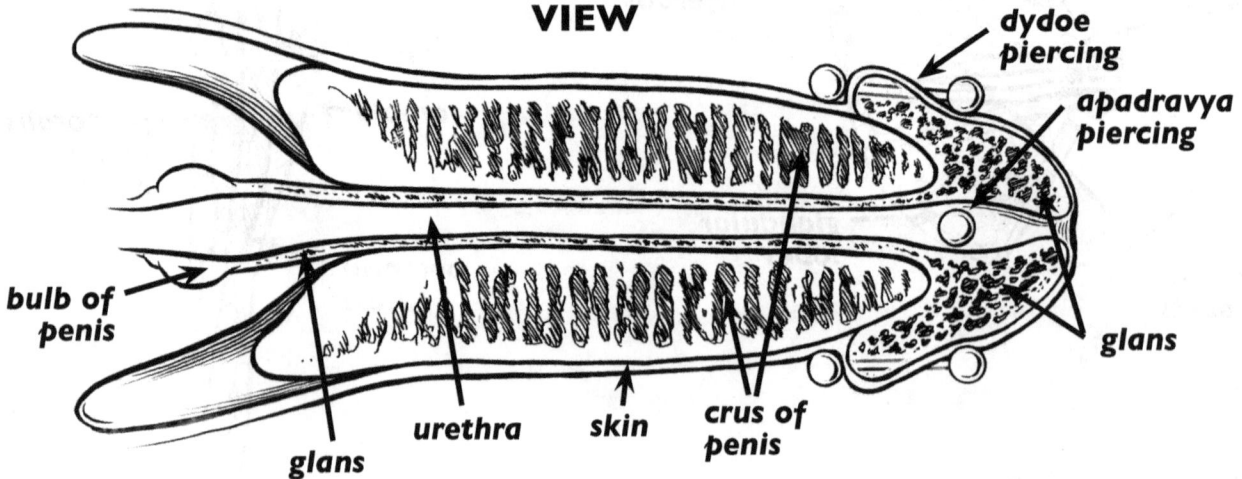

dydoe piercing

apadravya piercing

glans

bulb of penis

glans

urethra

skin

crus of penis

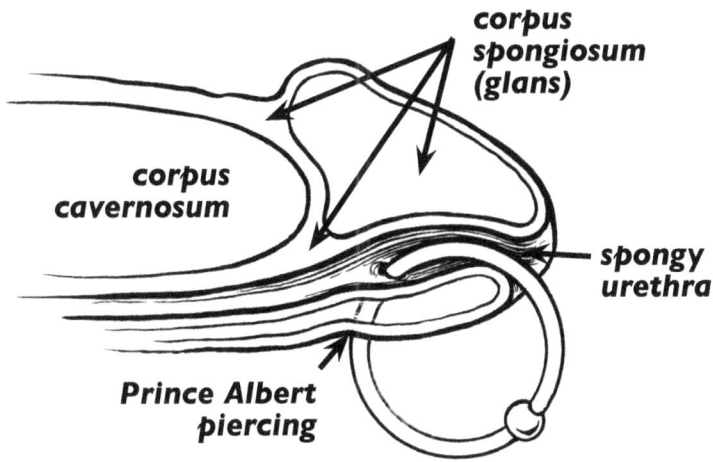

corpus spongiosum (glans)

corpus cavernosum

spongy urethra

Prince Albert piercing

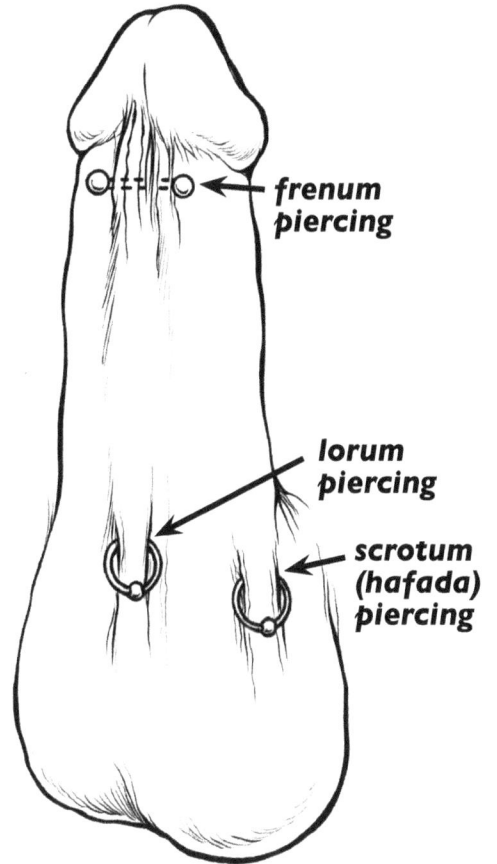

frenum piercing

lorum piercing

scrotum (hafada) piercing

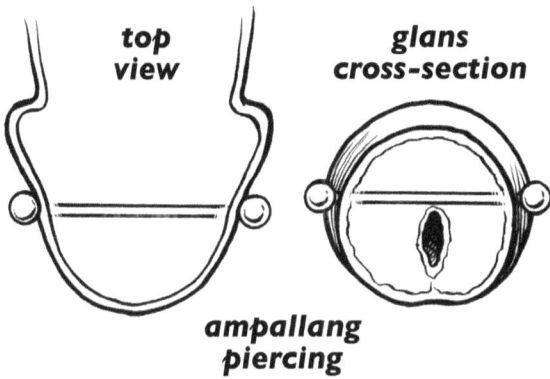

top view

glans cross-section

ampallang piercing

corona

dydoe piercing

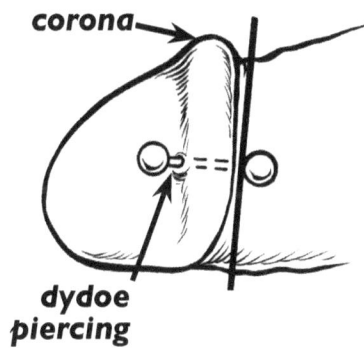

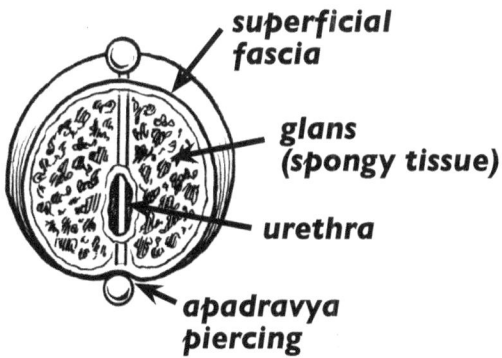

superficial fascia

glans (spongy tissue)

urethra

apadravya piercing

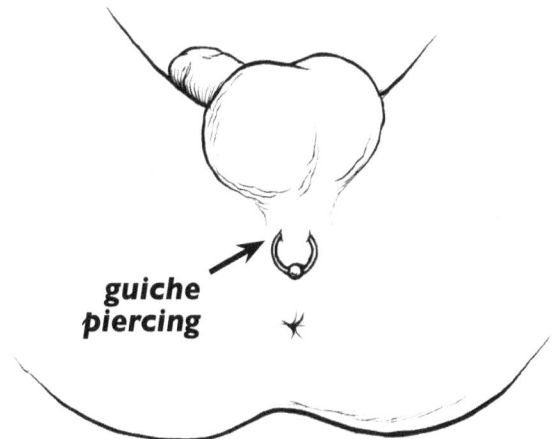

guiche piercing

✦ THE FEMALE GENITALS

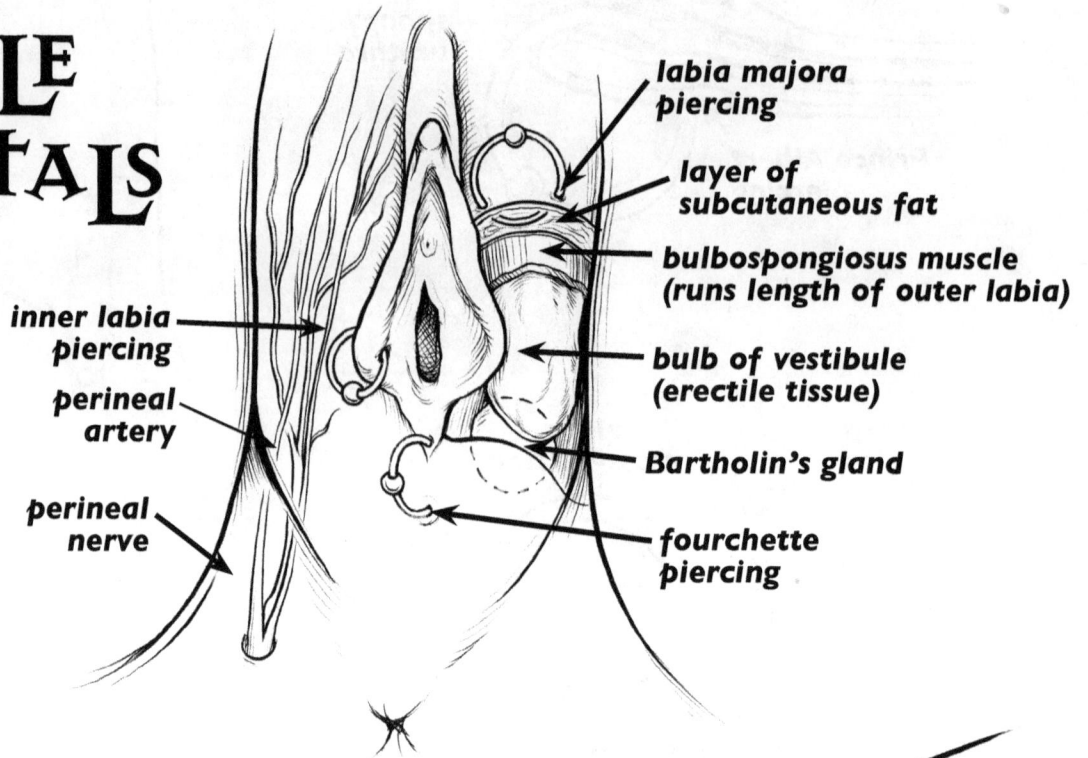

labia majora piercing

layer of subcutaneous fat

bulbospongiosus muscle (runs length of outer labia)

bulb of vestibule (erectile tissue)

Bartholin's gland

fourchette piercing

inner labia piercing

perineal artery

perineal nerve

1.

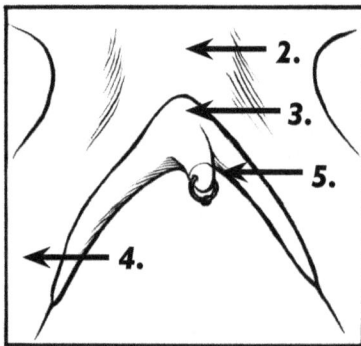

2.
3.
5.
4.

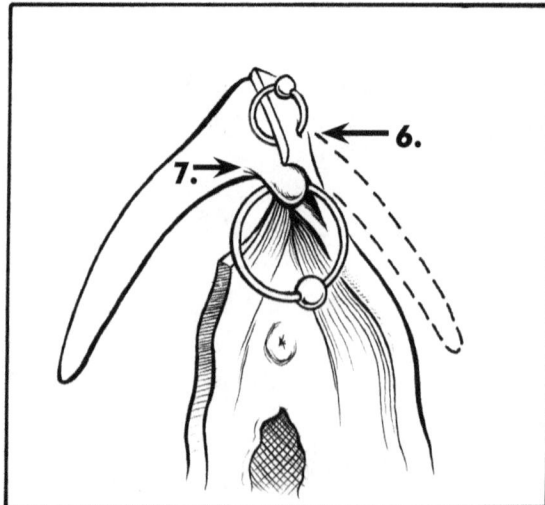

6.
7.

1. pubic bone
2. body of clitoris
3. glans of clitoris
4. crus of clitoris
5 clitoral piercing
6. clitoral hood piercing
7. triangle piercing

RESOURCES & SUGGESTED STUDIES

No single source could ever provide all you need to learn a skill. As you begin your apprenticeship, and as you continue to build your knowledge and experience, you will certainly want much more information than one or two seminars can provide. The scope of these seminars is inadequate to cover everything you might wish to learn about anatomy, psychology, history, spirituality, grounding techniques, and ritual. The more diverse your knowledge and experience, the more well-rounded you will be as a piercer.

What follows is a far-from-complete list of resources. Use them as springboards from which to begin what could easily be a lifetime's journey. We have also included a brief listing of equipment suppliers. Although many of the companies listed below do not care to whom they sell, it may be wise to refrain from disclosing the nature of your business when dealing with most of these suppliers. Some of the products that they offer may only be sold legally to medical professionals, in which case you will need the assistance of a sympathetic physician. Carefully consider your responsibility to the rest of the piercing community. Don't threaten their access to these much-needed health and safety supplies by breaking any laws or otherwise behaving irresponsibly.

• HEALTH AND SAFETY

Red Cross
The Red Cross CPR and first aid classes should be considered mandatory for piercers. Contact your local Red Cross for information and class registration.

Books & Publications

The Anatomy Coloring Book
by Wynn Kapit and Lawrence M. Elson
©1993 HarperCollins College Publishers
  Widely Avaliable, and highly recommended.

Atlas of Human Anatomy
by Dr. Frank Netter
Ciba- Geigy Medical Education & Publications
  Simply the best anatomy book ever. A must-see for all serious piercers, it travels layer by layer through the body. Distributed by Ciba-Geigy Med. Ed., PO Box 18060 Newark, NJ 07191. (800) 631-1181

The Ciba Collection of Medical Anatomy
by Dr. Frank Netter
Ciba-Geigy Medical Education & Publications
  See above.

The Point
Quarterly Newsletter of the Association of Professional Piercers, Post Office Box 1287, Lawrence, KS 66044
www.safepiercing.org

OSHA Guidelines
  A manual, or several volumes, detailing complete OSHA guidelines is available from each state's Occupational Safety and Health Administrations. Several magazines, such as *Compliance*, break the text up into more digestible portions and are recommended.

• HISTORY, CULTURE, PSYCHOLOGY, & ART

Book Dealers

Ethnographic Arts
  Booksellers in Marin, California. Their focus is on books about culture, particularly ritual, decoration, and historical information. Most of the books listed in this section are represented in the 12,000 title collection. (415) 383-2998 or (415) 332-1646.

Books & Publications

Marks of Civilization
by Arnold Rubin, ed.
©1988 by Museum of Cultural History, UCLA

The Penis Inserts of Southeast Asia: An Annotated Bibliography with an Overview and Comparative Perspectives
by Donald E. Brown, James W. Edwards, Ruth P. Moore.
Center for South and Southeast Studies, UC Berkeley

Mentawai Shaman: Keeper of the Rainforest-
by Charles Lindsay, Reimar Schefold, Phd.
©1992 by Aperture.

Man as Art
by Malcolm Kirk.
©1987 by TACO.

Tattoo, Torture, Mutilation, and Adornment: The Denaturalization of the Body in Culture and Text
by Frances Mascia-Lees, Patricia Sharpe, ed.
©1992 by SUNY Press.

• BEDSIDE MANNER/ GROUNDING
Local Massage Schools

These can provide an excellent resource for lessons in grounding, non-invasive touch, and pain management techniques. Many varied approaches exist, so if you don't click with the first method you encounter, keep searching. You won't be disappointed, and you may find your life taking some surprising directions.

Upledger Institute

Offers a one-day *ShareCare* workshop designed to introduce CranioSacral Therapy to the general public. It requires no understanding of anatomy or physiology. Participants learn about the craniosacral system and its influence on overall health. Techniques developed by Dr. John Upledger are demonstrated to provide skills that can be used to relieve headaches, reduce stress, control pain, promote relaxation, and lead participants to a greater understanding of the role they play in their own health.

Upledger Institute
11211 Prosperity Farms Road
Palm Beach Garden, FL 33410-4449
(407) 622-4334

Books & Publications
Your Inner Physician & You
by Dr. John Upledger.
©1991 by North Atlantic Books
Psychic Secrets by Ada
©1991 by Psychic Media Group
2280-152 A St.
White Rock, B.C. Canada; (604) 531-6160

Despite being saddled with a silly name, this slim booklet provides all the basic information you need to know on the subject of grounding.
Sacred Mirrors: The Visionary Art of Alex Gray
by Alex Gray.
©1990 by Inner Traditions International Limited.

A stunning visual exploration of the inner and outer spaces of the body. Provides clear explanation of the need for grounding and appropriate, non-invasive touch techniques. Widely available.

• SPIRITUALITY & RITUAL
Books & Publications
A Wiccan Bardo: Initiation and Self-Transformation
by Paul V. Beyerl.
©1989 by Prism Press.
Distributed in USA by Avery Publishing Group Inc.
Positive Magic: Occult Self Help
by Marion Weinstein.
©1978 by Phoenix Publishing Inc.

The Spiral Dance
by Starhawk.
©1979 by Harper & Row.

The three preceding titles are excellent basic texts on metaphysics, especially from the Wiccan perspective. Many concepts within translate well into the creation of personal rituals.
The Art of Ritual
by Renee Beck, Sydney Barbara Metrick.
©1990 by Celestial Arts.

Perhaps one of the best books specifically addressing the construction of individual, personal rituals. Highly recommended.

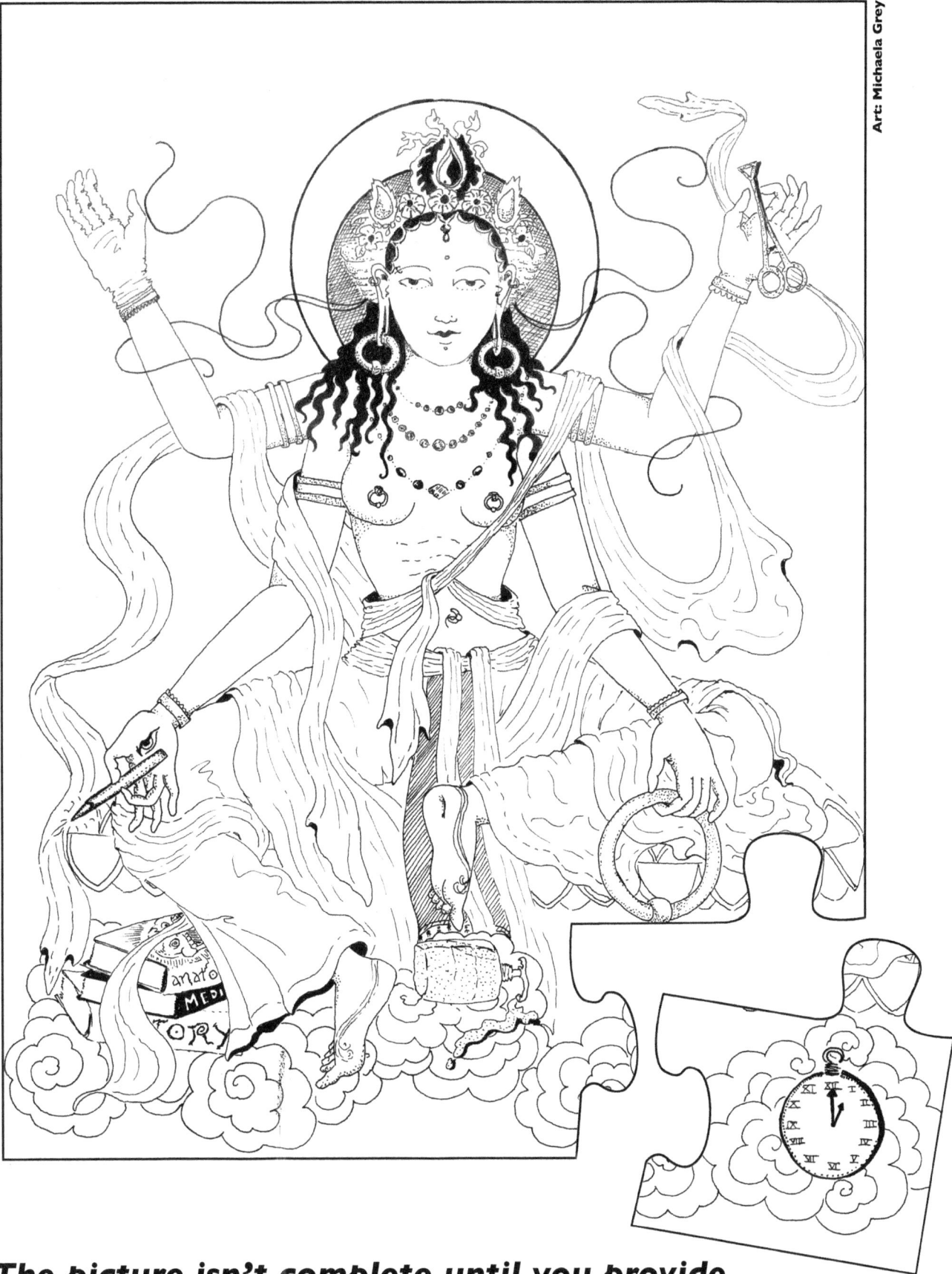

The picture isn't complete until you provide the missing piece... experience.

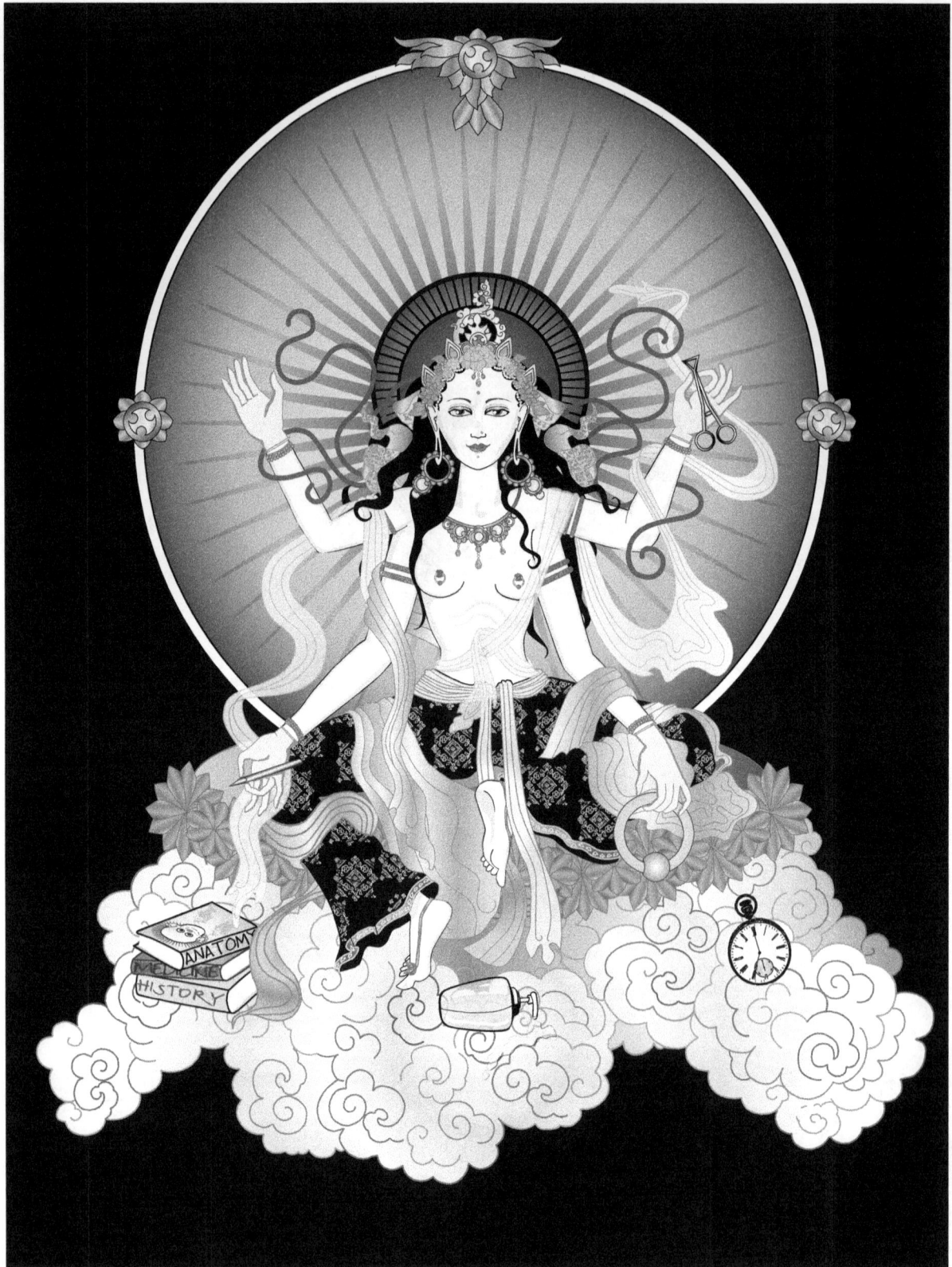

On the previous page is the image used throughout the original piercing manual. The artist, co-author Michaela Grey, considers the drawings a useful metaphor for the journey of a professional piercer. She says, "In the decades between creating these two images, look how time, training, and experience improved my skills." The original hand drawn, pen and ink drawing evolved into the computer generated, full vector image above and the full color version on the front cover. With time, schooling, and mentoring, your piercing skills can similarly improve and evolve.

• INDEX